FROM THE DIARY OF A
COUNTERREVOLUTIONARY

From
the
Diary

Translated from the Czech by
GEORGE THEINER

McGRAW-HILL BOOK COMPANY
New York   St. Louis   San Francisco
London   Mexico   Sydney   Toronto

Pavel Kohout

of a Counter-revolutionary

123456789 BBBP 798765432

Kohout, Pavel.
    From the diary of a counterrevolutionary. New york: McGraw-Hill, 1972
    First published in 1969 under title: Aus dem
Tagebuch eines Konterrevolutionärs.
    1. Czechoslovak Republic—Politics and government
—1968–   2. Czechoslovak Republic—History
—Intervention, 1968–   I. Title.
DB215.6.K648   320.9'437'04   72–38953
ISBN 0–07–035296–8

Designed by The Inkwell Studio

He who speaks the truth risks his head, he who is afraid of death loses the joy of life. Above all truth prevails. . . .

> Jan Hus
> in a letter to Rector M. Kristan of Prachatice

Go back whence thou camest, into the abode of thy heart, and close the door after thee!

> Jan Amos Komensky
> in *The Labyrinth of the World and Paradise of the Heart*, Chapter 37

Humanity does not mean sentimentality, but rather work and still more work.

> Thomas Garrigue Masaryk
> in *The Czech Question*

A nation whose every member is ruled both by his common sense and his conscience will not perish.

> Alexander Dubcek
> in his broadcast speech on his return from Moscow, 27 August 1968

Preface

Dear Mr. Young:

If your name happens to be Smith, Canelotti or Morgenstern, please excuse me; they forgot to introduce us.

One day you met a girl you didn't know. You didn't know her name, what she was doing, where and when she was born, who her parents were, what she likes and what she hates. You had your own joys and troubles, your job, your bank account, your friends and girls, your closed and defended space for living, to which she didn't belong.

Nevertheless, you started to talk to her, and only through this talk could you have found in her voice a long-awaited message. Today, this girl is Mrs. Young, Mrs. Smith, Mrs. Canelotti, or Mrs. Morgenstern, and two distant lives have merged into one.

One day—even today!—you opened this book. It relates hopes and anxieties of a totally alien country. Perhaps you have only a vague idea of what it is called, where it is, what its history was, how its future will look. You have your own anxieties and hopes—your flowering civilization and your moribund culture, your White House and your Negro problem, your flag, covered with glory on the moon and covered with blood in Vietnam. You are a citizen of one of the three major Powers ruling the world, and therefore possibly for you the problems of a small country in Europe are in a way equally as distant and ridiculous as is the spiritual behavior of hedgehogs to the elephant. After all, it is the hedgehog's duty to make way for the elephant.

Only, the world is not a zoo, Mr. Young! Elephantine countries as well as countries the size of a hedgehog have one denominator in common:

Man.

He has only one life, and therefore endeavors to create the best conditions he can for himself and for his children. Since human records began, men have been able to achieve this goal only

1. through collaboration with other human beings or
2. at their expense.

The first way is characterized by orchards, research laboratories, dams, large-scale undertakings, children's playgrounds, and concert halls.

The second way is characterized by mass graves.

Perhaps you are decidedly against socialism, Mr. Young, while I always have been against capitalism. Those are our own private convictions, and if it depended only on us, we would decide the quarrel by the results of our work. Unfortunately, there are too many lance corporals in the world, who can get their marshal's baton only in battles. Therefore they keep suggesting to us that blows are the best arguments. Also in the glorious days in which one could give blows only with cudgels or swords, they cost us quite a number of our great-grandfathers. In times when blows contain the power of several megatons of TNT, it may cost us all our sons and grandsons together.

Through our respective historical development each of us is enclosed in his own social system, but both of us have essentially only one chance, Mr. Young: by endeavoring to understand each other, to understand who we are, where we come from and what we want; by mutually comparing our intentions, our successes and failures; so that we are able to force the marshals to continue the quarrel only by means which do not destroy us. Means which will keep us above water, at least for the next generation. For, who knows—perhaps it will be *that* generation which will hear a long-awaited message and whose distant fates will merge, as your fate and Mrs. Young's have merged.

For this reason as well, I wrote this book, in which three diaries alternate with one another.

In the first one, the diary of a citizen, you will follow a number of characters who meet, separate, and meet again in the most important moments of the Czechoslovak history from 1944 to 1967.

In the second one, the diary of the writer PK, you will accompany me through spring, fall, and winter of that incredible Czechoslovak year 1968.

In the third one, the diary of a tourist, you will meet three characters who love and hate, lose and seek each other on the twenty-first of August 1968, when, in distant Rome, each has to experience the tragic hours of his homeland and the critical hours of his dreams.

This was the route of the book which even now you have in your hands, Mr. Young, and you ponder about whether, for its price, you will set off for the road which leads through the plain of distant joys and the mountains of distant sorrows, a road on which you will meet quite a number of unknown terms.

If you read this book, then both of us may hope that yet another thread will be spun, one of those threads which prevent our continents from drifting even further apart.

Pavel Kohout

CONTENTS

They tied me to a pillar in a huge hall. I could not see the ceiling. All around me hung heavy velvet curtains. One drew apart noiselessly. A sigh of many voices. No doubt: I found myself on a stage.

In the middle of the front row my father's face. I tried to call him, but the gag stifled my voice. Not even the privilege of saying last words!

A man in black came from the wings, a red-hot sword in his hand. Humiliation, rage, despair fused into a single tear. The outlines of objects and figures multiplied. Then the sword approached my eyes and the vision exploded in heat and pain.

I wrenched my head aside. The heat ceased, the pain vanished. I opened my eyes. A ray of sunshine, thrusting its way into the room between the slats of the Venetian blind, was scorching the pillow next to me. The morning sun must have been shining right against the room.

Tears were drying on my cheek. They had saved my sight, as they once had saved Mikhail Strogoff's. Why did my brain release this long-forgotten story of my childhood? I turned my head, intending to ask my dream interpreter. She lay at my side like a beautifully prepared corpse. She had felt hot during the night and had thrown the sheets off.

I crawled over her and crossed to the window to pull up the Venetian blind. Cool air was seeping through the open door and the slats. In Italy I always ached forward like an addict for these brief morning moments when one can finally breathe a little.

The blind would not budge.

I examined the mechanism. The cord vanished somewhere in the upper part of the window frame. I pulled gently, then more violently. The blind still refused to move.

I brought a chair over to the window, but even when I stood on tiptoe I was an inch short. Mounting irritation. Mornings are always extremely important to me. The first minutes decide the day.

I had to fetch the table. As always her things were scattered over it. Every evening I asked her to leave it clear. Cluttered tabletops remind me of my desk and with it of all the wasted hours of these last few years.

I picked up: her handbag, her comb, her cigarettes, her ball-point pen and unmailed postcards whose number increased with every town we visited, her Ronson lighter and her cigarette case, her purse, out of which had fallen Czech, Italian, and Austrian coins, her compact, gluey with some strange stuff she had bought to blow bubbles with, her note pad full of caricatures of me and realistic portraits of preening Latins, her broken watch, and a half-eaten banana.

I put the whole mess on the floor.

I climbed onto the table and tried to lift the wooden frame. It was nailed firmly to the window.

I started to sweat an hour earlier than usual, my mood darker every second. Frantically I tugged at the cords. Then I heard her laughing.

She must have been watching me for quite a while.

"What's so funny?" I asked coolly.

"You don't look exactly ravishing," she said.

"I'm not putting on a show. I'm just trying to pull these blinds, which only a moron could have pulled down."

"It seems to me that you lowered them yourself," she said. Slowly but surely my anger increased.

"You're asking a leading question, although you cannot have forgotten that we came here shortly before midnight, with a couple of bottles of Verdicchio inside us. In such circumstances it's not *me* who loses self-control so that the next day I don't know what I did. I took this room because they assured me it had the best view. Therefore I didn't have the slightest reason to destroy the blinds. Logically speaking, it's far more likely to have been you, since you destroy virtually everything you touch."

"If you really must reason like this, you shouldn't do it standing naked on top of a table," she said. "It just makes you look more ridiculous."

I stepped down from the table and, for the first time in a while, spoke an obscenity. It was that kind of a day. For the first time in many days she started crying.

We both began to dress in offended silence, with no thought of

2

making love in the morning or recalling dreams. Vengefully I didn't order breakfast.

While she sat painting her eyes I made one more attempt to raise the blasted blind. In vain. Not usually a morning smoker, I lit a cigarette and tried to catch even a glimpse of the scenery between the slats. The space was so narrow that the view I got of the much-touted panorama beneath the San Marino rock would hardly have satisfied a tank driver.

I turned around and looked at her. She had finished her make-up and was sitting on the bed, gazing silently before her. As usual I was suddenly sorry for her and I sat down at her side, my arm around her shoulders.

"Don't be angry," I said. "But you know it *was* your fault. You shouldn't have laughed at me when I was only trying to make things pleasant for you. And, worse still, you shouldn't have accused me of breaking that blind. After all, the only reason we came here in the first place was because I wanted to show you the view! Let's not spoil our whole day because of a damn Venetian blind."

"You're just like that precious Party of yours," she said. "All our life you keep promising us a wonderful view and inevitably a broken blind prevents us from seeing anything."

---

14 II 45 / Prague

When the sirens started screaming I was dreaming about A____. I was trying to unbutton her gray overcoat but my fingers trembled and the number of buttons multiplied all the time.

Then the air-raid warning, but I pulled the blankets over my head and tried to go on unbuttoning, but then Mother was in the room, urging me up. We dressed in a hurry, opened the windows to prevent them from being shattered by the blast, and picked up our specially packed suitcases. Outside on the dark staircase we heard footsteps, voices, children crying.

Before today no one had gone down to the cellar. At night in bed we would listen to the Allied bombers and in the daytime we watched them flying overhead. We felt no fear. The distant fronts we had been awaiting so long were suddenly close at hand. The small glittering dots left a white cobweb of vapor in the sky. We were up there, with the man who was pounding Germany on our behalf. An eye for an eye, a tooth for a tooth.

This noon a bomb fell on Prague. On bridges, squares, houses. I have seen it! I was on my way to school, walking across the Letna Park. In the winter sun the planes looked like Christmas-tree decorations. I was still wondering where these jolly firecrackers down in the city had come from when the air-raid siren screamed. Immediately afterward, a muffled horrible bombing noise.

Suddenly I realized that I was watching people die. Prague was slashed, a long fiery wound stretching from Smichov all the way to Vinohrady.

Vinohrady! I threw my satchel down on the snow and ran as if robbed of sense. I ran down the hill, across the bridge, through the streets of the center, with ambulances and fire engines rushing past me. Schwerin Avenue was cordoned off by the police right behind the National Museum.

"Let me through!" I shouted. "I must get to her! Let me through! Let me through!"

They let me through. In the street, dust was layered like black fog. Midday became midnight, full of fire and noise. I ran past the Prague radio building, miraculously undamaged, and into Manes Street.

Her house too was undamaged. I beat desperately on the door. I forgot the doorbell completely. She opened the door, still in her gray overcoat, just as she had come home from school. She was pale and trembling, speechless. I took her hand and led her across the kitchen into her room. There I embraced her.

"I love you. I'll always love you."

What I had so far not dared to do suddenly became possible. We fell in bed and kissed one another. I caressed her as I had always wanted to caress her, oblivious of the thick, rough material of her coat.

Her parents came running home very shortly afterward.

And so it was later, only in my dream, that I started to undo that endless row of buttons, and I would not stop until I had undone the last.

The cellar is divided by wooden lattices. Each of the twenty families has its own compartment. Like all the others, we had already shoveled all the coal into one corner last autumn. Down here we have Granny's old armchair, two chairs, and a small table. Mother is knitting a sweater by candlelight. I have seen her knit like this ever since I was a child. She had to earn money for the family when father was out of work. I would accompany her as she went to the neighboring districts, to sell the sweaters and cardigans she knitted to the wives of well-to-do shopkeepers. Never in our own neighborhood! She did not want people to see the difficult straits of the bank-manager's daughter who had married for love. They paid us mostly with meat, butter, and sugar. Sometimes Mother cried: when they cheated her, or when someone addressed her slightingly. When she got the money for her work she bought me a Linzertorte. After the war, if I have a little money, I'll take her to Linz. Linz is for me something very like paradise.

She sees that I am writing.

"You'll ruin your eyes," she said.

"So will you."

"But you have a longer way to look."

I could see Father's shadow flitting about behind the lattices and could hear him whispering with our neighbor, Mr. Jankovec. It's the latest news from London and Moscow this evening, no doubt. Father is the cleverest person I know. He speaks seven languages. I will never be able to understand how it was possible for a man like that to be unemployed two years. I once asked him about this and he laughed and said:

"A man has either money or convictions."

He must have read just about every book there is. And he is brave. But now is not the time to write about *this*. Perhaps later. Perhaps.

Here they come. The cellar is suddenly absolutely quiet. That all-pervading noise was coming closer and closer. Now the anti-aircraft opens fire. Windows rattle. Mother is still knitting, but I can see that her mind is not on her work; she is looking away somewhere, into a terrible unknown distance. Nobody wants to betray fear. Or is it possible that I alone am afraid? Yes, I am afraid. I can still see the merry, colored firecrackers and the black fog that followed. Maybe a bomb will fall on this house in a minute or two. That is one of the reasons I started to write this diary.

I am not quite seventeen. Of the world I know only war, hunger, and fear. People have flown across oceans, conquered the North Pole, discovered important medicines, written such beautiful books as *Cyrano de Bergerac*, *War with the Newts*, and *Mikhail Strogoff*. I have not had time to do anything, anything at all. Except for one thing:

I loved A——, loved her as much as anyone can love another. I knew I would never love anyone any more, even if by some miracle I survived this night. And what if I did not?

If I were killed, perhaps someone would dig up my diary with its three written pages, room enough to describe my life so far; perhaps he would dig up the diary, perhaps he would find you and perhaps give it to you.

If so, please remember from time to time the day that Prague was bombed for the first time: remember; and plant the buttons from your overcoat on my grave, my love,
my first and last love.

---

7 January 1968 / Prague
(*From the diary of the writer PK*)

When in October the rumor spread that at a meeting of the Communist Party's Central Committee Antonin Novotny had called Alexander Dubcek a nationalist, I said to friends in the theater:

"That's the beginning of his end."

"Whose end, Dubcek's?" they asked, not without justification, for fifteen years ago such an accusation would have been tantamount to a death sentence.

"No, Novotny's. I think that having included Dubcek he has finally managed to insult every living Slovak, including members of the Central Committee."

They did not really believe it until December, when we heard that the next plenary session was a very stormy one, although it had been convened practically on Novotny's own doorstep, inside Prague Castle. Yet for my own part I stopped believing it when the session was adjourned. The stated grounds were that "Communists too have a right to buy Christmas presents for their dear ones." Surely it was too good to be true; one could not expect this body ever to give birth to a decision truly in keeping with the interests of the Party and the Nation.

And thus the rank-and-file members of the Central Committee went shopping in Prague, buying sweaters and skating boots and Trebon goldfish for their dear ones, while the professional apparatchiks tore around the snowy countryside in their official Tatras, trying to re-establish the leadership's control over the district and regional Party organizations.

What it all boiled down to was this: were the Slovaks now really incensed sufficiently to become the first large opposition group in the Central Committee which would adopt the political proposals put forward by the Czech progressives?

Once more Antonin Novotny was to refute this hope when, as usual, he visited disappointed families on their TV screens.

"I am convinced that this is the beginning of a mighty process of universal development of socialist society, and that our road is the right one."

I switched him off, but his spirit lingered derisively in the flat. If the road of the plenum of the Central Committee was his road, then even this crossroads was nothing but a sham and our crisis would continue until the final catastrophe.

The January session of the plenum continued with unabated fury. Although Novotny fought tooth and nail—backed up, they say, by an ultimatum issued by a number of top Army brass—his supporters unexpectedly found themselves a minority. People who were present swear that the debate swung away from the person of Novotny to the inevitability of fundamental economic and political reforms as the only way of giving socialism any meaning and giving people confidence in it. Nevertheless, today's communiqué says:

"The plenary session of the Central Committee of the KSC approved Antonin Novotny's own request that, as President of the Republic, he be relieved of his post as First Secretary."

Not a word then that he had transformed a country with a great democratic and socialist tradition into a penal institute ruled by a police bureaucracy. On the contrary: gratitude for his unremitting endeavor is being expressed in the same breath as stress is laid on "the over-all conception of our politics aimed at the creation of a profoundly democratic, socialist society." *This we are now to achieve under the leadership of Alexander Dubcek, who is said to have created a more breathable atmosphere in Slovakia but who is also known to have the reputation of the notorious Soviet training and to have worked in the Party apparatus.*

The first to congratulate him was Leonid Brezhnev.

"The old comedy with a new cast" was Z____'s comment.

I do not argue with her. It is a detective story with an open ending. But when I consider that the year just beginning ends with an eight, which has always had a magic effect in Czech history, I nevertheless feel the urge, for the first time in years, to keep a diary again.

Wednesday, 21 August 1968 / Perugia
(Continued)

We did not speak to each other all the way to Perugia. I parked the car in the main square. It was noon and the heat was cruel. The population had disappeared without trace into that other Italy, which I imagine as something like an air-conditioned *ristorante* on the banks of the Styx, from which they emerge only toward evening to collect the dehydrated tourists. I sat down at one of the little tables on the scorching pavement under the walls of the Palazzo dei Priori. After a while a dark-haired waiter sauntered up to us.

"Want anything to eat?" I asked coldly.

She shook her head, although she must have been starving, as I was.

"*Mezzo bianco*," I told the waiter.

"*Va bono, signore.*"

He was not interested in details. The Piazza delle Quatro Novembre, framed by severe medieval portals, looked like a gigantic, overlit film set. From time to time an empty bus would slowly drive by, but otherwise everything was deserted and still, as if waiting for the next take. Pigeons were drinking from the Fontana Maggiore. It only needed St. Bernard of Siena to come and pray for peace.

Fortunately the man brought us some cool white wine, which we drank all at once. As usual, it only made me thirsty. I ordered a large carafe. I felt hot and sticky, the bitterness within me grew until it sought an outlet.

"I think we should have a talk," I said.

We were on our second liter. When she was drunk she was even more impervious than usual to argument, but I did not care any more.

"For four years I've tried to bear your whims and your selfishness, thinking that sooner or later you would change. I've wasted hundreds of hours and tons of energy trying to explain the most fundamental things. I could have found fifty young ladies who would gladly have given up everything to share my life and to help me. Not only didn't this ever occur to you, you haven't missed a single opportunity of humiliating me. You knew I was a Communist before you ever came to me; everybody knew it. For four years you have seen me fight for things which, after all, I needn't have bothered about. You saw how I was sticking my neck out and complicating my life when, as a writer, I might have lived in privileged comfort. Not only that, you saw that it made sense, that I was not merely tilting at windmills but that what I did brought on a chain reaction which gave rise to hope. And yet you wouldn't miss a single opportunity, however stupid, to trot out that 'you and your Party' routine. I'm only forty, neither bald nor fat; I keep getting love letters from twenty-year-old girls. But I've managed to live through a world economic crisis, Munich, the occupation, the Heydrich affair, air raids, the barricades in May 1945, February 1948, the political trials, the Twentieth Congress, as well as the Prague Spring. History has its protagonists and its onlookers. I no longer blame anyone if they choose to look on, but I can't stand onlookers who stand by and watch others being enslaved, starved to death, or fighting a war and then, from the height of their theater boxes, condemn revolution because it failed to knock on the door and change into slippers. For three years I fought for the victory of my revolution, twenty years for its purity. This struggle has lasted twenty years and it was more difficult than any other, because those on the other side had the same past as we did, they spoke the same language and carried the same Party card in their pocket. For twenty years Communists fought against other Communists to give revolution its final shape, and in this struggle the Communists in power used the gallows several times as the decisive argument. We accepted the confrontation and we have triumphed in it. And now that we have done it, for you as well as for ourselves, instead of appreciating what we have done you again lift up your clean hands and call us all 'You,' making no distinctions. For four years I have held you every night, for four years you alone read me like a book because I loved you and wanted you to understand me. And after these four years we are farther apart than when we started. Politics is lying between us in our bed like a naked sword, and it's your doing. You make me responsible for the shortage of veal, for the bad quality of shoes, for the fact that you can't travel when and where you want to. You blame me for the holes in our roads, for our dilapidated houses and boring newspapers, cowardly members of Parliament and omnipotent policemen. I accept this as a challenge, which forces me to neglect my own work even more than before, to concern myself with things that are, when you come to think of it, no business of mine. Then, at last, the day comes when those twenty years bear fruit, when life again becomes worth living. And on that day you, for whose sake I did all this, got up from your seat on the grandstand and, full of boredom and contempt, utter your allegory of the damn Venetian blind."

I was surprised that I felt neither anger nor sorrow. Suddenly I saw quite clearly that it was only defiance that made me carry on our relationship. I was intent on proving to her that I was right. Now it had happened. I was again free, at liberty, like my country.

"Let's part," I said. "And this time I mean it. I'll buy you an air ticket; or if you prefer, take the car. I'm sick of politics, of you, of everything. For the first time in my life I want to have a real holiday, take time off from life. And when I return I'll start again from scratch. It'll be my second half-time."

"You're right," she said. "Take my suitcase out of the car. Don't worry about *me*."

"But I have to arrange for your journey."

"I'm not going anywhere. I like it here."

"That's nonsense, and you know it. You can't speak a single foreign language."

"No, I can't. Didn't have much reason to learn them, did I? Thanks to you and your Party I grew up in a country where the farthest point you were permitted to travel was Slovakia."

"Correct me if I'm wrong, but I think you have seen half of Europe these last three years."

"Yes, with you."

"Thanks for the compliment. Fortunately now you know that you can travel even without me. So there's nothing to prevent you going home and finding someone more to your taste."

"I wouldn't dream of it," she said. "I only went back there on your account every time. Though I find it increasingly more difficult to understand why, I guess I must have loved you. Perhaps you interested me just because you happened to be one of *them*. When we had our first date I was terrified at the thought of what my parents and relatives, my friends, would say if they knew. You were one of those we hated. At school we learned your poems about Gottwald and the Party, about our great liberators, the Soviet Union. We had arguments whether you wrote the stuff out of simple stupidity or just for the money. I wanted to find out. Especially as you didn't look like a fool. I wanted to know what you Communists were really like. That was one reason why I started going with you. To my horror I discovered that you actually believed all that rot. Yet now and again you showed a spark of humanity. I tried to bring out that side of you. I wanted you to realize what we thought of you and others like you. You chose to interpret this your own way. And you tried to convince me that you were right. We spent our time with unbelievably boring people, you dragged me along to your stupid meetings, you kept fighting for something that was, when all was said and done, ridiculous. It took you and your Party twenty years to achieve a wonderful victory: you triumphantly brought us back to where we were twenty years ago. And now you again expect us to thank you for the lovely view. You go back if you want to; I'm not interested in the view. We know you too well by now to believe that we will really see what you've been promising us. Go on, don't worry about me, I can look after myself. I'm fed up with living in a cage. And luckily I am a woman. You can be certain that even without you I'll be in Rome before the day is out, within a week I'll be able to make myself understood,

11

and before the month is out I'll be married—and it won't be only for money, either. Thanks to you and your lot my generation has another advantage: in order that our hearts should belong wholly to the revolution they forgot to teach us that we had a homeland. Our national anthem could not be sung and our flag could not be flown without the flags and the anthems of our brothers. You told us what the First Secretary of the Communist Party of Mongolia had said about sheep breeding, but you forgot to tell us that our first President had been a philosopher. You made a museum out of a house which had once by chance been visited by Vladimir Ilyich Lenin, but you let us walk in ignorance past the house in which Franz Kafka had been born and had worked. Instead of the tomb of the Bohemian kings you showed us the embalmed corpse of Klement Gottwald, which you burned a few years later, pointing out reprovingly that it was a product of the personality cult. As if he had embalmed himself. And then came the era of leaders who did not even *have* a personality. No wonder you had to change the national emblem and deny national traditions so that the difference would not be so obvious. You insisted that we all become devoted internationalists. It took some doing, but it was worth it. We have at least rid ourselves of sentimental bonds. We can exchange Prague for any other city without missing anything more than a few beautiful façades, which you can find anywhere. We can adopt a new anthem, a new flag, a new language without losing anything but a few empty symbols, available anywhere in the world. To leave our homeland is no more difficult for us than to change trams. I'm not sure that's what you wanted, but you certainly have done it. And today I'm beginning to realize that losing you is not going to be particularly difficult either. Once you vanish down that street it'll seem as if you'd never existed."

That did it. I got up and put her passport on the table. Then I went to the car, took her suitcase out of the trunk, and her purse, and all her articles scattered in various parts of the vehicle. I put them all down on the hot pavement, got in, and banged the door shut. Once more I turned my head toward her. She was sitting there, immobile, with the two glasses on the table in front of her, all alone on that huge stage between the Palazzo dei Priori and the Cathedral, on the stage I was leaving after

12

having played my last scene. Now I was quite sure I could do it. She seemed as alien and distant as the women of my youth, somehow unreal and incomprehensible. I felt no vestige of love or responsibility. She did not want them, anyway. Already she belonged to another world. She had always belonged to it, but I had been naïve enough to talk myself into believing that it was otherwise.

I released the hand brake and the car started rolling slowly down the steep hill. The colored tables flashed past once more in my rear-view mirror. Nothing moved inside me. On the contrary. I began thinking about the beautiful young girls I'd meet the day after tomorrow in Prague. The fifty girls who would give up everything without hesitation to share my new life.

The sweat that poured off me was not unpleasant for a change. The heat of the sun seemed to cleanse me like a sauna. The rehearsal had gone very well; now I could try it in earnest.

"Well," I said, "here's to your liberation from your country, and to my liberation from you."

She drank the toast. I laid her passport on the table.

"Maybe you can still use it for a while."

I got to my feet, concentrating on the effort required to walk erect to the car, when I heard a strange voice. It sounded like a drawn-out wail, multiplied by echo.

Out of the medieval stage set a swarthy man came running with a bundle of newspapers under his arm. He ran right up to us and called out again in that wailing voice:

"*Cecoslovacchia è occupata!*"

The printed placard he was holding up right in front of my eyes showed the well-known silhouette of our frontier, pierced on every side by the arrows of military operations. From a large photograph in the corner a tank was pointing its gun at that frontier.

It came as a relief to me to realize how drunk I was. Often when I have had a little too much alcohol I fall asleep and it is then that I am most liable to have those grotesque, absurd dreams. But then I heard another curious sound and I turned my head to see what it was.

She was crying.

I took a closer look at the tank.

Our math teacher raised his arm as usual in the Nazi salute. He almost tore his arm from the socket. He is now the only one to do it. And the only one to put us through our paces even though he knows our days at school are numbered. The seventh forms have been called up to join the final war effort, and now it is to be our turn.

He began the lesson by telling us about a brave German soldier who had destroyed five Russian tanks. Does he really not know that at this very moment Russian tanks are pushing the Germans back from the Vistula to the Oder?

He has denounced a boy from one of the other sixth forms who last Christmas had painted red the star above the school crèche. He got sent to Dresden on Christmas Eve, and was missing after an air raid on 14 February. Who knows, perhaps he would have died the same way in Prague? They say our math teacher is going to swing after the war. Is he scared, I wonder?

Then the Principal came in to say that he was supposed to send some volunteers immediately to help clear away rubble. To spite the math teacher we all put our hands up.

Outside the Principal's study a blond type from the Kuratorium, a Nazi youth-front organization, was waiting for us. We felt betrayed. None of us was in the Kuratorium. Our mothers had our tonsils removed and medical certificates made out to show that we were weak and thus unfit for membership.

There was nothing to do. He took down all our names and off we went. In the tram we fooled around, creating as much disturbance as we could and laughing at the top of our voices. Since there were forty of us, he did not know our names and so could only shout helplessly:

"*Kameraden*, a little discipline!"

When that had no effect he added almost vengefully:

"The *joke* will be on you soon, I promise you!"

We got out in Strasnice, at the big crossroads by the three cemeteries. We protested that there had been no bombing here, but he took no notice of us and walked on ahead, holding the list of names in his hand. We had no choice but to follow him. He led us to the Jewish Cemetery. Inside the gates we were hit by a terrible stench, as if from a gigantic pile of rotting potatoes. Slavek said he thought we were going to dig up the graves. Robert added:

"The Germans are pigs."

A small table had been placed on the main path between the graves, and behind it stood a man in a white coat. On top of the table were stacked packs of cigarettes and glasses with a brown liquid in them.

"All right, boys," the man said, "come over. Ten fags and a swig each. It's good stuff, too."

Like most boys in the class I still did not smoke or drink. There were not enough cigarettes for those who smoked as it was; the ration was very small. I was glad that I would be able to bring some home for Father.

The boys began to drink. Their cheeks reddened and they started singing raucously. I drank mine too, to avoid ridicule. And I was curious to find out how it tasted. The first sip burned my lips. I was about to spit it out, but Slavek called out to me:

"You've got to gulp it down all at once."

I felt as if I had swallowed a nail. But the pain quickly passed and all that was left was a pleasant warmth and a strange feeling of lightness. I joined in the singing. Funny how my voice appeared to come from a great distance. Rob was saying something. He had to repeat it three times before he got it out properly and before I understood him. He wanted to leave because he didn't like the look of the whole business. I tried to reply but instead could only hear myself singing.

Suddenly we were all marching in twos. We marched up to a chapel, or perhaps it was a synagogue. Under the stone steps a lot of funny-looking boxes had been piled up. The man from the Kuratorium mounted the steps and started speaking in a very loud voice.

"*Kameraden*, inside this building some remains have been temporarily deposited, the victims of the barbarous air raid carried out by the Anglo-American pirates on 14 February. It is our task to transfer them into these coffins so that they may be laid to rest in a dignified manner. I hope you're men and not a load of old women! Anyway, it would be worse if it were summer. Let's show you how. You and you, pick up a coffin and come with me!"

Robert and I stepped out of line, the others gazing at us as if they were seeing us for the first time. I felt my head swim, a humming noise inside it. The box was made of thin planks and was not heavy. We entered the building. The stench almost knocked me over. Rows of bodies were along the walls, I could not tell how many, perhaps several hundred.

"Put the coffin down! Now lift the lid off. Take this one. One on each side, get hold of the corners of the sack; that's it, lift, carry it over here, one, two, go!"

A girl was lying on top of the sack. She had only a skirt on, and tied to her leg was a piece of cardboard inscribed HANA KORUNOVA, 19.

This was the first time I had seen a naked woman. Female breasts. They were quite unlike anything I had imagined, monstrously large and disgustingly yellow.

The next thing I remember is my first cigarette and the grave on top of which I sat, vomiting, while my schoolfellows retched all around me. And then the siren, which started wailing just at noon, as it had on 14 February.

We fled from the cemetery, crazy with fear. There was a single house in the vicinity and we all crammed inside, together with old ladies, pensioners, and children. The man from the Kuratorium showed up and started roaring:

"It's only a warning, you damn cowards! Back you come, this minute!"

No one moved, so he started tugging at the boys nearest to him. One of the old ladies said:

"You ought to be ashamed! They're only children."

"Boys their age fighting at the front in Germany," he retorted. "Fall in, *Kameraden!*"

Suddenly one of the pensioners put out his hand and caught him by the chin.

"Let's get a good look at you, so I'll remember your face."

The *Kamerad* hung his head and slouched away. Who, I wondered, was more afraid—they or we?

When the All Clear went we took the first tram home. We couldn't have cared less about anything. I did not even get off to go and see A——. I could not have touched her, not today.

Now it's evening and I'm writing this in bed. Mother found that I was running a temperature. I did not tell her anything. Why should she have to worry about two of us?

My friend Peter had just left, he had been home on leave. His seventh form was digging antitank trenches near Ostrava. He told me how two boys from another school had got themselves shot one night when they went to the latrines with a flashlight. Peter was very thin and completely changed. I told him what we were rehearsing in our drama group, but he didn't listen. He borrowed my *Cyrano*.

When would we be called up?

Father told me the latest news. The Russian tank divisions are continuing their offensive. All quiet on the Western front. I am alone again and I feel like crying. Nothing but death—death everywhere. Why can't they make faster progress? And why did that nineteen-year-old girl have to die? What if someone loved her as I loved A____? How many more of us will die? Will I be one of them?

What is the meaning of a life that could end so senselessly? And is there anything after life? Does God exist? The dead are like nothing else! What if Peter is right and there is *nothing* after death. I am scared. Scared for A____'s sake, for my parents, for myself. If we die, we will probably never meet again. Except maybe in that chapel. In that horrible chapel.

Our Father, which art in Heaven, hallowed be Thy name, Thy kingdom come, Thy will be done on earth as it is in Heaven, deliver us from those who sow death from the skies and bring quickly those who are coming on land, bless their tanks, oh Lord, and let the star of the East, like that of Bethlehem, illuminate our darkness, Amen.

◨

21 January 1968   /   Prague
(From the diary of the writer PK)

Prague Castle shimmers in the winter sun outside my window, the crowds out for a Sunday walk file through the Matthias Gate, it is a sin to sit cooped up at home, I am hungry as a bear, but I cannot tear my eyes away from my reading.

Two thousand mimeographed pages: the protocol of the December and January plenum of the Communist Party Central Committee, and I have to return it today.

I do not know what to make of it. It falls so far short of what was needed, yet it so greatly exceeds anything that could have been expected, particularly of them.

Are they really aware of what they are doing? Or am I again crediting them with something that did not ever occur to them?

Reading their words like this, you realize that almost every single one without exception was forced by an unexpected situation to reveal, for the first time in so many years, their true intellectual qualities, and you became painfully aware of the catastrophic consequences of the Stalinist model of the Party.

In this country where sixteen-year-old boys know how to repair car engines and your cleaning lady will discuss with you the situation in the Middle East, a good half of them would not be capable of so much as driving a tram.

The other half, in touching solidarity with the first, had only four months ago banned the Writers Union's literary weekly Literární noviny as a reprisal for the writers congress last June, and had expelled from the Party three honest, educated Communists.

With this other half, or rather through it, through these meritorious apparatchiks, a man had ruled this country for twelve long years, a man who could boast that he was absolutely average in every human endeavor.

His annual improvisation at the conclusion of the May Day parade, transmitted to the remotest villages by radio, is a cherished item in anyone's collection of tape recordings. I too have often amused myself by playing over that enthusiastic voice, hurling its famous message from the reviewing stand into the crowd!

"There'll be meat in the shops, comrades housewives, have no fear!"

I go through my papers to find the record of his discussion with Czech and Slovak writers in the offices of the Central Committee on 24 January 1963. Here are a few pearls of a statesman's wisdom, five years old almost to the day.

"Literární noviny is meddling in affairs for which it has no qualifications—such as economics and politics—instead of playing a decisive role in the struggle against decadent ideology in the arts, which is what the Party expected when it gave permission to publish."

He went on to prove his own qualifications to be the head of the state and the Party by the following statements:

"We were capable of fulfilling all the planned tasks for 1962 and starting out toward 1970, but then winter came."

"We have boldly decided to increase agricultural production by a full six and a half per cent—even if we fail to fulfill it!"

"We planned one butcher's shop per 800 consumers, but now that there are 3500 consumers, they stand in queues and people have the impression that there is a shortage of meat!"

Knowing that before making any decision members of the Cabinet must consult the appropriate official at the Central Committee and that all personnel changes are carried out by Antonin Novotny himself, that his sharp wits are directed at every single problem of national life, anyone might find it quite fantastic to read that he complains:

"You may well say, Why did you permit this harmful decentralization, decline of public services, bad management, why did you not do something about it when you saw that the government did not govern, since you were co-responsible? Well, we did try, Comrades, only the government did not listen to us. Some of its members couldn't even cope physically; the Prime Minister, for instance, can't climb stairs, he can't even sit!"

His face is that of an honest genius constantly betrayed by his unworthy collaborators.

"I'm no rebel, no Yugoslav, God forbid, but tell me, what harm would it have done us to have left cigarette stands and small shops in private hands?"

And those who would perhaps be inclined to believe stories about the large number of secret bodyguards who follow him around can listen to this tale, reminiscent of the old legends of the good King Wenceslas:

"There we were, my wife and I, just before Christmas, walking around Prague, and we looked inside a shop and what do I see: young people trying to buy a watch, watches being on sale. Not a single watch to be had anywhere in Prague, they told me. And so I gave orders for watches to be sent immediately from Bratislava."

What ingenuousness is needed to say this in front of our Slovak colleagues and not bat an eyelid. But there is more to come.

"When we let the bourgeois nationalists out of jail on an amnesty I said at once that there would be a second phase. And here it is already. Husak is asking for a retrial and we have eight resolutions from Slovakia which don't even try to formulate things differently from him. I offered Husak the post of Deputy Finance Minister. I'm no greenhorn in politics; I knew he would turn it down. And then I said, 'That's enough! This has got to stop! We won't let anybody confuse the issue. Once and for all we'll write off the past and mount an attack.' You should have seen how the Central Committee applauded!"

The last few pages of my notes are supplemented by doodles which testify to my growing mental collapse. A small detail, but a very characteristic one: though our meeting with him took seven hours, never once did it occur to him that anyone might want something to eat or drink.

And yet this man had secured without a struggle the top positions in both Party and State, had become Commander-in-Chief of the Army and the security forces, made official appointments, suspended legal proceedings against those guilty of judicial murders in the fifties, named members of Parliament, banned films, his will automatically becoming law.

He was the first Czechoslovak President who not only did not leave behind him volumes of his writings but also not so much as one remarkable thought or deed. Even his most devoted followers, when asked to state his contribution to history, would remind you that according to some Western magazine he had tied with John F. Kennedy as the best-looking statesman in the world.

What is the explanation?

With a past devoid of anything that might have placed him among the acknowledged popular leaders, Antonin Novotny was born like Venus out of the political foam of the fifties because, in the eyes of the rival, mutually suspicious authors of the political trials, he was the only one whom they did not credit with the ability to think for himself. And moreover he was sufficiently implicated in those trials to ensure that he would not one day use them against the others.

If he in the end became a ruler in spite of all this, it was with their consent because he deliberately relied for support on all the compromised and incompetent people in the State and Party apparatus, their only virtue being devotion. His occasional angry outbursts against particularly grave offenders did not spark off any revolts because they never endangered the 'Closed System.' And apart from this, it soon became evident that by his own unquestioning obedience Novotny had gained the absolute confidence of Czechoslovakia's Great Ally, who was able in all matters to deal directly with him.

Thus in the course of the years a patriarchal regime was created in what once used to be a modern European country. Just as Charles IV for similar reasons was known to his subjects as Father of the Country, Antonin Novotny was soon nicknamed Daddy, which in any event was the way his wife chose to address him even at official receptions.

And now this Central Committee, which he had once upon a time chosen personally with only a few necessary concessions to public opinion, this selfsame Central Committee deprived the omnipotent impotent of the more important of his two functions and heralded the introduction of what it boldly called A Process of Reform.

What was all this? A mistake? A trick? Just another slogan to camouflage a palace revolution?

Would it not be fitting to repeat the question put to the Central Committee by one of its members, Frantisek Vodslon—the question which in fact started the argument immediately after the acrobatic performance of Antonin Novotny in his opening speech as he tried for the last time to conjure up the illusion that the situation was quite normal and there was nothing to get excited about? Would it not be fitting to repeat this question:

"Comrades, who do you think we are?"

It must be admitted, though, that among all the blabber and bickering recorded in the protocol several speeches stand out in sharp contrast, the speeches of Dubcek, Smrkovsky, Slavik, Minac, Fierlinger, Indra, Bilak, and above all that of Sik, who managed to strike at the very root of the crisis. According to them the rescue operation which is to be mounted can be described in the following four terms:

Federalization, rehabilitation, democratization, and a new economic model.

Yes, but how do they intend to achieve all this when Sik alone went so far as to say that the Party and the country in general is in a state of crisis, which most of the others had tried very hard to stop him from saying?

By what miracle do they mean to achieve all this, when they were unable to get it into their resolution, when they permitted all the obligatory lying phrases to be used in the press release on this crucial meeting, including the compulsory gaffe about "complete unanimity and solidarity"? How do they mean to gain the confidence and support of an apathetic and utterly distrustful nation, when they fail to indicate what they are really after even by the wink of an eye? Or do they perhaps once again intend to fight it all out by themselves?

Dear God, shall we in Czechoslovakia ever find a politician enlightened enough to understand, on the basis of the country's past history, that these strange people will sacrifice the last shirt from their backs to the man who stands up and tells them the bitter, unadorned truth?

P.S. Is it possible that such a man has been found? To my great astonishment I have just come across, in today's *Prace*, Josef Smrkovsky's editorial "What Is at Stake Today?" In it he, as the first in the land, goes far beyond the resolution:

"This is by no means a merely personal matter, it interests and vitally concerns every single Communist and every citizen. The change in the person of the President is only a first step. We intend to act in such a way that there should be no discrepancy between our words and our actions. And we intend to be realistic about it. Not to make promises we cannot keep. To tell the nation the truth, whether it happens to be pleasant or not. And together with the nation to seek a solution. We intend to put right the distortion of socialism which took place in the past and to see to it that no such thing can happen again."

Well, if this really is a chance for us, then Marx have mercy on our souls, for it will most probably be the last!

I'm writing to you at the end of the day which has given me every-thing I've ever desired:

Freedom and you!

I'm sitting by the side of your bed and watching you sleep, lost in your father's pajamas. Not even the sound of gunfire wakes you. You sleep like a hedgehog, protected by the spikes of the barri-cades. And I am one of them.

It seems like several years but it was only this morning that my mother woke me with the wonderful news:

"They're speaking nothing but Czech on the radio today!"

She knew that our school recital society was to broadcast this morning.

"You shouldn't go. What if it starts?"

"But they gave me time off from school," I protested. "What would the others say?"

Fortunately Father was sensible about it.

"Well, the boy's almost seventeen. I suppose he knows what he's doing."

I found Peter waiting for me outside Studio 6, together with Robert and Slavek. He had run away from the trenches which he had been sent to dig. We exchanged news. The Russians in Brno, the Americans in Cheb. We argued whether Prague ought to rebel. Rob thought that it was a pity to spill blood needlessly. Peter, Slavek, and I opposed him. We had lived too long on our knees. Freedom cannot be accepted as a gift; a nation must fight for it if it is to deserve it. Then Rob said something that infuriated us.

"It must first of all survive if it is to be worthy of freedom."

"They can't kill all of us," I said, "and those of us who do sur-vive will be all the stronger for that blood. Surely a nation must not shrink from defending the truth."

A German patrol came toward us along the corridor. Two boys only slightly older than we, wearing overcoats and helmets that were much too large for them. For years the guards at the Radio had been two elderly Austrians, and it was said that they had promised to surrender if we let them go home once it was all over. Now they had been replaced.

The two soldiers stopped, one beside us, the other a little farther away.

"*Ausweis!*"

We showed them our passes—which stated, in German, that we were members of the school broadcasting group.

"*Wo ist hier des Ansageraum?*"

"We don't know," said Peter in Czech.

"*Scheisse!*" muttered the first soldier, glancing at us distrustfully. Then he shifted his gun threateningly, pushed Rob out of the way, and the two of them went on. Simultaneously we jumped them from behind.

What a pity that it was only in our imagination! We might have been the first!

But then I heard the clatter of your heels and forgot everything but you. You told us that your parents were out of town at a funeral and that you would like to go to the movies in the evening. We all agreed to meet at six and I felt sorry that we would not be going alone. Who could have known what fate had in store for us? Cruel fate? Glorious fate.

The broadcast was over by ten. Slavek played Icarus, the rest of us the chorus as usual. I don't envy him. I have you.

The corridors were full of station technicians with screwdrivers in their hands. They removed all the German inscriptions and we helped them. It was a joyous sort of rebellion and no one anticipated how useful it would soon turn out to be.

After we saw you home we caught a tram. The conductor told a German flyer that he did not take German money any longer. As the airman had no Czech crowns he had to get out and walk. The conductor shouted after him:

"Czechs can travel for free!"

We started to sing and all the passengers joined in. Everywhere shopkeepers were climbing stepladders and scratching out the German inscriptions over their windows.

When I got off Rob shouted after me:

"See you at six, then!"

A streetcar inspector was standing on the platform with a bottle in his hand.

"At six o'clock after the war!" he cried. "At six in the free Republic!"

The Germans seemed to have blown away. In Adolf Hitler Square, the German street names were disappearing from the houses. A large crowd marched toward the General Staff building, carrying a huge flag, once more complete with the blue Slovak triangle. They were singing the national anthem. I thought of a night in September 1938—I was ten and was holding my father's hand as a one-eyed general announced the results of Munich. That was the first time I saw Father cry. Then, too, people sang the national anthem. How many deaths and how many tears had come between those two anthems!

There was nobody at home. I switched on the radio. After six years they were again playing Sokol marches. Overjoyed, I placed the radio on the window sill and turned its volume full. Everyone else must have had the same idea, for in a few moments the houses in our street were shaking on their foundations. People waved to each other and hung rows of red-white-and-blue flags out of their windows. Then suddenly the spirited march stopped, shots, and an anxious voice:

"Calling the Czech police and the Czech Army. Come and help us in the Radio building! The Germans are slaughtering our people!"

I just had time to scribble DON'T WORRY, I'LL BE ALL RIGHT! on a piece of paper and then, for the second time this year, I ran as fast as I could to your neighborhood. The crowds were gone, trams had stopped. Shopkeepers were pulling the shutters down. A truck full of armed men drove past us. They were in civilian clothes and wore German helmets. A Czechoslovak officer was standing on the running board. I had not seen that uniform for six years. It was too small for him and he had it unbuttoned. I waved but they didn't stop.

The Germans were shelling Wenceslas Square, and it was impossible to get through by the viaduct. In the end I slipped across the tracks at the station.

In the Radio building it was almost all over. The dead had been laid in the passageway of a house across the way, their faces covered with flags.

The Germans had started to shoot when they failed to find the studio from which the Czech announcer was broadcasting. They did not find it because we all had removed the inscriptions that morning. Our people invaded the building by crossing the roofs of adjoining houses. And there had been a bitter fight for each story. The remnants of the garrison had retreated to the cellar, where firemen were even now flooding them out with water. This was a trick the Germans themselves had taught us—that was how they had got the parachutists who had assassinated Heydrich and had hidden in the Karel Boromejsky church.

One of those who had supplied the parachutists with food—I can say this now, and you are the first to hear—was my father, who was a friend of the priest Petrek.

There was an acrid smell of gunpowder in the building. Downstairs in the entrance hall, more bodies. I have seen far too many dead bodies for my age. Yet no matter how many I see, I shall never get used to the sight. In one corner a row of our dead, in the other the Germans. They were lying there like so many gray-green planks. A row of black boots, a row of heads. I recalled those two young soldiers. They might have been sixth formers like myself. I imagined them lying there in that row and felt a shiver run down my spine. But no pity. No, not that.

When Father Petrek visited us for the last time, a day before the assassination, he and Father talked about German guilt and punishment.

"After the war, when I meet a German in the street, I'll say to him, 'Out of my way, German, a human being wants to pass.'"

This slim, ascetic priest and scholar, who always reminded me of Jesus, daily lifted the concrete slab over the crypt in order to bring the hunted men food and to take out their excrement . . . yes, deeds such as this are also part of heroism. Like Jesus he was betrayed, tortured, and killed, without yielding. It was for his sake that I now struggled against pity. And for the sake of an uncle of mine who had been shot by the Germans. And for my favorite poet, the executed Vladislav Vancura, and the dead of the concentration camps. And also for our six years of despair, yours and mine.

The hall shook with explosions as hand grenades went off in the cellar. I tried to find someone who would give me a gun, but weapons were scarce and handed only to men who had done their military service. At last I ran into Mr. Karel.

"All right," he whispered, "since it's you. Come with me."

He has liked me ever since I brought him an old coachman's lantern for his collection. He led me to the props room, where German helmets, gas masks, belts, forage caps, and shoulder patches were piled in a heap on the floor. "This would otherwise disappear," he said triumphantly. "We must think of the theater at this time."

I chose a helmet, belt, and bayonet; all of them are now lying on your bed. Armed with these I hurried to keep our date. The streets were again crowded. Barricades were going up. Outside our movie theater a group of men was just overturning a pair of streetcars, the first coach already on its side in a welter of broken glass. You were startled.

"Where's Robert? And the boys?"

"I guess they didn't get through. I only made it in the nick of time."

"I'm so scared for my parents. No trains are running. Prague has been completely cut off."

"But the Yanks are in Pilsen," I reassured her. "They'll be here by tomorrow!"

For the next three hours we were two links in a human chain lifting and passing the cobbles over which I had so often accompanied you home. I would never have believed how heavy a street can be. It began to rain. The water ran down your cheeks, your hands were scraped by the stones. But you didn't slacken. I want you to know that I was happy and very proud of you.

Then we walked to your house. Shots on all sides. Flares lit up the foggy sky on the other side of town.

"Where will you go?" you asked.

"I don't know."

I could feel the pounding of my heart. There was a silence, and then you said it:

"You can sleep in the kitchen."

I sat up, fully dressed, on a bed made of sofa cushions which we had laid on the floor between the stove and the kitchen table. I sat there and listened to the water running in the bathroom. Then you came in, your father's pajama pants trailing underneath your dressing-gown. You looked touchingly comic, like a clown. I told you so and you laughed. The new intimacy brought us together.

"Why aren't you asleep yet?" you asked.

I got up.

"Can I ask you a favor? Just let me sit next to you and hold your hand until you fall asleep. I swear that's all I want."

And so, for the second time in my life, I entered your room, in which we had kissed three months before. How different it looked at night, by the light of the bedside lamp, and how different you looked with your head on the pillow. I put down my helmet, belt, and bayonet, but the war remained with us. The radio now played that old Sokol march, like the signature tune of a nation at war. In between they broadcast appeals, in English and in Russian, to the Allied armies. And a warning that German tanks were approaching Prague from Benesov.

We held hands a long time. And then I went berserk.

"I have two loves, you and the Republic. I am with one of them now, and I shall be going shortly to the other. Since God has granted me this evening, let me put my hand on your heart, I swear to you on my life that I don't want anything more than the gift of warmth which I'll carry away in the palm of my hand . . ."

You lay quite motionless. I was desperate. There was nothing for it now but to get up and go. And then I heard your voice.

"Put the light out."

I obeyed, hot all over. I heard the soft rustle of cloth, your arms embraced me and pulled me down, your father's jacket melted away, and there was nothing but your skin. I put both my hands on your left breast, which was warm and alive. I pressed myself against you and thought I might faint.

"Have you ever had anybody?"

"No . . . and you?"

"Me neither. . . . Come on, then, let's have one another."

My heart seemed to stop. I opened my eyes. Very faintly I could make out the silhouette of the various objects in the room. Distant gunfire obliterated the patter of the rain outside.

"No. . ."

"Why not?"

"Because I promised.

"I want you to know why I swore I would not touch you. I know you. I know how long it was before you let me even hold your hand. I desire you, but I don't want you to give yourself to me on this night of separation and blood. That would be like a sacrifice. And I don't want a sacrifice, I want love. I want to love you in June, on a quiet meadow with the smell of hay in the air. It's for that June that we're now fighting. Wait for me and I'll be back from the fight, for I am invulnerable when my virgin warrior is waiting for me."

You kissed me.

"You're sweet."

And now you slept, curled up like a child. "Don't go, stay with me," you whispered just before you fell asleep.

But I had to go. I had promised, promised you and myself. And the one who was yet to come and must never be ashamed of his father. If necessary, I'd know how to kill. And if necessary, I firmly believed, I'd know how to die.

I hate a world in which I must say goodbye daily not knowing whether it isn't forever. But today this world is still here and wildly struggling. That is why I have taken your school copybook, that is why I'm writing you this letter. I pray that you may never receive it, for if you do it will be my testament. Tell my mother that I ask her to forgive me. And my father that I had the sense to know what I was doing, but also honor.

As for you, please go on living, for me as well as for yourself. And should you ever have a son with someone else, at least name him after me.

I kiss you, my wife.

I don't want to wake you. I'll get out through the window.

Wednesday, 21 August 1968 / Rome
(Continued)

I did not need a map to find the right road out of town. I never need maps when I'm going home, like a dog finding his own trail.

The film is running backward: Ocher Gubio in a treeless landscape like a sun-besieged fortress, the lightning flash of a hairpin bend between the pink palaces of Urbino, then farther north, between the Scylla of Rimini and the Charybdis of San Marino, through Ravenna, passing by the ugly stone rocket of Dante's tomb, through Ghiogia, beyond which the famous rotting wreck of Venice rides a shallow sea, toward the Dolomites, which come at you like the tide, the film runs faster, there is a stone ebb, Linz as the springboard for yet another leap into the mountains, Grossglockner with its garland of mist, Salzburg with the castle as its tiara, boring Linz as a curious, vague childhood memory, the landscape a premonition, the antechamber of home, the last hundred meters, the film stops.

At the border a tank squats in the middle of the roadway, staring at me with the Cyclops eye of its gun barrel. I press my horn and my accelerator simultaneously, and the Renault charges forward like a warhorse, attacking the huge lance which bars the way home.

The hand on the speedometer steadily points to a hundred and fifty. The arrow of the *autostrada* has been aiming south for the past hour. My left hand on the wheel, I turned the radio knob with my right, releasing a flood of scrambling Italian. Like some magic formula the word *Cecoslovacchia* was repeated ceaselessly. She sat next to me, still and silent. Then she suddenly leaned forward.

"Look, a Czech car in front!"

It was a Skoda with a Bratislava number. As soon as I passed it, I lowered my window and signaled them to stop. They overtook us at full speed and waved. Either they did not understand or they did not want to. I accelerated and, catching up with them, drove side by side, waving all the time. I saw them talking together, and then the driver at last applied his brakes. I stopped immediately behind them. The man who got out of the car was tall and gray-haired, his khaki trousers the sign that he was an Army officer.

"Anything I can do for you?" he asked in Slovak. "We're in a hurry, going all the way to Palermo."

She spoke before I could.

"We have been occupied."

His wife, too, burst into tears. Women have a terrifying instinct. Even this woman, who did not seem to be the crying type. She was tall and gray like her husband; I could imagine her also in uniform. He turned and spoke sharply to her.

"Don't be silly, dear! The Warsaw Pact will intervene immediately. We'll drive them out within twenty-four hours."

The spontaneous reaction of a man who had experienced Munich. You could tell that he was quite ready to turn his Skoda round and go charging the Germans in it as if it were a Hussite wagon. I handed him the paper. He looked at the arrow-studded map without a word. It was only then that I remembered that officers were not allowed to travel in the West.

"You are in the Army?"

I had to repeat the question before he understood.

"I was demobilized last week. . ."

"This is our first trip abroad in twenty years," said his wife in a low voice.

Foreign cars raced past us in a foreign landscape, their horns sounding snatches of gay melodies. Somewhere above our heads artificial satellites flew about in space, recording objects over a meter in size. I tried to imagine Europe as it must look when viewed through those fantastic telelenses. Hundreds of thousands of immobile figures stood in silence from the Black Sea to the Atlantic, from the Mediterranean to the Arctic Circle. Czechoslovaks thrown out of their courses. Our destinies had become linked and had stopped.

"Where are *you* going?" the man asked me uncertainly, like a little boy hopelessly lost.

Suddenly I knew.

"To our Embassy."

"I'll follow you," he said.

Clusters of sun rays, as in Baroque paintings, pierced the crowns of the cypresses in the Villa Borghese. The rows of chairs in outdoor cafés, turned to face the sidewalk, made them look like so many little theaters, the customers leafing through their newspapers as if they were programs. And everywhere the occupation of Czechoslovakia was being performed.

I confidently retraced my footsteps of twelve years ago, when I was in Rome to attend some congress organized by the World Youth Federation. In order to obtain Italian visas we had had to pretend we were sportsmen, and every morning we trotted round Roman parks to reassure the police.

You could recognize our Embassy from a distance. In spite of the No Parking signs, the Via Luisa di Savoia was full of parked Czechoslovak cars. In front of the Embassy building itself, chaos, tears, and anger. Italian *carabinieri* with round rural faces were trying to disperse a crowd of people in track suits and beachwear.

"Why don't you go inside?" I asked a sunburned young man

who, in his striped jersey, looked like a genuine native of Rome but who answered me in genuine Prague.

"They've locked themselves in, the pigs! I guess they're already wiping the dust off Novotny's portraits."

I went up to the door and rang the bell. It rang loud and clear. I left my finger on the button.

"È, signore, basta, basta!"

The officer was young and zealous. I looked down at him from the top of the staircase and pieced together the sorry fragments of my Italian.

"Io sono alla ambasciata!"

He saluted.

"Escusi, signore."

The pealing of the door bell filled the entire building. My countrymen outside watched my experiment, tense with expectation. It took five minutes for those inside to lose their nerve. The door was flung open and the oh-so-familiar, dear face of a Czech porter appeared, the sort of face you want to hit on sight. A representative of the powers-that-be, he was getting ready to add some of his own gall to their indignation. Before he could open his mouth, however, I began icily:

"May I remind you that this building has not yet been occupied. Tell your boss to admit the waiting Czechoslovak citizens at once. He still represents the Czechoslovak Republic. If he does not do as I ask, we'll demand his recall."

The Prague Spring was still in bloom. He went straight to the telephone and spoke to someone very high up, for he was speaking very deferentially, his eyes fixed on the ceiling.

But by this time I was no longer taking any notice, for, coming down the staircase opposite me—himself.

---

16 V 45 / Prague

Hundreds of thousands of people are cheering on the radio. After six years and seven months President Benes is returning to Prague. How I have looked forward to this day. And yet here I am, sitting at home, dejected and empty.

I have seen many dead. But all this was not really Death. Death is perceived only when someone dies whom we have known closely. With him dies not only his body but also countless encounters, thoughts, and dreams in which we ourselves are participants. The lives of people who are close to one another overlap. Death tears you away from all the other lives. That is why today for the first time I feel it so personally.

Cruel irony of fate! Why did it not happen to me?

Only the Wednesday before last he was sitting here with us. The four of us were supposed to be cramming for school, but instead we argued about the meaning of Czech history.

"It's time to realize," he said, "that not Jan Hus but Hieronymus of Prague was our real prophet. With all due respect, Hus was, after all, a heretic, who counted on being burned at the stake. A martyr's death became the cornerstone of his philosophy. But how many martyrs are born in this country in any one generation? Hieronymus, on the other hand, twice recanted before his judges so that he might be allowed to return and continue preaching. That seems to me far more purposeful."

"And yet he, too, was burned at the stake," I cried triumphantly.

"The example of born martyrs," he went on quietly, "convinces the weak multitude that it is futile to oppose brute force. The weak can only be roused by people like Hieronymus, who stipulate a sensible dividing line between weakness and conscience. In the decisive hours, Hieronymus refused to recant just as Hus had done before him, but he first gained time to develop his arguments. Hus gave the Bohemian reformation its banner, Hieronymus its brain."

"But which of the two became the Czech saint, which of them gave the nation the strength needed to survive both the Habsburgs and Hitler?"

"I admit there are times when the nation needs apostles more than anything else. Those who were tortured by the Gestapo in an effort to make them betray their resistance organizations had to cling to Hus. But a nation does not live permanently in a state of emergency. Its program is formed by those who think ahead and take practical steps to prepare its dinner. The Hussites simply over-estimated their possibilities. Instead of securing their victory politically, they decided to convert the whole of Europe to their faith. Their twenty-year-long permanent revolution exhausted the nation and created its own opposition. We have all been told in school that in the fratricidal battle of Lipany the faithful Hussite yeomen fought against the treacherous nobility. Hardly anyone knows, though, that it was also a struggle between generations, between a generation of fanatics and a generation of realists."

This infuriated us.

"You think that counterrevolutionaries are realists, then?"

"Why this demagogy?" he protested. "Why can't you look beneath the surface of words? According to the classical formula, the Chiliasts were the most revolutionary wing of the Hussite movement because they weren't content to have communion in both kinds but demanded absolute social equality as well. And what did the Hussites do? They massacred them. Were they therefore counterrevolutionaries? No, not at that time. The Chiliasts had advanced ahead of their time and their revolt threatened the unity of the revolution just when it was in greatest danger. But history moves on. Fifteen years later the revolutionary movement turns into a military dictatorship which leads the country to disaster. That is the reason why the Hussites had to leave the political scene and make way for the Czech Brethren. That is why a Hussite king appeared as a symbiosis of the old and the new. And Jirik of Podebrady not only consolidated the country, he also saved the reformation. By means of his diplomacy he won for a weakened Bohemia a political standing such as it had never gained by force of Hussite arms."

I almost shouted at him.

"Yes, but that wouldn't have been possible without the victories at Vitkov, Usti, and Domazlice! It was Zizka who taught Europe to respect the Czechs. Everybody knew that even after Lipany Zizka's spirit lived on in Bohemia, and that if need be the people would instantly take up arms again and fight."

I can still see his stern face, hear his thoughtful voice.

"Certainly, there are times when a nation needs a fighter like Zizka. I'm glad we had him, only Jirik of Podebrady knew how to look ahead; he saw what Europe would be like five centuries later. Sometimes it seems to me he even foresaw Munich. And how did Zizka help us then?"

"Do you mean to say you agree with capitulation?"

"No, not exactly . . . just that I don't see any alternative."

"To stand up and fight—that was the alternative. We had a fine army, frontier fortifications. It was our duty to fight."

He did not look convinced.

"Maybe. But if we had, we should most probably not be sitting here today, arguing about the future."

"I see, so according to you we should let ourselves be occupied every twenty years or so and then wait for someone to come and liberate us? Where, then, is the meaning of our national existence, what have we done to deserve it?"

"I can't help thinking that there is nothing left of Zizka's militant legacy in an age of devastating air raids and Panzer engagements. Yet you will find the legacy of Comenius in every schoolbook in the world."

I am trying to record what I remember of his thoughts. That is the only thing I can do to prevent him from leaving us completely and irretrievably.

Our friendship with him was, when you think of it, just one long argument. He would argue about everything, casting doubt even on his own ideas. He used to say that even the profoundest truth loses its currency by the evening and has to be proved once again in the morning. Frequently—just as that last time—we were firmly convinced that he was wrong, yet we invariably lacked arguments to prove him so. He was terribly well-read; he'd gone through more books than the three of us put together.

Yet when he was put to the test he refuted his own words with an irrevocable deed. I still cannot understand it.

I'm sitting in my room, happy and miserable at one and the same time. Outside in the street there is wild jubilation. For a week I felt sick at the memory of all the "heroes" who came crawling out of the safety of their cellars to let themselves be photographed on the battered barricades. Today, in the sharp light of Rob's sacrifice, I'm beginning to think that I am one of them.

What did I do to help the liberation? I was helping to move our broadcasting equipment to the Hus Chapel when a bomb crashed through all the floors of Radio House and exploded in the entrance hall. Then for three days I acted as an ordinary courier, carrying messages which may well have been of little use. The only really creditable thing I did was that I refrained from taking time off to visit A——, fearing that she would suspect me of weakness. And the only exceptional occurrence of those momentous days merely serves to make me feel ashamed.

On Tuesday night I took a message to the technicians working at the Strasnice transmitter station. The journey used to take ten minutes by tram. On foot over the barricades it took me three hours. As soon as I got there we received a report that the road back to town had been cut by German tanks. We heard gunfire. I had to stay.

The men who were due to go on night shift were sitting in the chief technician's office, twiddling the knobs of the wireless instead of sleeping. On every wavelength cathedral bells could be heard pealing to celebrate V-Day. Yet we were in the midst of war. Schorner's army was trying to take Prague in order to turn it into the last German fortress. The aerial above our heads sent out nothing but depressing news. In the suburbs of Prague the Germans were setting fire to apartment blocks with the inhabitants inside. At one of the main railway stations they lined up the railwaymen and passengers stranded there by the outbreak of the rising last Saturday, counted them off, and shot every tenth person right there on the spot. And now they were coming for us.

I lay on a camp bed, unable to sleep. I heard midnight chime and made up my mind. I got up, went outside, and told the man in charge of the guard:

"An urgent message for the Hus Chapel."

I ran through the streets, across the deserted barricades. Her window was open and I climbed in. She woke immediately. Everything was the same as last time down to the last detail, even her words:

"Come on, then ... let's ..."

This time I did not leave. I stripped off my clothing and, holding her close to me, penetrated her exultantly. A hot pain stabbed within me. It lasted only a short moment, then I felt myself falling into unfamiliar depths....

A tremendous din woke me. Her father ran into the room and brutally squeezed my shoulder.

"Get up, quick!"

One of the technicians was bending over the camp bed.

"The Germans are here!"

Slowly I came to, conscious of a wet warmth on my thighs. I have promised myself to be absolutely frank in writing this diary, to be sure that when time changes the present into a legend I may find my true image in it.

This, then, was how I spent the last minutes of the war: bayonet in hand, I crouched under a window behind which I could hear the rumble of approaching tanks. Someone somewhere was praying. I was incapable of thought. All I was aware of were my trousers, sticking to my thighs, and my humiliating fear that I would die an embarrassing and futile death.

The menacing silhouette of the first tank loomed suddenly out of the darkness.

This was it. Now I could write The End to my glorious life. . . .

And then someone down in the yard yelled to us:

"The Russians!"

What followed is a kaleidoscope of impressions. My triumphal ride on a tank, with the barricades quickly dismantled to make way for us. Me ringing the bell on the door of our house and my mother's tears as she scolded me and rejoiced at the same time. A stroll with Father through the city, in which unending columns of tanks had replaced the familiar streetcars. The defeated masters of Europe escorted in large numbers by a young soldier playing a mouth organ. And the victors, making up for a thousand nights of war, curled up on the steps of the National Museum like pigeons. Collaborators with the swastika painted on their backs, removing the debris. And a dead Gestapo man, burned alive and slung up from a lamp post by a leg. The sight turned my stomach.

"Is this justice?" I asked Father.

"No, that's barbarousness. Those who did it are no better than he was."

I say goodbye to Father. I pluck some lilacs in a park and run to A____'s house. I throw the bouquet up into her window. She appears. No, she is sorry but she cannot come with me because her parents have just arrived. I did not object, but I waited for at least a word that will confirm what has passed between us some nights before.

"Come by again, won't you?"

I am disappointed, but at once curse myself for being a fool. Did I expect her to tell the whole street that she loved me? I simply have to wait.

Again I crossed Prague on foot. People were dancing in Wenceslas Square. Under the Charles Bridge, Cossacks water their horses. On the grass plot in front of the Rudolfinum a Soviet soldier is being buried. A girl in uniform holds his head in her lap and weeps in long drawn-out tones. It sounds almost like singing. A song of love and grief. Standing around her in a semicircle are unshaven soldiers with automatics, and they too weep. An island of woe in a sea of joy. I cannot look on.

Then I meet a convoy of Army trucks. Sitting on benches along the sides are Red Cross nurses, holding curious creatures round the shoulders. Toothless mouths try to smile under clean-shaven skulls. It takes some time before I realize that these beings who looked anything but human are actually women. Concentration camp prisoners returning home.

WE MUST MAKE SURE NOTHING LIKE THIS HAPPENS AGAIN!

I stopped at Peter's house. He, too, had come home not long ago and was now fast asleep. I did not wish to wake him, and so I went on to Robert's. There I found only his terrified mother. Like the rest of us, Rob had left home at lunchtime on Saturday. Only he had not yet returned.

I got the others and we started to search for him.

It was not until the day before yesterday that Slavek found him, in the Sokol gymnasium at Pankrac, which had been converted into a huge morgue. Robert was wearing an Afrika Korps uniform with a Revolutionary Guard armband. He had stayed on his barricade to the end, until a hand grenade tore away a piece of his skull.

He had waited there for us in the heat of May for six days.

His mother collapsed when she heard the news. We tried to arrange a funeral, but there were so many dead that the gravediggers were dropping with fatigue, and we borrowed some spades from the Civil Defense people and this morning dug the grave ourselves at Olsany, Peter, Slavek, and I. We found a coffin in a German Army store. We buried him and over his grave we sang the national anthem. A_____ stood opposite me in a borrowed black dress. She looked beautiful.

Even at this moment, I felt tempted to go and kiss her. . . .

Forgive me, Rob. The fate that I had feared so much for myself has been yours. We recognized that you left us. You, who more than any of us had clung to life, had volunteered to fight and had died a martyr's death.

I feel deeply ashamed.

President Benes is speaking in Old Town Square about the country's future. A future that no longer concerns you, although you more than any of us have deserved it.

Goodbye, Robert.

I PICK UP YOUR GAUNTLET AND SHALL CARRY IT AS MY BANNER.

□

Wednesday, 21 August, 1968 / Rome
(Continued)

He   This is the third and most terrible shock of my life.
I   Which were the two previous ones?
He   Stalin's death and Khrushchev's speech at the Twentieth Congress. The first meant the end of a myth, the second the loss of a certainty.
I   And what have you lost today?
He   I don't know. I don't dare to name it.
I   Are your parents still alive?

He stopped turning his glass in his fingers, which had made the ice clink rhythmically. He nodded, obviously at a loss to understand this digression. I went on:

You're older than I, but, unluckily, I am more adult than you. I distinctly remember March 1953 and the spring of 1956. I, too, was sure the world had collapsed about my ears. But I buried my parents shortly afterward, both of them. And only then did I begin to see life in proper perspective.

He   You're trying to reconcile the irreconcilable. I am forty like you, I have been through the mill. A divorce ... why drag that into it. It's not that I underestimate the human aspect of life—but ours is a kind of special generation. Politics have become an inseparable part of our lives, and political catastrophes affect us no less than personal tragedies, per-

39

haps more. Just think of all those suicides this last spring. They were people older than we, people who had been in concentration camps; they, too, must have had their private sorrows. And yet it was the collapse of a political concept that toppled their equilibrium.

I   You are putting forward the gravest argument against us. Unless you are thinking of honorable men who slammed the door behind them because they were unable to bear the responsibility for having destroyed the equilibrium of others.

He   Are we guilty just because we strove to do things for others and not only for ourselves?

I   We elected Communism as a weapon against Hunger, which had sat at our table ever since our childhood, and against Death, which went even to school with us after the assassination of Heydrich. We elected Communism as a cure for fear. As the highest form of economic and spiritual freedom. In short, we elected it in the name of life. However naïve, however emotional, however dogmatic we may have been, even though we were quite sincerely prepared to make every conceivable sacrifice for the sake of world revolution—under all that abstraction there remained concrete human desires. To create, to love, and trite as it may sound, to live in happiness. Doesn't it seem absurd to you that we almost managed to deny the most fundamental human values?

He   Oh, nonsense! We didn't deny anything. We only misjudged the international effect of our revolution, that's all. We thought that a world shocked by the horrors of Fascism would immediately take appropriate steps, as Czechoslovakia did in the first postwar elections. We believed that it was a question of a few years. We underestimated the ability of imperialism to survive. And in our own Party we underestimated the human element. We were pure and expected everyone else to be like us. How could we foresee that the leaders of our revolution would turn the class struggle into an inquisition?

I   Yes, that's what it is all about.

He   If you're thinking of the Moscow trials, then at the time the overwhelming majority of European Communists was taken in by them, and with good reason. Moreover, the traditions of our Party were deeply democratic.

It was still early and atmospheric interference made it impossible to get Prague on the radio. We therefore waited for the news on the Italian TV in a room which even here, in the heart of the Eternal City, all too plainly showed by its impersonal character that it was a Czech official's residence. It too gave evidence of our decline. The country famous throughout the world for its china and cut glass supplied its diplomatic representatives with chain-store crockery. I went on:

> I'm not concerned with individual details but with the substance of the problem. We chose Marxism because it offered us a scientific approach to nature and society. How can we shrug off our responsibility by pleading that we believed something, overestimated or underestimated this and that? If a surgeon is to operate he must be absolutely certain both of the diagnosis and of his own skill and possibilities. Otherwise he is committing a crime. And for Marxists who aim to carry out an operation on society this is doubly true.

He   Are you trying to say that we were criminals?

I   I am trying to say that we weren't Marxists, and that if we are ever to be punished, then first and foremost for our crimes against Marxism. We behaved like quacks pretending to be experienced surgeons. It is possible to find extenuating circumstances in our good intentions, but one thing we cannot do and that is plead not guilty. We subjugated objective laws to our pious wishes, permitting the substitution of an unscientific ideology for revolutionary scientific thought. That is how it came about that even this most pure, just revolution of all devoured its own children.

He   Well, I unfortunately am no poet...

I   But you used to be! For God's sake, stop talking like a Party official all the time!

He   I *am* a Party official, even though at the moment in something like exile. You see, somebody had to do the job. But perhaps we can leave that for some other time.

It was obvious that he did not wish to speak about it in front of her. She was sipping her Campari, the ice quickly melting in the glass. It was impossible to tell whether she was listening to us. Just as well if she wasn't, I thought. While on the one hand her exaggerated anti-Communism forced me to defend my fundamental beliefs, I found myself, when debating with other Communists in front of her in the grotesque position of someone who was arguing along her lines. I recalled a Prague psychiatric clinic whose inmates include former concentration-camp prisoners as well as wartime collaborators, victims of the political trials of the fifties as well as some of their interrogators. It occurred to me that my generation would provide a large new contingent of schizophrenics for this institution.

He A revolution, scientific or not, is above all a revolution. A conflict between concrete reality and an ideal concept. This concept can be brought to life only by people who have been marked by that reality. A revolution may be planned by a scientist or a saint but it has to be carried out by millions of miserable sinners.

I It's good to hear that not even twenty years of Party political work has cured you of purple prose.

Just as in the past, he was intent on his train of thought and would not be deflected from it:

Perhaps you and I can still agree that capitalism has fulfilled its historical mission and has come to the end of the road.

I Why perhaps? Of course we can.

He Good. It took over from the colonizers, replacing medieval methods of exploitation by modern ones, war still remaining the answer to its recurrent crises. But the capitalists had learned one lesson, that brutal force only helped to bring nearer the end of capitalism. That is why *they* had to devour their own child—Hitler. And that is why defeated Germany became a show window of goods and freedoms aimed at the hungry victors. We knew that it was a shabby trick. But did everyone know this? Ignorance and fatigue are also political factors. They help to smother class consciousness, they breed premature liberalism and even anarchy, bourgeois sentiments against which the proletariat is not immune because it does not live outside time and space. The work of the leading revolutionaries is all the harder because they have to accept responsibility for those who have not understood . . .

I   And sometimes even against them . . .

He   Yes, because it's in their true interest, if they only knew it. What right had we to give up our truth for a full stomach and the fiction of democracy? Could we risk a new version of the prewar Republic, with its unemployment, shooting at demonstrating workers, and Munich? Could we, in the name of a relatively higher standard of living and relatively democratic traditions, betray the newly created community of East European nations which had started out on the road to socialism straight from a feudal or even a Fascist past? After all, the fact that such an industrially and culturally advanced country as Czechoslovakia had so spontaneously joined in the revolution was of supreme importance for the whole of Europe. The West was not slow to see this. They paralyzed us with embargos and surrounded us with propaganda, declaring a cold war that turned out to be more than hot enough, as it included subversion, sabotage, and the brutal assassination of rank-and-file Communists. Or have you forgotten the dead men in the schoolhouse at Babice? It was the West which forced us to drop the Iron Curtain. That was our only chance of gaining the necessary time for what we had to do. And if all this helped to create a climate in which vigilance grew into suspicion and class justice sometimes became unlawful persecution, that is certainly a tragedy but we can hardly be blamed for it. As long as a revolution has to defend its very existence it invariably contains a latent conflict between conscience and necessity. Just think of Rolland's *Wolves.* I am of course all in favor of punishing those who staged the mock trials or abused power for their own selfish ends. But I refuse to join in the fashionable craze for flagellation which in this world of Vietnams and Biafras seeks to put hundreds of thousands of honest Communists on trial. I can regret my mistakes, I'm ready to pay for them, but I have nothing to be ashamed of!

I realized how little he had changed. Despite the gray hair and sharper features he looked just as he did twenty-three years ago. And he still conducted monologues, though in a quieter fashion, without gesticulating, as if he were merely thinking aloud.

I saw that she, too, was watching him. With interest rather than with the disapproval I would have expected. He must still be quite a ladies' man. I became conscious of an old aggravation.

"Isn't it difficult to live alone in this city, of all places?" I asked him. "Or has the Party turned you into a monk?"

This took him by surprise. But then, for the first time, he laughed, almost boyishly.

"It *will* be difficult from now on, when I see that there are, after all, beautiful women who don't mind listening to this kind of talk."

"Isn't it time for the news?" she asked brusquely.

As if she were afraid I might tell him the truth about her. Yet a look at the clock confirmed that it really was seven. The Italian newscaster was reading the TASS communiqué, which he translated for us.

"Party and State officials of the Czechoslovak Socialist Republic turned to the Soviet Union and the other allied countries with an urgent appeal for military aid against the counterrevolutionaries."

Then the statement by the presidium of the Communist Party of Czechoslovakia:

"The invasion took place without the knowledge of the President of the Republic, the Party presidium, the government, and the National Assembly. It is an act in direct contravention not only of the basic norms of international law but also of the principles governing the relations between socialist countries."

Now we saw pictures from Prague. A film taken from a car. Driving up Wenceslas Square, a slalom among the crowds of people and the tanks. What does it all remind me of? I want to slow down, but the brakes fail me. The familiar façade of the National Museum is speckled with white. What is this—a bad quality in the picture? The building vanishes to the right. I feel helpless as a horse with blinkers, forced to look straight ahead. He goes on translating:

"The National Museum became the target of a short, concentrated burst of fire."

She cries out, horrified. "Why?"

But I know why. These shots were fired prematurely. They were meant for a different target. We are now approaching it, traveling up Vinohrady Avenue behind the Museum. The street had been given back its innocent original name after having served as a temporary relic of three regimes—Foch Avenue, Schwerin Avenue, Stalin Avenue. Or the Street of Three Marshals, as the inhabitants of Prague called it. Now five others had left their visiting cards here in one brief fusillade.

An overturned bus with shattered windows, a lonely, futile barricade. A tank was on fire in front of the well-known building with the inscription CZECHOSLOVAK RADIO over the door. And in the passage of a house across the street there were lifeless bodies covered with a flag.

Again! In God's name, how was it possible for history to repeat itself in this absurd manner?

"Yes, that's our punishment," I said. "*That* is our punishment!"

He turned to face me.

"All this needn't have happened," he said. "If it hadn't been for people like you."

□

29 February 1968 / Prague
(From the diary of the writer PK)

In the morning I went to the Vysehrad cemetery. This year I miss him more than ever. How many men have the good fortune to have their own father for a friend? Or on the contrary had his death deprived me of my most important protagonist?

I don't know. All I know is that he would have found this last winter most exciting.

Just as well that this year February has an extra day. Last year at this time the weeks went by without leaving any more trace on the life of my Czechoslovakia than on the life of hibernating bees. Will there come a time when we shall look back on those days with nostalgia?

The first public reaction to the January plenum is one of excitement. Professor Eduard Goldstucker has a TV interview in which he uses the term "enlightened socialism."

A mimeographed letter is being circulated in Prague, signed by five old Party members led by a man called Josef Jodas, who "has done a great deal of good work in the physical culture movement." It is said that he previously did a great deal of good work in the secret police.

The fourteen crammed pages are literally a requiem for Antonin Novotny, who "is now the only one to defend the legacy of the Gottwald leadership of the Party, who alone takes a stand against reaction and advocates unquestioning friendship with the Soviet Union." Even the Party Secretary in charge of ideology, Jiri Hendrych, known as the Second, who only last summer manipulated the writers congress so adamantly, is here denounced as "a man of two faces" who had "proclaimed ideological tolerance stretching from the Communist Manifesto to Mein Kampf." Beginning with him, the members of the Central Committee are singled out, one after the other, for accusations of "ideological miasma."

"What was the December and January plenum of the Central Committee really about? This has now been made abundantly clear. It was the so-called theory of the elite. We can all remember how what was called the elite used to be a joke for us Communists. These were the Preisses, the Petschkas, the Batas, Bernas, Görings, Himmlers, Heydrichs, and similar scum. This elite is now ostentatiously joined by a group of our intelligentsia, led by some writers, journalists, and professors. This elite has the following theory: there exists an elite of power and an elite of influence. The Communist Party is an elite of power but has no influence. Writers, journalists, and artists are an elite of influence but possess no power. And that is what the Central Committee session on 5 January was all about, to give the elite of influence, our bourgeoisie and neo-bourgeoisie, the power it lacks. If our reactionary element was to become an elite of power as well as of influence, it first had to dominate the Party. And that, with the aid of the Central Committee Secretaries, is what it succeeded in doing, working against

Comrade Novotny. That and nothing else is the result of the plenum."

With each added page, the argument becomes increasingly ingenious.

"This entire period is one of domination by the writers, poets, and artists, who find their model in the perversions of the West and of Hitler's Fascism. And, conclusively, they have proved this quite clearly by placing at the head of the Writers Union the German scholar Goldstucker, who belongs heart and soul to West Germany. . . ."

"The Trade Union daily Prace has published two articles, by Smrkovsky and Hubl, which are full, especially Hubl's, of the obscenities of which only a professor is capable. . . ."

The document names dozens of politicians, economists, philosophers, journalists, and writers. For the benefit of the reader these are described by a variety of escalating epithets: provocateur, liquidator, pseudo-intellectual, scoundrel, henchman. And from behind all emerges a clear accusation that seems to have arisen straight from the mausoleum of the fifties: Zionists.

Yet almost at the same time as this pamphlet was circulated, that gray eminence Comrade Mamula left the Security Department of the Party, to be replaced by General Prchlik, a decent chap under whom I served during my military service in 1954.

It cannot be said that the citizens of Czechoslovakia are dying of boredom.

Two speakers addressed the People's Militia in Old Town Square during the celebrations to mark the twentieth anniversary of February 1948: Antonin Novotny and Alexander Dubcek.

Everyone can make his choice.

I took part in that glorious February twenty years ago with the firm resolve to become, sooner or later, the leader of the world revolutionary movement.

Now, after exactly twenty years, I had been honored with my first Party office: I became the chairman of a Party organization.

Nevertheless, it was something out of the ordinary, on two counts: first, it was the Party organization of the Writers Union, and second, I had been nominated and elected although no one had yet revoked the reprimand for caution with which I had been punished less than half a year ago by the Central Committee itself after the writers congress.

The short newspaper announcement of my election had immediate repercussions. Yesterday afternoon I received a letter posted, with no sender's address, in the industrial district of Prague 9.

In this letter a certain Comrade Moravek informs me in the name of the working class that I am Zionist and revisionist rolled into one. Apart from this, Comrade Moravek has reliable information that I am also an agent of international imperialism. Now that my henchmen had carried out a putsch in the Central Committee of the Communist Party I would shortly issue directives for Czechoslovakia to be affiliated to West Germany.

Comrade Moravek goes on to say that he, together with the working class, will soon put a stop to that and he ends by assuring me that a lamp post has already been selected for me.

However, the other side, too, has come out of its long sleep and is showing encouraging signs of life.

Today, at two in the morning, I had a phone call from a certain Mr. Novak—or so at least he introduced himself—who said impatiently:

"All right, where do you want to hang, you red pig?"

I thought for a while and then answered truthfully that in fact I did not wish to hang anywhere.

He chuckled, saying that maybe my wishes and opinions counted for something while Novotny was in power, but now that freedom was about to break loose no one was going to take the trouble of asking me.

By this time I had come completely awake and I asked him why, in that case, he bothered to ask me about such details.

He started to swear at me and said I need not think that any kind of trick with Dubcek would save us from a second Budapest. He, Mr. Novak, had been assigned to take care of me.

I asked whether I was to come down into the street or whether he would trouble himself to come up to my flat.

Whereupon he warned me that I would soon be laughing out of the other side of my face and rang off without so much as saying goodbye.

Well, at least nobody can complain that the political situation in this country is uninteresting. My own position certainly seems complicated enough.

Mr. Novak and Comrade Moravek evidently share the same noble sentiments. The problem, as I see it, is which of the two am I to accommodate.

I try to imagine what would happen if by some coincidence the two of them arrive together. Comrade Moravek, I recall, promised to come accompanied by the working class, nor did Mr. Novak explicitly state that he would come alone.

Let us therefore suppose that we shall have two lots of people congregated outside my house.

Should I be asked, I'll of course have to admit that Comrade Moravek has priority, since he got in touch with me first. Then it will all depend on whether Mr. Novak will agree to abide by this.

But what if no one asks me? In that case both sides will have to present their arguments.

Mr. Novak will base his claim to me on the accusation that in my literary output I glorified the Party.

Comrade Moravek on the other hand will contend that in my literary output I denigrated the Party.

Mr. Novak will argue that I had been a member of the Central Committee of the Communist Youth Union.

Comrade Moravek will counter this by saying that I was a member of the Central Committee of the anti-Communist Writers Union.

Mr. Novak will state that I am a lackey of the Kremlin.

Comrade Moravek will state that I am a lackey of the Western imperialists.

Mr. Novak will shout that I have betrayed Democracy.

Comrade Moravek will shout that I have betrayed the Revolution.

Mr. Novak will grow angry.

So will Comrade Moravek.

The two crowds will begin to murmur ominously. Now they must surely come to blows any minute.

That will be my great opportunity.

I'll lean out of the window and shout that I am a Jew.

Both sides will see eye to eye at once, and my hanging can then proceed without any further impediments, everyone cheerfully doing his bit.

The joke, of course, is that I am not Jewish at all.

But I'll not tell them that. I'll shuffle off this mortal coil with the comforting knowledge that I had played a significant part in uniting the two extreme wings of our society.

---

26 V 46 / Prague

On the day when you and I both buried Robek, that evening when the blackout regulations were lifted and we both watched from Letna as, after six years of darkness, the lights went up again over liberated Prague, that night when a Soviet officer invited us both over to their bonfire and offered us some vodka—that night you and I drank to our brotherhood.

That was 375 days ago.

All that time I thought of you as of a real brother. We read our verses to each other, we both read Fucik's *Report from the Gallows* for the first time, out loud so that we would memorize it.

Together we tried to discover what it was that gave him the strength to be brave even under the executioner's axe, the strength that had sustained those tired soldiers who had come to Czechoslovakia to die in the last hour of the war. And we found it in the same source, in the source which Robert had begun to probe when in that last winter of the war he had brought us *The Origin of the Family* by Engels.

And since, to our regret, we had still not come of age, we founded our own Communist Party. It boasted four members: Stalin, Fucik, you, and me.

We turned up at school with the five-pointed star on our lapel, and we got the same treatment as the first Christians in Rome. Our dear masters from that good old bourgeois district put us through our paces, but we crammed until all hours of the night so that we ended at the top of the class. And a number of other boys began to study Marx.

On Saturdays, instead of enjoying our weekends by the river, you and I both went on night shifts in the Klando coalmines.

Together we mastered our fear of the low workings overhead, the creaking props; together we swelled with pride when, in the morning after work, genuine coalminers took us with them to eat salt herrings and drink beer like real proletarians. Once we even persuaded Slavek to join us, so that during the tea break we gave them an underground reading of Nezval and Blok.

We were also together on that day in November when the Red Army withdrew from Czechoslovakia. We stood on the pedestal of the St. Wenceslas statue, climbing as high as we could to catch a better glimpse of the soldiers inside the trucks. And we also saw the faces pressed against the windows of the coffee houses, big business firms, and banks. In them we read the hope that now at last it was their day.

Together we presented ourselves at the Central Committee of the Party. We were too young to be given a Party card, but at least they gave us some work to do. While our schoolfellows played games and went to the movies, we two entered the struggle for a better world. The victorious Allies put the Nazi murderers on trial at Nuremberg, but in Greece Communists were again dying. In the pages of our newspapers, the first bombs were fired in the pre-election campaigns. The right wing no longer made any secret of its intention, if elected, to denationalize the industry and to return the country to the old, pre-Munich days. We were only seventeen and we had our loves—you several, I just one—and yet instead of love lyrics we wrote propaganda leaflets and militant slogans. It was also partly for her sake that I did all this, wishing our children to live in a world free from poverty and misery.

We both rejoiced as we stuck our own verses, still fresh from the printer, underneath the billboard posters urging people to vote Communist.

We were still together only this morning, when full of anxiety we went the rounds of the polling booths; not allowed inside, we tried to judge from the appearance of the voters as they entered who was likely to vote for the revolution and who against.

Now it is long past midnight. I can hear the glasses clinking in the kitchen; I can hear Mother's laughter and the voices of Father's friends.

The battle is over. The Left has won, the Communists alone gaining 38 per cent in a free, secret ballot. Klement Gottwald is to form the next government.

And I feel like crying.

Again and again I keep rereading the note written in her hand which I found among the pages of my *Cyrano*, the book you once borrowed from me and today brought back at last.

"Why this long silence? Is it again because of him? Surely you know he is not and has never been anything more than a friend to me. I talk with him because he tells me about you. I feel sorry for him, but if you don't want me to, I shan't see him again. It's the fifth of May, exactly a year since you whistled under my window. Death was all round us, but you taught me to live. So why do you torture me, mon petit Pierre! A____"

And so, in a way, you and I, we both were together on that night as well. Only I went away, because I loved her. You knew that well enough. Yet you stayed.

You even drank to our brotherhood, and then for 375 days you lied to me. And you taught her to lie too.

I am full of disgust, for I cannot live by halves. I gave myself without reservations and that's why I know this—never again will I love anyone as long as I live.

> *And never again do I want to have a brother.*
> *Yes; all my laurels you have riven away*
> *and all my roses; yet in spite of you,*
> *there is one crown I bear away with me.*

No, I shan't jump in the river, or take an overdose of sleeping pills. I want to live for the sake of those who suffer, I want to be with those who fight. I desire no high office, no exalted titles. Not even a poet's laurels.

All I want is to be a Communist.

A private in that army which today set out on its march in our country too, to bring the world peace and justice, to rid it of baseness and lies.

I have lost a brother. I'll have comrades.

They do not betray.

I hope you will understand why you have no business among us. The Communist revolution needs people of a high moral fiber. Only they can bring about a new era of mankind.

And so goodbye. We part company, irrevocably and forever.

Go forth and multiply.

And as for me?

Once more Cyrano:

These have I buried now: a friend and my happiness!

He said we were welcome to spend the night in his flat. I declined politely. His accusation was too grating, a blow below the belt. I felt no inclination to continue our discussion and I did not want to be indebted to him in any way.

He shrugged his shoulders and turned to her.

"Well, at least let me phone a small hotel I know. It's near the Embassy and they put Czechs up at reduced prices."

"If you would," she replied with a smile.

As I got into the car he asked me:

"What are your plans?"

"To call on the Pope," I retorted. "He alone can absolve me of having caused our national tragedy."

I was very tired and fed up, and the unfamiliar one-way street system was confusing. After we had driven in circles for a few minutes she said:

"I can't really see why we couldn't spend the night with him."

"I would have thought that today of all days it would have been even more unacceptable to you than to me."

"Why?" she asked. "I wasn't listening to your talk."

The hotel which gave special terms to Czechs turned out to be a sorry testimony to Czechoslovakia's foreign currency reserve situation. Although it was in the center of the city, its rooms had neither telephones nor running water. There was just a tin washbasin next to the iron bedsteads and ancient cupboard. The thought of people famous throughout Europe spending their nights in this dingy hole saddened me. I promised myself that we would find another hotel first thing in the morning. I usually spent the larger part of my foreign royalties on decent hotel accommodation since I found it unendurably embarrassing to let the world see how broke our country really was.

Though for years she had been in the habit of sleeping naked, she put on a nightgown in the stifling heat. I did not even know she had one. Why did she? She fell asleep as soon as she got into bed.

I went downstairs and asked the night porter to get me Prague on the telephone.

I had to repeat my request three times before he understood.

"Maybe you wait entire night, maybe not get at all," he said in atrocious English.

The hope that I would hear my children was stronger than my desire to sleep. I stripped off my sweat-drenched shirt and, stretching out on the bed in my pants, I switched on my transistor radio. Coming down some narrow channels between Italian stations I caught Czech voices fighting their way through to me only to fade away again. One of them, laden with a heavy foreign accent, was monotonously reciting an unbelievably long article from the Moscow *Pravda* entitled "The Defense of Socialism—the Supreme International Duty."

Its authors worked on the premise that if a lie is to become truth, it must be as absurd as possible. The article was a fantastic collection of false "proofs" and distorted quotations, evidently intended to convince the European Left that the fraternal Soviet move had averted a counterrevolutionary *putsch* in the very nick of time. Some of these arguments were based on lies of our own currency, whose instigators had never been publicly repudiated by Dubcek and his colleagues because they were Party members of many years' standing. Thanks to this practical naïveté hurtled back now like boomerangs at our heads.

I tuned in to another station. A familiar voice was reading a statement issued by the Czechoslovak government:

"Thus for the first time in the history of the international Communist movement the allied armies of the socialist countries have carried out an act of aggression against a state run by the Communist Party."

I began to lose track of the sense of what he was saying, hypnotized by that voice. It must have belonged to someone I had known intimately. I closed my eyes and at once saw his face.

Had I stayed the night in the flat and listened to Prague, the three of us would have been together again. The three musketeers after twenty years.

It was almost midnight. The reception had improved; there was now only a strange staccato in the background, seemingly not caused by atmospheric interference. It took me a while to realize with horror that it was a burst of gunfire. In spite of the temperature I shivered.

Where was he speaking from? Had they again moved the studio to the Hus Chapel? What was he thinking about, in the intervals between his announcements, in that makeshift studio whose walls let in the sound of machine-gun volleys? About his six wasted years doing forced labor in a uranium mine? How did he manage to live through them?

On that single night shift we got him to join us just after the war, he had been so scared that his face was chalk-white under the coal dust. What was he frightened of today?

His voice sounded calm and grave.

"Dear friends, it is still in our power to bring to a successful conclusion the great task of resurrecting socialism which we began last January. Refrain from taking violent action against the invaders. Don't allow yourselves to be provoked by those who wish to furnish evidence to show that the intervention was justified. We are passing through very difficult hours. Let us do all we can to come through them with our heads high and our backbones straight!"

The news gave a staggering account of the events of the past twenty-four hours. Dubcek, Smrkovsky, Cernik, Kriegel, and others were missing. The Chairman of the Czech National Council, Cestmir Cisar, had been arrested by a group of Czech secret police collaborating with the invaders. The President had been made a prisoner inside the Castle. At that moment the country was an unguarded barrel of gunpowder which anyone could explode. Of all the voices that could prevent an explosion, only one remained.

His voice.

I found it fantastic to think that of all people, *he*, with a dozen valid reasons for locking himself up at home and waiting for things to quiet down, was tonight holding that difficult and dangerous guard, protecting the national reserve of common sense and conscience.

A thousand kilometers away, across three frontiers, condemned to helpless security I resolved to stand guard with him.

At six in the morning I was awakened by the porter. He saw

it his duty to come and tell me that they had not managed to get Prague for me. Another voice swallowed up by the dawn.

"Come," I said to her, "we must *do* something, or else we'll go mad."

We tried to carry on with our vacation. The attempt ended when, on the stone floor of St. Peter's, with the longitudes of the other world cathedrals we found the one for St. Vitus, Prague. I closed my eyes. I turned around. Like a sleepwalker I took those two hundred steps through the cathedral door and across the Castle courtyard to the Matthias Gate. In Hradcany Square, with its delightful baroque and rococo façades, crouched a pack of steel monsters, their guns aiming at the windows of my flat. The pink-and-white faïence chandelier from Karlovy Vary gave off a delicate glow against the blue ceiling that has been with me since my childhood—like a small private piece of my own sky. Then a booming sound.

The peal of the bell reverberated inside the dome of St. Peter's. She was kneeling next to me on the mark showing the position of St. Vitus' Cathedral and she was praying with the humility and earnestness of those who after years of anxiety are trying to rediscover a forgotten God.

One more attempt at evading the present. The Colosseum, titanic, two thousand years' struggle of a human effort against the heat of the sun, might perhaps make us forget for a few minutes our more immediate concerns. But no . . . all I saw there was a depressing monument to relativity and transience. If even the great Roman Empire crumbled into dust, what earthly chance did we stand?

In the ancient interior, whose damp stones seemed still permeated with the mortal sweat of man and beast, we found a hideous bar with a refrigerator, shade, cool Coca-Cola, and above all, newspapers in a language I could understand. The *Neue Züricher Zeitung* devoted a full six pages to Czechoslovakia. I translated excerpts for her. Our depression increased. Surely that newsboy's cry in Perugia had told us everything—and yet it was only now, learning the details, however banal, that we found the reaction setting in, paralyzing us.

The bus carried us back, along the banks of the Tiber. But the Eternal City flashed past the windows for the second time a boring, flickering film without sound or subtitles.

Moving like automatons we again reached the Embassy. We felt a need to be among our own, to hear a familiar language. It was an age-old atavism, to share despair as well as hope with the other members of your tribe.

The tension and uncertainty had left marks on us all: the women's hair was a mess, the men were unshaven. I ran my hand over my chin. For the first time in years I hadn't shaved in the morning. The demobilized Army officer from Bratislava had aged visibly overnight.

The Embassy had only just been opened. We squeezed inside the hall and squatted on the lowest step of the huge staircase. An Embassy official was holding forth. The powers-that-be were evidently panic-stricken that this horde might be dumped in their lap. You could tell that by the way the fellow spoke to us, as though the occupation were no more than a minor domestic bother.

"Why should you be unable to return?" he called out to us optimistically. "What do you think can happen to you? After all, you were all abroad on holiday. What is there to be afraid of? It's not as if any of you had been involved in politics..."

He caught sight of me and at once grew less enthusiastic.

"But of course everyone must do as he thinks best..."

Several of the other tourists now recognized me, and they crowded round us.

"What are *you* going to do?"

Such a simple, basic question. Why hadn't I put it to myself before now? What was I doing in Rome, anyway? I could have been at the border by now. Why hadn't I driven there straight from Perugia? I felt utterly confused, yet I replied with conviction:

"I want to go home."

I could see how relieved they were. And I was relieved too. I still did not know whether I *could* go home, but now at least I knew that I must. I had no choice in the matter. In certain situations a writer is nothing but one of the actors on the national stage. Certainly in Bohemia he is. And that included me. To abandon your role in the middle of the play would be to betray your audience and forever lose face.

Their reaction was spontaneous.

"That's what we all want. But shall we get there?"

A long argument ensued between the enthusiasts and the skeptics, the former suggesting that we all go together, leave our cars in Austria and walk across; that we send a delegation ahead of us; that we ask the Swiss Red Cross for an escort; that we cross the river Dyje in boats and prevail on our border guards to let us through.

The man who put forward this last suggestion was, of course, from Moravia. He and his family then accompanied us to our hotel. He, his wife, and his daughter were all in their bathrobes, the girl carrying an absurdly long cardboard box. They looked eccentric even in uninhibited Rome. We stood interminably in front of the hotel, while he clamored for support of his idea.

I could see that his wife was very tired, and out of politeness I asked the whereabouts of their car.

It had been stolen yesterday in Venice, together with all their belongings, while they had stopped off for a swim in the sea. All that remained was their beachwear and a big gondola they had bought shortly before as a souvenir. Stunned, they went to the nearest police station, only to learn that apart from their car they had also lost their country. The second blow had made them forget the first. When I now asked them how they thought they would get home, they replied:

"Oh, Lord, surely our people won't stop us!"

They refused my offer of help. We discovered that they had the room above ours. The Embassy had apparently come out of its torpor at last.

When I asked for my key at the desk I was handed a letter.

"Terribly sorry. I didn't mean to offend you," he had written. "I'd very much like to talk to you. We're negotiating with the Italian Party. I'll drop in after lunch. You'd better stay for the time being, as the border is guarded by the Russians. Give my love to your wonderful woman!"

She was reading the letter over my shoulder.

"Go to bed," I said. "I'm going outside for a coffee."

She laid the key down on the desk.

"I'll come with you. I feel hungry."

I was too weary to comment.

The *ristorante* was right next to the hotel. The tables by the wall were in the shade, such as it was. I ordered an iced coffee.

I could not have stomached anything else. She asked for *spaghetti milanese* and a half-bottle of white wine. No social or natural catastrophe could ever spoil her appetite.

Since our dialogue in Perugia we had talked together only when it was absolutely essential. Now we had fallen silent completely. I did not mind. I kept thinking about those three people in bathrobes with their absurd gondola, about the tired man in khaki trousers and his weeping wife, about the entire fortuitous sociological cross-section of Czechoslovak citizens besieging the Embassy. How many of them had been caught up and wounded in the inhuman machinery of the distortions; how many had waited all these years for an apology, for compensation, for a decent job, for a passport? And yet during these long hours I had not heard a single reproach. They had an almost fanatical confidence that it would be the Communists, yes, above all the Communists back home, who would fight for and save the hope of us all, the hope which went by the name of socialism with a human face. How many times during the day had I heard the sentence: "If only the Party Congress could meet!"

Of all the countries in which the bourgeoisie had been defeated, Czechoslovakia was the one where socialism had taken root most naturally. What irony! Of all the errors and shortcomings of the revolutionary movement from the time of the October Revolution until today, this was by far the most tragic.

Who in our country were the counterrevolutionaries?

Was it she?

True, she reproached and insulted me, blaming me for the deadly sins, from our dependence on Moscow to the low yield of milk by our cows; and hers was the voice of a whole generation, asking why we should be condemned to socialism on a continent which held countries like Sweden and Switzerland.

But was it really socialism they rejected—that conspiracy of incompetents, that tsardom of mediocrity created in the image of Antonin Novotny?

As soon as we had proved the obvious truth—the Emperor is naked—as soon as politics came out of the Novotny's kitchen into the public view and liberated brains began to give the revolution back its purity and its program, she was on my side, on our side, for that opportunity of sending our message to the whole world, the kind of message that a nation is sometimes permitted to convey only once in its history.

For a moment I saw her again as she had been on that night in March, again I heard her astonished voice:

"Look, the lights are on in all the windows. . .!"

And that venomous remark in Perugia?

Sad . . . if I were a banker she would have attacked capitalism with equal vehemence. Politics at that moment only took the place of love.

And that was a different chapter. I did not want to think of it. I was too tired.

13–22 March 1968 / Prague
(From the diary of the writer PK)

Wednesday, 13 March

Today I received an invitation to a public discussion that was to be held in the Slavonic House tonight. I don't think I would have gone if it had not been for Z——'s remark that it was still more worthwhile to spend an evening with a parrot than with the Communists.

There was a swarm of young people outside Slavonic House. Dancing lessons, no doubt. I recalled the meetings we had held here twenty years ago. All that boundless enthusiasm. And all that deadly naïveté which had helped to make us the last political generation. Après nous the big beat.

I was welcomed by an official of the municipal committee of the Youth Union. I had had no idea that it was their show. He led me to an empty meeting room. My premonition of a wasted evening was turning to certainty. I wondered how to make my excuses and go home. So she had been right yet again.

Just then a tall man with a crew cut entered the room. His face seemed familiar. He pressed my hand, making me wince with pain. I introduced myself.

"Ah, so it's you," he said. "I am Smrkovsky."

"Oh, so it's you," I replied, genuinely pleased. This was beginning to look interesting.

A strange procession was filing into the room. Member of the Party Central Committee Frantisek Vodslon, the former Chairman of the Youth Union Zdenek Hejzlar, who had been expelled from the Party and for ten years had not been allowed to live in Prague, the rehabilitated Marie Svermova, economist in disgrace Radoslav Selucky, and the writer who enjoyed Novotny's favor, Jan Prochazka. I greeted them all cordially, but I failed to understand what was happening. Were we to talk to one another? Was this an illegal meeting?

A pale attendant came rushing in.

"Comrades, there are several thousand people out there unable to get in! Traffic in the street is completely blocked!"

Dancing lessons indeed! What an ass I was. Smrkovsky went out to put things in order. And then we were all led into the big hall. It looked as if some of the audience were even hanging from the chandeliers.

Smrkovsky was the first to speak into the mike.

"My friends, boys and girls. How am I to begin? Perhaps by saying how glad I am to be present at this meeting, unlike any seen here for a very long time. We had to turn several thousand young people away. I told them they couldn't get in here now, the place was packed, but we would all meet as soon as possible in the Congress Hall. We must all start making preparations for that meeting tomorrow, the Youth Union, everybody. We've got to get things going!

"You mustn't expect anything sensational here. You are going to ask questions and we, as senior Communists, are going to answer them. And we're very happy that you too want to participate in the running of this country in the years to come."

Again there were some derisory exclamations from the gallery, but now members of the audience in the hall jumped to their feet and called out over our heads:

"Provocateurs! Thugs! Why don't you go and joke elsewhere?"

The atmosphere was suddenly reminiscent of the big annual Slavia–Sparta soccer match, the air charged with electricity. It was clear to us that the mortally offended secret service was sounding the alarm. The angry old man at Prague Castle had a unique opportunity. Would we learn tomorrow morning that he had saved us from another Hungary?

Written questions deluged our table, Jan Prochazka bringing the first bale.

Question: "Aren't you afraid that it'll all end the same way as in Budapest in 1956?" Answer: "That would be a bit of a luxury where we are concerned, our houses are crumbling without any help from anybody!" (Laughter.) Question: "Will censorship be tightened up again?" Answer: "There is no censorship, my friends, it has been eliminated." (Thunderous applause and cries of "Hurrah!") "That's enormous progress; the last time we achieved something like this was exactly fifty years ago!"

Burst of laughter. And more laughter greeted practically every answer.

"It's illogical for man to spend so much time learning to speak and then not to be allowed to. And in any case, the free expression of views will do this country a lot of good. Maybe it will show us our direction to get back into Europe."

We took turns. Newspapermen from both East and West scribbled in their notebooks, looking bewildered. Was this a revolution or a music-hall act? We felt a wonderful sense of relief. The electricity had gone out of the atmosphere, the police chiefs would wait in vain. The spirit of the Prague Spring had just been born. If there was divorce Italian style, why shouldn't we have politics Czech style?

From outside we heard whistling and shouts from those who had not been admitted into the overcrowded hall. The ushers were at their wits' end. No one had thought of providing loudspeakers. I reflected bitterly how the experience of our younger days stood us in good stead. But then I realized that the young generation of today could hardly have had that experience, and it was our own fault.

All we had to do was place a table at the top of the stairs. Here again we took turns answering the questions that came shooting out of the crowd, using our two cupped hands in place of a megaphone. The answers had to be honest: empty rhetoric was rewarded with catcalls.

"Do you still mean to defend the leading role of the Communist Party?"

"You are just witnessing an attempt to put it into practice according to our original ideas."

Applause. At long last the sense of fair play was again being reborn in Bohemia. Solid argument and humor were winning the day against mass hysteria. But the crucial test was yet to come.

It was almost midnight. Suddenly someone in the main hall put forward the motion that Antonin Novotny be deprived of his position as President of the Republic. The young man who was in the chair and who, until now, had given the impression of being timid and even scared, suddenly flared into life and put the motion to the vote. It was carried immediately. Smrkovsky got up and marched to the microphone. We realized what a tricky position he was in and wondered how he would extricate himself from it.

He was again welcomed with applause. Any run-of-the-mill politician would have cherished this newfound popularity as if it were a winning lottery ticket, yet Smrkovsky told his audience that they had disappointed him. It just wasn't possible to replace illegality with more illegality. Only Parliament was entitled to recall the President.

Someone in the audience whistled. (In Czechoslovakia this is an expression of protest.)

"All right, you just whistle, Comrade; I know how to whistle too. But you must see that an elephant has lots of courage but not much brain. It's exactly a proposal such as this that some people want so they can show that it is the mob which is taking over in our country." (Whistling.) "I know how you feel, only don't forget that politics out of control is just as dangerous as politics conducted behind locked doors. I can promise you that I'll convey your wishes to our Parliament and the Central Committee of the Party. And I beg you to withdraw your resolution."

For most of the audience it was the first time they heard a politician begging them to do something. The packed auditorium voted in his favor.

Outside the hall Z_____ was waiting for me with her bearded fellow students.

"It could have been worse," she said.

Thursday, 14 March

A meeting of the presidium of the Writers Union.

To prevent me from becoming a member of that organization,

Jiri Hendrych ordered last year's writers congress to cross my name off the list of candidates. Now I was back as the new chairman of the Party organization. I moved that the playwright Vaclav Havel, chairman of the non-Party writers' group who had likewise been crossed off the list, be invited to take part in the meeting.

P_____ was sitting at the opposite end of the table. We had not seen each other since last autumn. He was still head of the cultural department of the Party secretariat, and I could see that my colleagues virtually ignored him: a logical consequence of last year's events. They weren't linked to him by a friendship that went back more than a quarter of a century. I nodded to him and he nodded wearily in reply. I had never seen him so gaunt, lighting one cigarette after another.

Drahomir Kolder, member of the presidium of the Communist Party's Central Committee, was answering questions.

"When people speak of opposition inside the Party, many feel that this is unacceptable. Yet there have always been divergent views in the Party, even though we may not have wanted to admit it. The Party must function on a truly democratic basis, otherwise it cannot fulfil its historic task. And although we had many reservations toward Togliatti's testament, I believe that we must solve the theoretical problems of our movement. We in Czechoslovakia are called upon to formulate them anew."

For years we had regarded Kolder more as a right back; it was strange to see him play on the left forward wing. But he spoke with conviction.

I said: "After twenty years even politics has become risky. In these new conditions, talented people are bound to come to prominence and they can easily outstrip you. Isn't it possible that in such a case you will again use force to defend your positions?"

"If we prove inadequate we must make way for others. That is the iron logic of the democratization process. Speaking for myself, I have every intention of proving adequate. If I fail, I'll go and study, I'll try and gain the necessary qualifications to return to my post."

God Almighty! Is this really a miracle we are witnessing?

I meant to invite P_____ over to my place for a glass of wine, but unfortunately he had left before the meeting ended.

Friday, 15 March

The deputy director of the State Security investigation department made an urgent request to reply to the questions of an angry public on the pages of Literární listy. A black limousine was to come tonight to take Ludovik Vaculik and myself to the political prison at Ruzyne. Z____ forced me to take certain precautions. And before we set out she three times made the sign of the cross on my forehead.

The car's headlights picked out the bulletproof gates of the prison, which opened in front of us like an accordion. All around us were tall buildings full of dark, barred windows. The gates closed silently behind us. Suddenly we were blinded by strong beams of light.

"In the name of the law, you are under arrest!"

Someone seizes me, many pairs of hands which blindfold me and drag me across a courtyard, up some stairs, along a corridor. I am pushed from behind and fall on the floor. A heavy door slams shut. I'm in a concrete bunker without any windows, with a hole in the floor in place of a lavatory. I crawl toward it, trying to loosen my trousers; when you are in a state of shock, you lose control over your bodily functions. The peephole clicks. I hear a distant voice:

"What's yours doing?"

"Pissing."

"Mine's shitting!"

Laughter.

From the pages of Josefa Slanska's diary I came slowly back to the present. I realized how much more terrible it must have been for Communists persecuted by their fellow Communists than for the wartime victims of Nazi persecution. Lieutenant Colonel K____ and Major V____ were both careful to point out right at the outset that they came to Ruzyne long after the political trials of the fifties. They also told us that Dr. Ivan Pfaff, the author of the spurious Manifesto of Czechoslovak Writers, which I had denounced as a forgery in Hamburg, had been released from prison at noon today. Was that supposed to be a peace offering? At any rate a good beginning.

We stated our questions. On the Manifesto, Jan Benes, Mnacko, the writers congress, my interrogation at the border, postal censorship, the bugging of telephone conversations. They replied succinctly, or at length, after evasively, occasionally attempting a forced joke. They both smoked heavily. Major V_____ sweated. I tried to imagine the many faces that had sweated here in front of him. After all, we were grilling them in their own office. We tape-recorded all the questions and answers.

Question: "You have acquainted us with some of the statements and articles that were the subject of your investigations. They are an innocuous collection of words compared with the things we can hear today quite officially on the radio or television or that we read in the daily press. I can therefore only conclude that one and the same law has been interpreted in two different ways within a mere six months. . . ."

Answer: "The work of our State Security is closely linked to the existing political trend. A murder committed before the war is still a murder. That which was called espionage in 1948 may be only a misdemeanor today. By all means condemn interrogators who treated people inhumanly. But don't condemn them for investigating things which were an infringement of the political line of the time."

Conclusion: "It looks as though we have one constitution known to us all and a second, secret one composed of internal directives and Party resolutions. I think two constitutions are something of a luxury for such a small country and the sooner the second one ceases to exist the better for all concerned. I imagine that even your investigators, prosecutors, and judges would welcome this, for the status quo can only lead to schizophrenia."

The meeting was over. We were all very tired. They offered to show us their new cells, which were to provide the prisoners with a "cultural" environment. We declined courteously.

"On consideration," they tried another lame joke, "it's rather careless to come and visit us at night like this."

Silently I gave thanks to Z_____.

"Not really," I replied. "You see, all our friends are waiting for us at the Viola. If we're not back by two they'll all come to collect us."

A car was quickly summoned to take us home.

The annual conference of Communists from Prague 1 in the large hall of the Lucerna. Yet another of my belated life premières. I was asked to speak as the eighth out of a hundred and fifty who wished to address the meeting.

"... The District Committee's report is once again nothing but hot air. It's a sobering thought how many people worked on it day and night, all that labor producing such a lean mouse. And how horrible to think that we have been building socialism for a whole twenty years in much the same way as this report was put together." (Applause.)

"... Nobody can overlook the fact that those who stood up against those Communists who had led our society into a blind alley were also Communists. If, moreover, we offer people proper guarantees, not only cannot we be dropped from the team but, on the contrary, only then will we really gain a leading position, this time a respected one." (Applause.) "We must do everything in our power to make the Party's Action Program not only a Czechoslovak but a world best-seller for 1968." (Applause.)

"... If Czechoslovakia breaks off diplomatic relations with Israel but does not break them off with Indonesia, where hundreds of thousands of Communists have been murdered, and does not break them off with the United States, which is conducting a far more dirty war in Vietnam, then all I can say is it isn't logical and something ought to be done about it." (Applause.)

"... In this conflict between two concepts we can see the person of Comrade Novotny coming ever more clearly into the foreground, although he himself has been persistently standing in the background. In the past our organization used all the means at its disposal to inform him of the grave errors committed by the Party leadership not only in cultural matters but also in its work of directing the Party and our whole society. We can produce the necessary documents to prove this. Comrade Novotny took no heed of our warning but, on the contrary, conducted himself in a way that disqualified him. We do not hold him solely responsible for the crisis in which we find ourselves, but we have reason to state that he has become the chief support of all who want to throw us back into the past to preserve their own power. Apart from this, Comrade Novotny has till now not clarified his part in the staging of the political trials, as is evident from the official documents of the fifties. We therefore suggest that our conference send the following letter:

" 'To the President of the Republic and member of the Presidium of the Communist Party of Czechoslovakia, Antonin Novotny.

" 'Dear Comrade, it is becoming increasingly more evident that the comrades whom time has found guilty of serious political errors do not intend to provide the progressive forces with the necessary conditions for overcoming the crisis in our Party and society, that they are creating an organized counterpressure. Communists in Prague 1 find this extremely disturbing. The history of the postwar years, and in particular the events in Hungary, warn us against such a development, which could have the gravest consequences. There are times when the interests of society as a whole must take precedence over the interest of an individual. We therefore ask you, Comrade Novotny, to give the Party and the entire nation proof of your feeling of responsibility and voluntarily relinquish your participation in the running of this country, both as a member of the Party's Central Committee and as President of the Republic. May this serve as an example to all the others!' "

The motion was carried by 924 votes to seven.

Sunday, 17 March

Next day the conference continued with a number of sharp clashes. A vote was taken on whether the conference was to go on longer than originally planned. The first secret ballot in the history of the Party became a silent, fierce battle. The right mercilessly canceled out the left and vice versa. The only people not to lose any votes were the unknowns who did not even take part in the discussion.

None of the former Party secretaries survived in the election of members to the District Committee. Almost all the progressives were elected, though in some cases with very narrow majorities.

In the election of delegates to the Prague Municipal Party Conference I was one of those who failed to gain a majority, losing narrowly with three hundred votes against me.

That was the requiem for Antonin Novotny.

The conference ended in the early hours of the morning with the singing of the Internationale.

Monday, 18 March

I slept an average of three hours a night this week. My writing desk was a sorry sight with its abandoned manuscripts. Oh, for the golden days of oppression, when I was allowed to be nothing but a writer. Now I am engaging in politics, at my own expense. But I feel I owe it to somebody.

"You bet you do," was Z____'s comment. "But I think you ought to forget about it soon, before you and your Party make a mess of it again."

There has been little enough danger of that. The awakened millions had almost the same power as a kindergarten. There was still time to humiliate us all.

A meeting at Smrkovsky's office in preparation for another evening of questions and answers. My first visit to the Ministry of Forestry and Water Economy. The porter in a gamekeeper's uniform, Smrkovsky's secretary in that of a chief forester. I reached the Minister and survived his handclasp.

"No wonder they're after you," I told him. "You're the only one who has any hope of carrying out a successful putsch."

"How do you mean?" asked Smrkovsky.

"How many forests are there in this country?"

"Oh, about a hundred thousand."

I told him that he could take every single strategic point in a night and then celebrate victory by giving away carp to the populace.

"Well, what shall we do, boys, to make things go smoothly?" said Smrkovsky.

He conducted the improvised meeting with skill and pace. It went easily enough, everybody speaking succinctly. And with humor. I could not help remembering February 1948. What would happen if I now climbed on top of a desk and started to sing a revolutionary song? At best they would give me a tranquilizer. And yet, surely there was as much at stake as there had been twenty years ago.

The conference was almost over. Then someone said:

"We'll have at least ten thousand people there tonight. What if some fool stands up and shouts 'Let's go to the Castle!'? Shouldn't we take precautions against something of that sort?"

"The best precaution you could take would be to send all the policemen to the movies," I said.

Smrkovsky grinned.

"I understand."

We finished up with dinner at the Golem. The notorious lovers of wine and women stared uncharacteristically past the waitress for two hours, at the TV set above the bar, to watch the highlights from the discussions at various District Party conferences.

Tuesday, 19 March

For the first time I presided over a plenary session of Communist writers. Dr. Frantisek Kriegel, member of the Central Committee of the Czechoslovak Communist Party, reported on the results of an international Communist Party meeting in Budapest. He could not stand still behind the speaker's table, walking back and forth instead, sipping tea and smoking his pipe. His squat body, rolling gait, and slow speech recalled a submarine captain rather than a head physician at one of Prague's main hospitals.

The questions soon showed that the writers were concerned with matters more immediately connected with themselves.

"Comrade Kriegel, you're one of the best-educated of all the members of the Central Committee, as shown in your speech at the January plenum. Why then, as late as last September, did you vote in favor of punishing the writers who spoke out at the congress and for the abolition of Literární listy?"

"I knew that the progressives in the Central Committee were still not strong enough at that time. If our disagreement with Novotny had come out into the open, we would have furnished him with more arguments against us and helped him to win over the hesitant centrists. It was necessary to wait for the Slovaks to form a united front and be ready to fight. Should it all happen again, I would vote just as I did then. And anyway, I knew that you had enough stamina to survive."

His words evoked courteous disagreement, yet everyone smiled. His calm frankness made a good impression. I was glad to see that he did not excuse himself by saying that Smrkovsky, Sik, and others had voted exactly as he had. Nevertheless I wondered how frightened he was at the time.

But I supposed that we would find out one of these days.

It was the last night of winter. For the last time, now only symbolically, I lit the fire in the fireplace. Z____ later opened the window and leaned out.

"Don't be so naïve!" she told me. "Kriegel will still be in his place when I'll be visiting you in prison."

"Optimist! What makes you think they won't throw you in jail too?"

"They'll deduct the years spent with you from my sentence."

Exactly opposite, almost within reach, I could see, flying above the rooftops of Hradcany Castle, the presidential flag of Antonin Novotny.

Wednesday, 20 March

The last day of winter. At two-thirty a meeting with young workers in the works canteen of CKD-Elektrotechnika. Here the questions were even franker than at the other meetings and conferences.

"Let us try to free words like 'the leading rôle of the Party' or 'friendship with the Soviet Union' from the connotations they were given in the fifties," said Professor Goldstucker, Chairman of the Writers Union and a leading Czech Kafka scholar. "If politics are not to lead to catastrophe, they must not be ruled by emotions but rather by a constant reassessment of all the social factors and forces, the short-term as well as—and above all—the constant ones. One such constant factor is the world-wide movement in the direction of socialism. Our task is to overcome the distortions that have arisen in the past and to find ways and means of preventing new ones. If, on the other hand, we wished to prevent the further development of socialism, our humanist endeavor would change into its negation and the best people in the world would condemn us for it. One extreme cannot be removed by substituting another in its place. To give up the Party's leading rôle and to abrogate our friendship with the Soviet Union would mean that we were leaving the field open to anyone and anything. What we have to do then is to give these concepts a new meaning."

We parted from them at five, but not for long. A number of buses were already running their engines in the factory yard. Our audience was to follow us to the big public meeting in the Congress Palace.

On the stroke of seven we mounted the rostrum, our team considerably reinforced. We were welcomed by an ear-splitting din. Slavonic House was a school picnic by comparison. Each of us had a large name-card on the table in front of him. We were introduced like the finalists in a wrestling match. I almost expected them to raise our arms in the air. The gong sounded.

Smrkovsky: "We promised those who didn't get in last time that we would hold our next meeting in a larger hall. Now it seems that not even the biggest hall in Prague is big enough." (Laughter.) "We have opened the second wing as well and it's still not enough." (Applause.) "There are over twenty thousand of us." (Uproar.) "But the Republic has fourteen million inhabitants. In order that everyone may hear, Czechoslovak Radio is going to broadcast the whole proceedings." (Hurrah!)

In front of the speaker there was a row of microphones bearing the initials of all the major world radio networks. On the right side of the hall were several dozen cameras, including those of Czechoslovak television.

What an incredible scene! A procession of names that only yesterday were still accursed, opinions that only yesterday were still forbidden.

Professor Goldstucker seemed to be carrying on where he left off that afternoon: "We have to realize a fundamental thing. What is happening in our country today is not an attempt to bring back the old social order, it is a movement intended to carry socialism to a higher stage of development. We must not forget that we are in the midst of a revolution which started twenty years ago. The assumption and fortification of power are unthinkable without a revolutionary dictatorship. But then there comes a time when it is necessary and possible to bring back into the structure of society those freedoms which the revolution had temporarily invalidated. All the revolutions in history came to grief on this very count. We for the first time have a real chance of solving this problem which has wrecked so many revolutions in the past."

Academician Ota Sik: "Some individuals in power did not put

people in important posts to serve the nation's requirements but so that they could create favorable conditions for their own position. That is why experts who held different views than the First Secretary had to go. That is why there was an artificially created gulf between expert knowledge and political conviction. But those capable of getting work done properly can be left in charge politically. We must see to it that elected Party organs give orders to the secretaries and not vice versa, that the plenum is able to put forward a number of different suggestions as regards both the solution of problems and the appointment of people to various functions, that the members of elected bodies have the possibility to choose between several candidates by secret ballot. Only in this way can we prevent an individual from misusing his position to strengthen his own personal power above that of the collective."

Dr. Husak (Slovak): "I have been handed a question. 'Is the Constitution still valid? If it is, how is it possible that portraits of the President who is still the head of this state are defaced?' It is a fact that the Constitution is still valid, and it is equally a fact that the portraits are defaced. I think this is a paradox between the Constitution and the real state of affairs, but the reason for this is that we have at the head of our state a man the majority of the people no longer want. We shall have to introduce mutual control of State, Party, and other social institutions so that no single person or group of persons can make us a flock of sheep."

The hall was full of cigarette smoke; you could not see the rear wall. Here it was, that bugbear of all socialist (and not only socialist) politicians, the immense, uncontrollable mass of young people without the vigilant supervision of teachers, school caretakers, watchmen, and "ushers" from the ranks of the secret police. If there were any of these present, then only as timid spectators surrounded by the crowd. And what was the crowd doing? Laughing, clapping its hands, stamping its feet, and whistling to show its disapproval, but remarkably fair-minded and restrained.

The only conflict occurred toward the end of the long meeting, when voices from the audience demanded that a sentence be deleted from the resolution, the sentence that spoke of Czechoslovakia's "indissoluble friendship with the Soviet Union." Smrkovsky again sailed into battle.

"When you get home, Comrade, take a look at the map!"

There followed a heated hour-long controversy. As a result the following wording was adopted:

"We want our foreign policy to respect the geographical position of this country in Central Europe and to give expression to the wishes of the Czech and Slovak people for good and equal relations with all our neighbors, in particular with the Soviet Union. The history of our two nations provides adequate justification for our alliance treaties with the Soviet Union and the other socialist countries. However, we are of the opinion that they should be stripped of all the taboos and conventions of the recent past and instead consistently honor the principles of sovereignty, socialist moral and humanitarian principles, which means that our relations with all countries should be conducted on a basis of absolute equality."

CARRIED BY SEVERAL THOUSAND AGAINST SOME FIFTY VOTES.

We were among the last to leave the hall. The sky was full of stars and there was not a policeman in sight. Thousands of people had dispersed in front of our eyes without the slightest noise, with a somehow noble dignity. As we got into my car Z____ said in an astonished voice:

"Look, the lights are on in all the windows!"

"Well, so what?"

"But it's half past two in the morning."

That is how spring came to Prague that year.

Thursday, 21 March

To crown it all I accepted an invitation to a meeting in Tabor. Not so much because it was the town of the Hussites, but rather because my mother was born there. I was accompanied by Karel Kosik, the philosopher. The local movie house was filled to overflowing.

Last night's seven-hour broadcast had caused a sensation. Until now news and information had been strictly rationed, filtered in the last instance by the local functionaries, and filtered the more severely the farther away you were from the source. We who lived in Prague and were at the center of events had somehow failed to grasp that the majority of our fellow citizens had until last night still been living in December darkness. Nevertheless, the response showed that in Bohemia even the harshest truth does not kill but, on the contrary, vivifies.

Karel Kosik's participation raised the debate to a higher level.

"The way it entered history is very important for every nation. There are nations which started out as conquerors, warriors, and colonizers. Our nation entered European history with a message by means of which a great fifteenth-century Czech intellectual lighted its path for centuries to come, for all of eternity: Uphold what you know to be true. It is what we know to be true that we are now concerned with, rather than with what we are told is the truth."

This was his first appearance at a public meeting of this kind; he lacked the experience and the mannerisms of the professional politician, even of amateurs like me. He acted as though he were giving a lecture at the university, but the occasion made his somewhat pedantic delivery easily understandable to everyone.

"The democratization process must not be halted before it has led to the institution—legally, constitutionally, and organizationally—of a system of socialist democracy. Should it stop halfway, should it founder on half-hearted measures, it will merely result in something modernized and refurbished but basically still the same old system of police bureaucracy, in which all our present problems will be multiplied and will erupt in tragic conflicts."

That evening Prague was tired and nervous. Antonin Novotny had telephoned to the offices of Vecerni Praha, the city's only evening paper, to explain why he had been silent for so long. He had been ill with flu, he told the newspaper.

"I am prepared and ready to take my stand at any time."

Coming from the Commander-in-Chief of the armed forces, these words assumed a special significance.

Friday, 22 March

At noon I gave an interview to Austrian television. The telecast was meant to show that socialism was no less socialist for having a human face, but rather the contrary.

The interview was filmed in my flat with me standing in front of the window. The presidential flag could be seen fluttering in the breeze behind my back.

The interview over, the TV men started to dismantle their equipment. It was exactly twelve-twenty when I turned round to look out of the window.

The flag was just being lowered.

Ten days. . . .

Someone had once written a book with that title.

The Austrians almost cried with vexation that they had not started filming a few minutes later. They could have had a historic shot.

I was glad.

An epoch that had threatened to end in bloodshed ended in silence.

This era of the deaf-and-dumb could hardly have had a more fitting curtain.

---

26 II 48 / Prague

I am looking at the last page of my diary, written five days ago, and I feel as if between it and this page the ocean had swallowed up Atlantis, the lava had scorched Pompeii, and the plebeian tide had swamped mighty Rome.

A mere hundred and twenty hours—and yet these lines are being written by a different person in a different country. If I were John Reed, I would write a book entitled *Five Days That Shook Czechoslovakia.*

It is noon. I can't remember when I was last home for lunch since the time Mother started working. The sun is shining outside the frosty windows. Everything has a festive air about it. I made the fire and took a bath. Lying in the warm water, pleasantly tired, I felt drowsy and nearly fell asleep. But I kept my right arm above the surface.

It had been coming for some time. The workers employed in small factories and the farm workers on large estates had clamored for further nationalization. The soldiers demanded that reactionary officers be dismissed from the service. Soviet wheat drove out the specter of last summer's drought. The Communist Party had waged a successful struggle for the introduction of a millionaires' tax and was growing stronger every day.

They had to do something before it was too late.

The Communist Minister of the Interior dismissed several right-wing police officers whom he accused of preparing a *putsch*. On 20 February the Cabinet met with only half its members present. The ministers belonging to the Czech Socialist, People's, and Slovak Democratic parties had resigned.

"If they do it," my father had said the day before, "it'll be an attempt to bring down the whole government. The President can then appoint a caretaker government and thus take the key ministries away from the Left. A similar thing happened when we tried to create a socialist republic back in 1920."

The news of the resignation reached me at the school. I went at once to the Central Secretariat of the Party. Special editions of the right-wing papers were already on the streets. They had thought it all out well.

They had chosen their moment and were therefore ahead of us. But we were catching up fast. The house next to the Powder Tower had been transformed into a huge brain which was directing operations. A machine gun had been placed behind the iron gates. In the courtyard fires were burning, sailors warming their hands over them. Couriers hurried up and down stairs carrying ticker tapes. I heard a tumult of voices. Elbowing my way into a large hall I saw, through a mist of cheap cigarette smoke, a shadowy figure mounting the rostrum—Lenin!

Today, worse luck, it was all far less dramatic, but still the same revolution pulsated to repel the attack and to triumph.

Dozens of people crowded the three small rooms of the propaganda department. I recognized the faces of well-known writers, painters, actors. They were on our side. They were on the side of the people, as artists have always been in this country. I almost cried for joy at the thought that I was privileged to be here with them.

At last Jiri Hendrych. A smallish, stout man with glasses, he gives the impression of wisdom and calm. He speaks slowly, choosing his words carefully and frequently repeating himself in a search for the right word.

Comrade Gottwald had sent his greetings and thanks. The Party would never forget that the artists had come to her aid in these difficult times. The Party needs their help: A list of things to be done. Posters. Articles. Verses for leaflets. Speeches on the radio and in factories. They raise their hands asking to be heard, they make jokes, they shout, and soon they are making such a din that you cannot hear yourself think. It occurs to me that the Party is bound to have a lot of trouble with the artists in the future. This makes me even more determined to work hard, to become a real writer as soon as possible. I shall never cease to be a rank-and-file soldier of the revolution. My heart and my pen will always be at the Party's disposal.

"Tomorrow the Party is organizing public meetings throughout the country, in every town and every village. Comrade Gottwald is to address the meeting in Old Town Square. His speech will be broadcast; the overwhelming majority of the Radio employees stand behind us. We hope that the right wing is not going to prevail in the Social Democratic Party, which with us forms a majority in the government. But with or without them we are determined to implement the will of the workers: the President must accept the resignation of the treacherous ministers! The bourgeoisie wanted to scuttle the ship of socialism, but it will find itself sinking instead. The Party will bring the nation's hopes to fruition, fulfilling the revolutionary legacy of former generations. The Party will not disappoint the fighting proletariat in capitalist countries. The Party will not betray our loyal friendship with the Soviet Union. Comrade Gottwald has given us our slogan: Forward, not one step backward!"

That was all. I ran over to him.

"And what do you want me to do?"

"We need you in the Youth Union. Both of you."

He gave a tired smile.

Both of us?

"You will reinforce their propaganda department. The comrade here knows all about it."

Peter was standing right behind me. We had not seen each other for a long time. He knew what I was thinking.

"Are you coming with me?" he asked.

Despite the resignation of the right-wingers, the Youth Union was still a junior National Front in which tens of thousands of young people met, regardless of their political conviction. It was true: we were needed there.

"I'll come," I said.

In the Youth Union headquarters on Gorky Square there was chaos. They sent us to bring straw mattresses to hold the building during the night. We helped turn the offices into billets. And then we were again vainly looking for something worthwhile to do. But I had an idea, which even Peter had to admit was a good one.

"Let's get together a front-line revolutionary theater!"

That is how FLRT came into existence. The Union's chairman, Zdenek Hejzlar, gave us a room to rehearse in and promised to get us the necessary props. Peter went off to recruit people for our group while I had to find plays for us to put on. At home Mother had left me a message that she and Father would spend the night at the district Party committee headquarters. I added my own note:

"I'll be back after the revolution. Long live the Party! Comrade son."

I had an idea Peter would bring Slavek. What I had not anticipated was that he would bring A——— as well. I had heard that she was having an affair with one of her teachers at the Drama School, but evidently she had stayed with Peter. Never mind, I said to myself. I would treat the whole thing as a test I have to pass.

Slavek was accompanied by his girl friend, a medical student like himself, who was fond of the theater. He called her, affectionately, Ofinka. I decided to stick with them.

Night. Motorcycles roared to life under the windows; in the corridors the voices of the organizers of tomorrow's demonstration. We rehearsed a program of revolutionary verses until about two-thirty in the morning. I managed to behave quite normally. I believe I was even wittier than usual.

Then we put three mattresses together and took piles of folders full of papers from the tables to put under our heads. We lay down fully clothed, Slavek, Ofinka, A———, Peter, and I, covering ourselves with our coats. It was pitch-dark. The two couples whispered together, and for the first time in many months I recalled that night during the Prague rising of 1945.

I think Peter and A——— were arguing next to me. Peter suddenly rose and went out into the corridor. Then I felt her hand in mine. She pressed it and I withdrew my hand and crossed over to the stove, which I tended until Peter came back. But I knew I still loved her. I felt uneasy.

But next morning we took a barrow to Old Town Square and, using two stepladders and some planks, we erected our front-line theater. I was quite calm again. We had a tremendous success. And when my voice merged with the voice of Prague to welcome Klement Gottwald, I felt that certainty: Yes, here was the hope I sought once, in despair, in God and then in love, here in this multitude which had set out to seek justice and in this man who was leading it into the decisive battle.

This was the *centrum securitatis* which Comenius had sought in vain and which now I have found instead of you, my poor Rob.

Our little stage had become a grandstand thronged with people. Snow was falling sparsely, and on the balcony of the Kinsky Palace Comrade Slansky—or was it Clementis?—lent Comrade Gottwald his Russian fur hat. Wearing it, Gottwald announced the formation of Action Committees of the revived National Front, which were being joined even by honest members of the right-wing parties.

"Reaction will not prevail in Czechoslovakia!"

In contrast to the conspirators in governmental circles, the Party explained its policy in the open street without exception to everyone. This decided the issue.

Three more days passed like a single intoxicating minute. We dragged our Thespian cart all over the city. While the President still refused to accept the ministers' resignations and the bourgeois world sounded the alarm, we stood on our stepladders feeding the hungry with the verses of Mayakovsky, Blok, Wolker, Neumann, as well as our own. Peter and I wrote them on our mattresses at night, and even forced Slavek to do the same; a revolutionary actor had to be able to turn his hand to anything. We were alone, just the three of us, for after that first night the Youth Union leadership issued an order that girls were to sleep apart. Nothing was to be allowed to sully our flag. And all our thoughts had to belong to our cause.

A——— spent the nights at home. At home . . . ? Well, that was no concern of mine. Peter was nervous. No doubt he, like us, saw the paradox: she, a girl from a working-class family, slept at home, whereas Ofinka, the daughter of a wholesale merchant, slept with young factory girls one floor below us. On the morning of the second day she came up to us, pale, slim, and pretty even in her creased dress, and she asked Slavek to get her an application form for Party membership.

He almost had a fit.

"But what will your father say?" he asked.

"It's my life, isn't it? And I want to live it my way." No wonder we gave Ofinka all our new verses to read that day. Even Peter. As if he wanted A_____ to realize that the Drama Academy was not everything, that conviction was also part of revolutionary poetry. Perhaps it was cruel, but it was in her own interest.

We were standing on our stepladders in front of the Industrial Palace when hundreds of delegates arrived for the congress of works councils. They decided to declare a general strike, with only ten votes recorded against. Standing between the gates of the Praga and CKD factories I recited my "Ode to Red Army Tank No. 23" when the strike began. The shriek of innumerable sirens was a mantle covering the entire city—and yet it in no way reminded me of the horror of wartime air raids. It was a lofty sound, like the voice of the organ in St. Vitus' Cathedral. Perhaps, I thought, a revolutionary composer would soon be found who would write "Gottwald's Concerto for Sirens and Proletarian Choir," which would be played on every anniversary of this day.

And we were standing on our stepladders in the middle of Wenceslas Square that evening when a menacing crowd advanced toward us from Mustek, chanting their slogan of hate:

"Kill the reds! Kill the reds!"

So they were on the march. Reactionary undergraduates, office workers, shopkeepers, all those deluded pawns who were expected to shed blood for alien kings.

We tried to send the girls away, but Ofinka refused to go. I glanced at A_____. She too remained, but I could see that she was terrified. At that moment it was as if some chain that had held me these past three and a half years had suddenly snapped. How could I ever have loved her? I longed for a girl who would be my companion not only in love but also in battle, someone like Anna the machine-gunner in *And Quiet Flows the Don*.

The crowd drew nearer and we could now distinguish individual faces. Peter climbed onto the top rung of the ladder and, waving our red flag, shouted:

"Kronstadt does not surrender!"

After this invective, what would happen next? Would they spit at us? Attack us? Or would I perhaps become the first casualty in a civil war? I did not care. I had chosen my fate. I had no regrets.

Just then we heard a well-known revolutionary song, sung by thousands of voices. We turned round in amazement. From the statue of St. Wenceslas at the top of the square a human sea was advancing toward us, covering the whole width of the boulevard right up to the walls of the houses on either side. In the first row marched members of the People's Militia, without their rifles, arms linked. Behind them came students, members of the Youth Union, postmen, railwaymen—the People!

They surged past us, hundreds of clenched fists raised in greeting. The bottom half of the square was almost empty now. We wept with joy. All of us. A____, too.

Were A____'s tears ones of regret at the distance that separated her from us? At the gulf she knew she could no longer bridge? Or had she come to recognize the emptiness in herself which would prevent her from giving life to the characters of the revolutionary plays to be written?

She failed to turn up next morning. Peter was taciturn but otherwise remained calm.

"I'm sorry, forgive me . . . ," he said.

"You took my cross on yourself," I replied.

Together we drank a little rum, this time to comradeship. May she rest in peace in her teacher's bed.

Then came the most dramatic hour of all. We attended a meeting at Slavonic House in the middle of which a delegation of young Social Democrats turned up to ask our assistance. Their leadership was holding a stormy conference, with Minister Majer requesting that he be allowed to withdraw from the government. Once that happened, Gottwald's majority would be lost. They wanted to prevent this and called on us to help them occupy the Social Democratic headquarters. Slavek asked why they did not do it themselves, and they replied that they were too few.

"But we're not Social Democrats," he objected.

"Nobody'll know the difference."

"But that's not fair!"

In the ensuing argument several people backed Slavek's standpoint. I thought Peter would say something, but he was not himself today. I spoke up instead.

"Comrades, what if the right-wing Social Democrats really get what they want and resign from the government? That would mean civil war! You all saw what happened yesterday in Wenceslas Square. What if by this we save thousands of lives? Perhaps the whole revolution? They have come to ask our help as Marxists. Have we the right to deny it? I suggest that we go with them. We needn't lie; let's simply act!"

My suggestion was adopted unanimously. We ran the short distance to the Social Democrat headquarters on Prikopy, where a small detachment of the Workers Militia had just arrived for the same purpose. They were carrying guns. It was beginning to look like a real revolution. We held a quick discussion and agreed what to do. Each of us went into a different room and said to the person in charge:

"Comrade, please stay where you are and don't touch the telephone."

"About time, too," said the chap in the room I entered. "I was about to go and bash their teeth in myself."

He opened a bottle of beer and offered me a cigarette. A man came running out of the conference room where the Party Presidium was in session and engaged in a scuffle with the young Social Democrats. We left them to it and did not interfere. I asked one of the militiamen whether they had been given live ammo. He nodded.

"Six bullets each. In case the Army officers start something. But Comrade Pavel told us that if anyone fires otherwise, he'll be thrown out of the Party double-quick."

There were some hot moments for us when sixty policemen arrived, sent by the Social Democratic police chief Pros. They ordered the building to be cleared, making no secret of their determination to have us arrested if necessary. Fortunately someone had time to phone Minister Nosek, so that soon a hundred Communist policemen arrived. They all left together, arguing heatedly. It was all over, and the government majority had been saved.

I felt on top of the world, thinking that my words had succeeded in bringing about action.

Wednesday. Perhaps in a year or two I'd write a novel about this day. Now I could think of nothing else but this one particular moment.

President Benes at last accepted the resignations and agreed that Klement Gottwald should form a new government. The hundreds of thousands who had been waiting in Wenceslas Square since early that morning sang the *Internationale* for what must have been the fifth time. Thanks to our stepladders, which by now were well known to all, we managed to make our way right to the speakers' platform, which had been set up on top of an ordinary truck. It occurred to me that the truck ought to be taken straight to the museum. Leaning against the sides next to the Party Chairman were Comrade Slansky, Zapotocky, Kopecky, the chief of the Workers' Militia Pavel, the entire general staff of the revolution.

I thought that there could be no greater happiness than the happiness experienced by these people at this very moment. I would have given the rest of my life for the privilege of being up there with them.

Then Comrade Gottwald came down among us. Thousands of hands reached toward him, mine included, across the cordon formed by militiamen.

And it was my hand he shook! Only mine!

As if in doing so he was symbolically saying thank you to the Party, the people, to us all.

I shook hands in turn with my comrades.

And then we went home in a tram chock-full of people and we felt a little sad that it was all over, knowing that we should never again live through anything quite the same. Socialism had won. A straight and shining road to Communism had opened in front of us.

"Come to my place," said Ofinka, who was alone at home, her parents having gone for a ski holiday in St. Moritz. I had to laugh at the thought that they would come back to a country of the victorious proletariat and a daughter who had turned Communist.

We arrived at a palatial villa, a typical stronghold of the Prague bourgeoisie. In the hall there was a huge fire burning in the fireplace. On a tiger-skin rug in front of it, just like in a film, a girl in a red dressing gown was lying on her stomach, sipping her drink. Ofinka seemed embarrassed.

"I thought you were with Ivan."

"I left him last night. Told him to fuck off."

She said this as one might say "Good evening." We stood rooted to the spot. Perhaps she had not seen us. Her long hair fell across her face, covering her eyes.

"You've had a long weekend, haven't you?" she said.

"I was at the Youth Union."

"Oh, had a good lay, did you?"

Slavek seemed about to faint. We had all turned a deep red by this time. Ofinka, however, regained the upper hand and said:

"Yes, thank you very much. May I introduce my lovers? This is my sister; she is in her last year as a medical student."

The girl turned her head toward us at last and I saw her face. It is hard to describe—beautiful and cruel, as if two different persons existed in it.

"The gentlemen are Bolshies, I hope. Have they come to take over our house and property?"

"That's right, Miss," I replied. "But you can finish your drink. We'll wait."

"How very gallant of you! In that case perhaps you'll join me."

I drank Scotch for the first time in my life, diluting it with soda like the girl. She now ceased to take any further notice of us, but we did not mind that. We stared at the fireplace, as we watched a speeded-up film of the past few days and nights. Excitedly we recalled the most memorable moments.

"Do you remember how . . . ? And what about . . . ?"

How curious! The day was not yet done and already it belonged to history.

Peter, who had drunk more than any of us, started to recite his "Red Rhythms" in a very loud voice:

How I hate your If and But,
Your goldfish, your budgies, your animal slobber,
Your banks, your tanks, your gold-greedy goblins,
Your saints, your private Mass, your panders, your whores,
Their breasts, their loins will find consummation soon—
In the fires of the revolution.

It sounded a little forced. However, the girl's comment bowled me over with the rest of us.

"You are so revolutionary that I imagine you must be impotent."

I jumped to my feet. But Peter only took one step, then he fell. She was at his side in a flash. It surprised me to see how matter-of-fact she could be.

"Alcohol poisoning," she said. "Give me a hand."

We carried him to the bathroom. She stayed there with him, and we could hear him retching. *Mon petit Pierre. . . .*

When I next opened my eyes she was again lying in front of the fire and looking at me. I got up quickly. It was ten o'clock. I had slept for three hours.

"I'm sorry—"

"Oh, that's okay."

"Where are they?"

"I took the vomiting poet home. The other two, I expect, are fucking."

I was quite fit now and I felt a sudden anger.

"Have you no shame?"

"Shame? What's that?"

"It's a natural human trait which distinguishes man from animals. An accidental quality that prevents us from returning to the jungle. But you, I can see, have shed your skin . . ."

"How is that?"

"Your real one is under you."

She looked at the tiger rug and laughed. I was now fully launched.

"You're cruel and heartless. You love offending and humiliating people, don't you? You insulted my friend, who is worth a hundred times more than you because he knows how to sacrifice himself for a cause. You're a typical daughter of a class which is incapable of creating anything of real value, which only knows how to make money. Can you wonder that we hate you so much?"

"I don't wonder a bit," she said. Strangely enough, without a trace of irony.

"Good night."

She stretched out her hand. I took it, and before I realized what she was doing she pressed it against her left breast. I leaned over her, unable to speak or move.

"Now I feel as if Klement Gottwald himself were caressing me," she said.

I saw red, and for a fraction of a second I thought I would strike her. I fell upon her, ripping open her dressing gown. I wanted her to cry out, to hit me, I wanted to humiliate her. But instead I heard her murmur in a strange, almost childish voice:

"Darling, be careful, won't you ..."

Afterward we lay quietly next to each other, and she put the question I had been afraid she would ask.

"How many times have you ...?"

My throat was parched and I needed a drink.

"Was it so bad?" I asked.

"Silly! You're fishing for compliments," she added in English. "You were just wonderful."

She laid my head on her breast and stroked my hair. I could not help wondering at her unexpected gentleness.

"I don't know, it must be your influence," she said.

"Nonsense, you can't just become gentle like that. You must have had it in you."

"Well, maybe they forgot to tell me."

"I'm telling you now."

"Yes, you are. Go on telling me."

"You're wearing a mask that doesn't fit you. Why?"

"After all, I'm a typical daughter of my class, aren't I?"

"Are you fond of them?"

"Of whom? All those idiots, drunks, and skirt-chasers? They make me sick! I'm glad they flopped today, let them go to hell. The trouble is I'm going with them."

This was no pretense. All her cynicism merely covered up her despair at what she saw as a catastrophe. I could not bear to look on at a stranger's suffering. A stranger? Suddenly she seemed very close to me.

"But you're wrong! Your ship is sinking, but don't you see that we are sending lifeboats out? Communism is intended to make people happy. Every human being, so long as he does not exclude himself from a society of equals. This is your chance. Abandon the wreck."

"How does one do it?"

"Look, both my grandfathers were capitalists—one was the

manager of a mining company, the other of a bank. But my father and mother revolted, they wanted their lives to mean something. And your sister has decided to join the Party."

She drank some whisky. I could see she was thinking hard.

"I don't think I could do that."

"Your sister has come to understand what you should understand as well. The revolution needs not only workers and soldiers, it also needs poets and doctors. Why shouldn't you be one of them? You're needlessly letting yourself be paralyzed by your class-consciousness. Your parents are an anchor tying you to your past. But you also have a harpoon aimed at the future."

"What on earth are you talking about?"

"Your children. For they are going to live in Communism."

B_____ was silent. I could see her eyes in the dim glow of the smoldering logs. They were humble and wild at once.

"Virgin Mary of the wild beasts . . ."

"And what's *that* supposed to mean?"

"That's a prayer I am addressing to you. Have mercy on yourself and on your future children. What are you afraid of? I too am the revolution, you know. I'll be there with you, if you wish, and I'll teach you everything. I'll teach you how to live."

"And in return I'll teach you how to love!"

I raised myself on one elbow, but she pushed me back, whispering:

"No, just lie there."

I had not realized that it was only on the borderline of shame that the wide country of love begins. Thanks, B_____. Without you I'd have been like a blind man all my life.

Suddenly my entire body, my soul, my memories, and all my desire were compressed into a vacuum.

Then the long, soothing murmur of blood, through which I heard as if from afar the sound of B_____'s low, husky voice.

"You know, I think I'd like that . . . to have a child by you."

Five days that shook Czechoslovakia.

It is getting dark. I'm back home. On the table stands a bottle of wine, put there in readiness yesterday. Soon my parents will come back. We'll open the bottle and tell each other the history of February 1948. But I'll keep one chapter to myself. For the time being.

Tomorrow I'll ask B____ to marry me.

What does it matter that she is five years older than I? On the contrary—that's all to the good; we'll be both teacher and pupil to one another. She'll make a man of me. And I'll make a Communist of her.

I gaze at the palm of my hand. It still holds the memory of Klement Gottwald's handshake and the warmth of her body. I have nothing to be ashamed of. The fight for our cause and the fight for my love—two phases of the alternating current which gives me strength, which forms my whole life.

For you, my Party.

With you, my love.

Thursday, 22 August 1968 / Rome
(Continued)

Although we had taken our separate beds, I awoke in her embrace. Our bodies had come together in sleep, as they had over a thousand nights. The nightdress had rolled up to her tanned stomach when she assumed her usual sleeping position with her knees drawn up almost to her chin. Invariably she lay like this, touchingly reminiscent of an embryo. Why is it that we so quickly abandon this pose for one that is more suited for the coffin? Every night throughout her twenty-six years she returned to a state of prenatal bliss, as if by so doing she wished to protect herself against death and all the world's evil.

Both the shutters were closed, but the sun was so strong that even the narrow rays that penetrated the chinks filled the room with light. She gave a sigh and came awake. Befuddled by sleep, she thought it was morning.

"All night I dream that you and I go underground and want to get in touch with Dubcek ... all we know for sure is that he has hidden himself in a shop where they sell wool and knitting needles ... so we go there to look for him, thinking he is there among the shop assistants, perhaps even disguised as one of them, but we can't find him, we search the whole place but there is no sign of Dubcek, and then we see that he is cleverer than that, because he is standing in the shop window, pretending to be a dummy and holding a . . . what do you call it?"

"A ball of wool?"

"No, no, a skein. Yes, that's it, he is holding a skein in his hand, and it keeps unwinding. There is a spinning-wheel and a chair in the window, too, and Dubcek says: 'No one wants to sit down at the spinning-wheel and to spin my yarn,' And then he cries."

"And you sat down."

"I woke up just then."

"Well, and what does it mean?"

"A very sad dream. My granny dreamed about a spinning-wheel when my grandfather was in Russia in the First World War. And next day she got a letter to say he had been taken prisoner."

"But surely your grandfather came back, didn't he? Otherwise your mother would never have been born."

"Mother could have been born even if he hadn't come back. But perhaps Granny's dream didn't include the thread."

"What does a thread mean?"

"A thread means long misfortune. And if it breaks, it means death."

"It didn't break, though."

"That's because I woke up."

"Well, that doesn't matter. After all, it's only what's in the dream that counts. Fortunately you happened to wake up just in time."

"I *always* wake up in time . . . unlike others I could mention."

Reality returned as the effects of sleep wore off. Slowly and as if automatically she stretched out her legs, the rolled-up night-dress giving her a pretext for freeing her hands. The cool waters of Suez, dividing two hostile shores, again began to flow soundlessly between our beds.

"What time is it?" she asked.

"Almost four."

"What a reliable friend you've got."

"He promised to come and see *me*, not you."

"That's right. And I couldn't go for a swim because of him."

"I had no idea you wanted to go swimming today of all days."

"Maybe you've forgotten that that was the reason we came here in the first place."

"I thought we had other things to worry about."

"Well, I can go for a swim even if I have other things to worry about, can't I?"

"Who's stopping you?"

"I don't go swimming alone even in Prague."

"You could hardly have expected me to come along today."

"Of course not. I was waiting for that friend of yours."

"I guess he too has other worries just now."

"Think so?"

My irritation increased. I felt tempted to tell her that the liking she had shown toward him was utterly illogical and that, in any case, she didn't need to show it so blatantly. But before I could say anything somebody knocked on our door and opened it—the hotel receptionist. He looked at her with obvious pleasure. She squeaked and then, unable to cover herself up with the blanket since she was lying on it, she slid behind the bed and lay on the floor.

"*Buon giorno. Un signore vuoli parlare con lei.*"

The receptionist stepped aside to let the visitor through and with a smile closed the door behind him.

"For Christ's sake, tell him to go away!" she moaned, still lying on the floor behind the bed.

"*Kruzinal . . . !*" the visitor stuttered in Czech. "Sorry, I had no idea . . . I'll wait in the restaurant downstairs. God, that fool receptionist!"

"I'm attending a congress at Naples," he told me a little later. "What do you drink at this time of day?"

"Nothing when I'm at home, here Campari."

"*Cameriere!*"

He ordered our drinks in what seemed to me perfect Italian. Then he stopped the waiter.

"*Un momento* . . . what about your wife?"

"Oh, Campari too, I expect."

And since she was not there I could put the record straight.

"She isn't my wife, by the way."

"Oh, I understand," he said, winking.

"I don't think you do, but never mind."

"Anyway, she's a peach. Is that the proper Prague slang? But I expect they have other things to think about there just now.

You know, yesterday I realized to my horror that I was still very much a Czech. We were having our normal briefing when my boss came in and told me about the invasion. I was completely knocked out. And so today I decided to drive to Rome and go to the Embassy to see if any of our people needed help or advice. I heard someone mention your name and I remembered at once."

He was still talking but his eyes were fixed somewhere above my head and he got to his feet with a rapt, admiring expression on his face. The shadow of her wide-brimmed summer hat lay like a strip of lace across her breasts, almost bare in the low-cut dress without a bra. And miniskirts must have been invented by a man who had seen her legs.

It was quite fantastic how little I cared. He kissed her hand and apologized once more for barging in on us.

I explained that he was the husband of an old friend of mine and had come to offer us his help.

"That's awfully nice of you," she said. "Where is your wife?"

"She died last year. Lung cancer—and yet she never smoked a single cigarette."

Although he gave the impression of being tough, his eyes filled with tears as he spoke. The thought flashed through my head about when would I again be able to see the grave of my parents.

He had fine, trustworthy eyes, broad shoulders, a jutting chin, and a crew cut. It is incredible how nature and tradition mold a man in their image.

Now it was her turn to apologize. He only waved his hand and changed the subject.

"When I came to Canada in fifty-one all I had was my diploma from the Technical College. I read in the papers that in Saskatchewan they were looking for an expert in hydrology, so I thumbed a lift up there. A matter of four thousand miles. There were ten of us who applied, a Jap, an Englishman, two Americans, five Canadians, and me. When the interviews were over they called me in and asked: 'Where did you say you come from?' 'Why, from Czechoslovakia.' 'Never heard of it. Here are the maps, keys, and a gun, and you can start out at once.' 'What are the keys for?' 'For the car out there in the yard. It'll be deducted from your salary.' 'And the rifle?' 'The rifle? To shoot bears with, of course.' Good, isn't it? Today I look after a province that's as big as half of Europe and my boss, when the two of us watched the evening news on TV last night, cried like an old whore."

He had been in Canada for seventeen years, yet his Czech sounded as if he had come straight from Prague. The Prague of seventeen years ago, that is.

"We spoke nothing but Czech at home. Even my son speaks it, although otherwise he might be a born Canadian. Now he is at college, so I have my work cut out. America is splendid, but the women aren't worth a shit, if the lady will pardon the expression. Why, for heaven's sake, has that nutty Czechoslovakia got a monopoly on the right sort of women? And why do so few of them run away?"

"Now's your opportunity," she told him. "This year practically all the attractive girls are abroad, holidaying by the sea."

She was scribbling something on the back of the menu.

"I don't mind telling you that that's one of the reasons I am here, to pick me up a Czech girl. Wouldn't you say I was right? I'm almost forty, work like a dog, so why should I live alone like a backwoodsman? What's the meaning of life after all?"

"Will she adjust to the life over there, though?" I asked on purpose.

"Oh, sure. To tell you the truth, that's not the problem."

"What is, then?"

"To readjust. I got used to the different climate, to the work, the money, and the bears very quickly. But to this day I can't help remembering how, at home, you could talk to just anybody you liked and be sure to have an interesting, intelligent conversation. The Czechs are simply a wonderful people. Over there you can only talk to hydrologists about water, to a dentist about teeth, and with strangers about the weather. But as long as a girl isn't too culture-conscious she'll settle down all right. Culture is groggy in America. She needs to be interested in iceboxes, automobiles, air conditioning, and so on. A gym teacher would do fine. Do you happen to know of one?"

We didn't. He ordered another round of drinks.

"When did you leave Prague?"

"On Saturday."

"My, you were damn lucky."

"That depends how you look at it."

"Look at it just the way it is, that's all. You see, there ain't no such thing as democratic Communism; that's one thing the Russians are absolutely right about. What Mr. Dubcek was trying to do had nothing in common with Communism, and that's a fact. The firm had changed both its owner and its wares but had kept its old name for the sake of its regular customers. There's only one Communism, and we saw it go into action once again in Prague last night. I guess you know what has been happening there. All that fine talk about the convergence of Western and Eastern socialism is just a lot of babble. What we in Canada are doing for the social welfare of people and what the great teacher of nations Leonid Brezhnev has in mind simply cannot converge. For one thing, the Russians have been so brainwashed by now that nothing can help them except a cosmic fluke or—pardon me —a swift kick in the ass. This is simply 1938 all over again, and when they have done their bit in Czechoslovakia they will march right on because for example in *this* country you'll find quite a few boys who will welcome them with open arms just as we did in May 1945. Listen, pack your bags and make a new home in Canada. There are plenty of Czechs there already, and some of those whom you for years had denounced as traitors have given Czechoslovakia such a good reputation that we could have a whole province for the asking, so to speak. The Czechs have a right to exist because wherever they go they leave something worthwhile behind them, and at least over there across the ocean they can be sure that no one will run down what they have achieved in later years."

The receptionist called me to the telephone. As I went, his monologue kept ringing in my ears, naïve and a little absurd perhaps, but at the same time magnificent.

"Hallo. Did you get my message?"

"No."

"I might have known. I have only just finished work and I'm coming straight down to fetch you. Tell your lady friend that I'm terribly sorry but will make it all up. Tell her I'll lay nocturnal Rome at her feet."

I returned from the telephone feeling that I was one of the few normal Czechs left. It seemed that the attraction was mutual.

94

When I reached the street I saw the Canadian Czech leaning across the table and kissing her hands, which he held in his own. He smiled at me with zest.

"You see, I keep telling you our women are fantastic. No Canadian girl would carry off a situation like this. Sweetie, you'd be the first lady in Alberta."

On the back of the menu she had drawn a quick caricature: The Canadian, returning home with a whole flock of Czech girls, warmly greeted by a number of bears. I felt like remarking that for a thousand lira any of the student painters on the Piazza di Spagna would do as much in five minutes, but then in all fairness I had to admit to myself that the drawing certainly had something undefinably Czech about it. I therefore limited myself to giving her Peter's message. As I had expected, his apology was accepted graciously and his proposal with evident satisfaction.

The Canadian took his leave at once, leaving his visiting cards with addresses in Naples, Montreal, and Edmonton. She got up to go, wishing to take a bath before we went out, and he kissed her hand once more and said:

"Should you meet a girl friend, put in a good word for me. I'll be here until Sunday, at the Hotel Parco dei Principi. And if she's anything like you, tell her she can wake me even in the middle of the night."

I accompanied him across the road to his huge car. He was carrying the menu with the caricature as if it were a sacramental wafer. As we passed my car he bent down and put his hand on the number plate, hot from the glare of the sun.

"Just a damn ordinary car and you feel you can smell the meadows of South Bohemia!"

At long last I was able to ask him:

"Your wife had an older sister—"

"That's right, she did."

"What's she doing?"

"Oh, she went nuts and married a doctor from Havana. Ran off to Fidel with him."

Friends,

Forgive me, for addressing you in a way we haven't used for some time, but the word *Comrades* would be even less fitting. It is to you that I am writing my last letter.

I recited your verses because I believed in them. Because, after everything we had been through by the age of seventeen, I too thought that Communism meant freedom and justice.

The same applies to her, even though she had grown up in an environment beyond even our dreams. She had something to lose, she gave up comfort, luxury, her home and whole way of life. That is why I think she was the bravest of the lot of us. I remember that you, too, considered her to be a living proof of the potency of our ideal.

> We're sailing together
> To a future bright
> As we work together
> On our building site.

Underneath the verses the author had written by hand: For Ofinka on joining the Communist Party of Czechoslovakia. . . .

When I came to tell you that the Party Committee at the University had refused her application you were indignant, speaking of dogmatics and idiots. You, Peter, promised to intervene on her behalf. Later you explained to her that the Party was going through a critical period when it had to be a militant organization of the working class. I asked you how, in that case, we could remain members and you said that it was probably because one had to distinguish between those who had joined before February 1948 and those who always join the winning side for their own selfish purposes. The Party had to protect itself against careerists even at the cost of perpetrating some temporary injustice.

This sounded logical enough, and Ofinka accepted your view, even though at the same time the Party took in people I wouldn't even ask to save me from drowning. And she went on reciting your verses. Among other places, in the square which I can see now from the window of my hotel, in April of this year, the day her parents and her sister defected to the West. They waited all night for her at a prearranged rendezvous not far from here, yet she elected to stay with us.

She offered their villa to the state, to house the homeless, in exchange for a room in a student hostel. She moved there with her books and a single suitcase of clothing, having only one desire— to finish her studies and then go to work as a doctor in the borderlands.

All this you knew. What you don't know is that we came back from our voluntary stint on the Ostrava building site on September fifteenth. She insisted on doing manual work with me, although she could easily have gotten a job as a medical worker at our headquarters. I asked her not to volunteer for night shifts, but she told me she wanted to liberate herself completely from her class. That she wanted to gain the Party's confidence and find her real self. A day before we left for home she was decorated for her exemplary work.

The day after she came back to Prague she was told at the school that she would not be allowed to continue her studies. She pointed out that she had been an excellent student; she spoke of her work in our drama group, she showed them the award she had won in Ostrava. The Action Committee, composed of her fellow students, replied that she was not the only one left behind by reactionary elements to keep an eye on their property. The bourgeoisie was clever, but the Party was cleverer and would not tolerate the formation of a fifth column.

She would not let me go to you in case I got you into trouble. I obeyed her, being afraid that you might tell her the same things as the Action Committee. That same day she had to move out of her room at the hostel. The villa has been taken by an official from the Ministry of the Interior. So I took her home. She slept in the kitchen. Still she did not give up, she went to the Tesla factory and asked for a job on the conveyor belt.

You see, she still hoped that in time she would convince us of her good faith and sincerity.

The factory evidently asked for a report from the school. When she had been there a week they told her that they could not have bourgeois elements infiltrating the working class because they were manufacturing radio and telephone parts. She asked what she was to do. Whereupon the man in charge of the personnel department asked her why she had not left the country with her parents.

When she recounted this interview to us that evening she started to cry for the first time. I said at once that I wanted to marry her.

I thought my mother would have a fit. She lamented that I was only twenty-one, that Father didn't know what was going to happen to us tomorrow because he owned a small business, that they both had to work hard for me to study at the Drama Academy and now I had to make things even more difficult for them. She said the man at the Tesla factory had been right, so many people were running away. Why didn't she follow her parents, she would have a soft life of it and would never have to lift a finger...

Yes, that is exactly what my mother said. And then she sat down next to Ofinka, stroking her hair and begging her to stay as long as she wanted to. The times made us all so inhuman....

The times, my friends, to which we have all given our hearts, our energies, and whatever little talent we may possess.

And now I am sitting here in a little hotel in the town square of Domazlice, writing my last letter from Bohemia to the two of you. By the time you receive it I'll be over the border. I know you'll call me a traitor. But I'm not leaving to fight against you and what you stand for. I just want to go with her. It is my duty.

You have allowed your Party cards to drown the voice of reason and conscience. I cannot do that.

I feel dreadfully depressed and ask with Comenius' Pilgrim:
Oh God, if any God there be, have mercy on me, a poor sinner. Yet no one answers me.

Goodbye. The future will decide which of us was right.

Yours,
Slavek.

Domazlice, 2 October 1949

I had promised to take C_____ to see *Maxim Gorky's Childhood*. She would now be waiting for me outside the Alfa cinema. Instead, I was sitting with Peter in the Slavonic House, at the table at which the three of us had many times pooled our resources to buy a single lunch, toasting our successes with a bottle of soda water. Today we drank wine, feeling gloomy and miserable.

"What's he going to do abroad? An actor who doesn't know any foreign language. What a tragic mistake, Peter. I can never think of him as a traitor."

"Nor me."

"He did more for her than was good for him. You and I are cowards."

"A coward is someone who acts out of fear. Are you afraid of anything? No, it's Slavek who lacked courage."

"Courage to do what?"

"To leave her."

"But he was in love with her!"

"Perhaps this was his mistake."

"But he had good reason to love her. Ofinka was one of us. I can understand why they felt unable to take her into the Party, but why couldn't she continue her studies? We both know a certain young lady who is not fit to tie her shoelaces, and yet she can do anything she likes just because her father happens to be a stoker."

"That is our own hurt feelings talking. And our upbringing. Let's be glad that we have grasped the need for a revolution. But that's about all. You and I aren't proletarians, we grew up in soft homes, read books, never knew hunger."

"I did. My father was unemployed before the war."

"But it's still not the same thing. Read your Marx and Plekhanov more carefully. Whether we like it or not, we have been molded by the traditions of the class we both hate. That is why we alone could never have defeated it. Just think how many revolutionaries from our ranks failed when it came to the crucial moment. Some just caught a cold, others had a fit of sentimentality. The proletariat is simply tougher. They have nothing to lose and as a result they don't mind taking risks. They know that any defeat has to be paid for with blood. That is why they lack sentimentality. They have to rely on themselves alone, and for that reason cannot trust even us completely. Remember the Trotskyites? How are the workers to distinguish between their allies and their enemies in the midst of battle? The tragedy of the French Revolution is not that it devoured its own children but that it shrank from shedding further blood before it had liquidated all its opponents. A wave of sentimentality caused a little man to become head of the state who then cost France a thousand times more dead than the revolution."

"Ofinka is no Napoleon. She loved this country and wanted to be a doctor, to heal its citizens in a region where doctors won't go for love or money."

"She was just as nontypical a bourgeois as Slavek was a Communist. Only the worker who considered her application for Party membership, and the worker whose job it is to decide who can study at the University, and the worker responsible for the personnel department at Tesla—only they have their class experience. This may seem rough to us, but as you can see it was not unjustified. In the end Ofinka showed that she couldn't persevere. She remained true to her class origins."

"That's all very well, but what did you expect her to do?"

"You know that as well as I do. We would have arranged for her to go back to the building brigade in Ostrava. Or got her a job in a factory that does not make military equipment. Or perhaps she could have worked on a farm for a time."

"But you forget she wanted to be a doctor."

"So did thousands of others before her, who might even have had more talent but never made it to the University because their father happened to be a stoker."

"Does that mean we are only trying to replace one injustice by another?"

"No, it doesn't. That's something we certainly don't mean to do and mustn't do. Only before we can do anything else, the original injustice has to be completely eliminated. The proletariat has a right to its own doctors, its own teachers, its own Army officers—even its own artists, come to that. Maybe one of these days they'll come to us and say, 'Look, boys, we want you to spend a couple of years working in a factory so that you will know how and what you are to write for us.' What'll you do if that happens? Will you skip the country too?"

"Don't ask silly questions. You have known me long enough to know that I'll always go wherever the Party sends me."

"Because you have come to realize that revolution is not just a game to be played for kicks. Maybe that's how it seemed when we were still at school and came into the classroom wearing the five-pointed star in our lapel. We have chosen revolution as our lot, for life and with all that this implies. One of the possible consequences may well be that only our children will reap what we have sown. We cannot hope to earn the glory of great military leaders; at most we'll have the satisfaction of knowing that we did our duty and, like ordinary soldiers in the ranks, marched without complaining and reached our goal. If he really loved her so much, he should have convinced her that this was the right thing to do. And if this proved impossible, he should have had the same courage and strength as you had."

He was obviously referring to B_____, forcing me to think about her again. Now I can face it once more, thank God.

The mistake I made was not in falling in love with her. I had, after all, managed to remain my own self. But I tried to make her see things our way. That was why she embraced me. And it was also why she left me. Not I, but she found the strength to refuse me admittance one night last May. And a lucky thing for me she did, too. I still tremble when I recall those ten weeks of spring when she gave me all the keys to her body. I was beside myself with love. What would have happened if she had asked me to go with her? Of course I would have refused. Would I, though? Perhaps.

And so it was a mistake to fall in love with her.

Peter was right. We had chosen our lot, and everything else was secondary. A soldier could not love someone on the other side of the barricade.

Perhaps I have at last found my real love in C_____. Mustn't count my chickens, though. I have been deceived twice already. For the time being I lend her books and take her to see my favorite films. In the semi-darkness of the cinema I often glance her way and am happy to see her react just as I have. Her father, a Communist, had been executed by the Germans during the terror that followed Heydrich's assassination, and she cannot remember much about him. She also wanted to be an actress, but mainly because she hoped to help people to live better by showing them the example of the greatest heroines. I made up my mind not to kiss her or to commit myself in any way before I could be quite certain that she would say the same thing to the Gestapo commissioner Bohm as Gusta Fucikova did when he threatened her with death:

"That's no threat, Commissioner, I beg you to do it: if you execute my husband, execute me as well!"

Today I know B_____ would never have said this. Nor Ofinka. Oh, Slavek, you set out on the road to treason the very first time you took her out.

Did I write treason? I did.

For the second time in my life I am drinking to a dead friend. The difference is that Robert has remained forever with us. You did not.

---

24 April 1968 / Prague
(From the diary of the writer PK)

I have read the complete protocol of the April session of the Central Committee. It lasted six days with 144 members taking part in the debate, and it approved the Party's Action Program and the composition of the new Cabinet. It was a performance worthy of sportsmen.

Although for the first time the discussion had been published in toto, I had hoped to find in the protocol an unpublished paragraph or two giving more details about the Dresden meeting of six Party leaders. I found no such thing. Did they really travel all that way only to give us a friendly warning against antisocialist forces and then to "wish us every success in our work, assuring us that we had their full backing"?

How in that case was one to explain that the press in the German Democratic Republic had stated that Antonin Novotny had retired for reasons of health? And what was one to make of the incredible pronouncement by Professor Kurt Hager, who claimed that Dubcek's policies were "a consequence of the efforts of the West German government of Kiesinger and Strauss"? That was a new one. Surely the German comrades, more than anyone else, kept in line too habitually for it to be supposed that they had committed a faux pas of their own accord.

Did perhaps our big brothers demand something else, something so completely different that our leadership did not dare tell us about it? Whatever the truth of the matter, one gained the unpleasant impression that even our "process of democratization" was still built on two floors—one to which the common man was admitted and another with a salon for VIPs only.

The district conferences held in March had made an unexpectedly strong assault on the foundations of the bureaucratic pyramid. These bureaucrats had for years translated the wishful thinking of the leaders into a political system. Now regional conferences had demolished the middle layer, the rising wave carrying away with it officials whose only qualification for their job had been loyalty, and in many cases even this was just a sham. The new candidates for their places were educated, intelligent men who enjoyed the voters' confidence and who had a background of nonpolitical careers that made them independent of the powers-that-be. It was a foregone conclusion that this flood would soon reach the gates of the Central Committee itself. That was why some of its members delivered speeches that showed how concerned they were to stem the tide before it was too late.

"The most disturbing fact is that this time the process of democratization is no longer confined to the Party but has become a public affair unparalleled in the Party's history. . . ."

Truly a disturbing thing in a country that has been fighting for civic and social liberties for exactly five hundred and fifty years!

If there is anything disturbing about the whole thing, it is the situation inside the Central Committee. This body, which in January gave its approval to the new course, was now paradoxically becoming the last bastion of the old guard. Had it reached its Waterloo, or was it still only on Elba? In spite of all the oaths taken on the banner of democratization, the Central Committee was still theoretically capable of voting the sad Bonaparte of Cakovice back into power.

"There will be meat in the shops, comrade housewives, there will!"

What if we were to hear these words once more in the May Day procession next week?

No wonder there is a growing clamor for an extraordinary Party Congress. No wonder the Central Committee, in its April session, only agreed half-heartedly to convoke it "at such a time as is consistent with its thorough preparation."

As the chairman of the Prague organization of the Writers Union

—and of course also for purely personal reasons—*I* found the following two paragraphs of the Central Committee resolution the most interesting of all:

"A short discussion took place regarding the disciplinary action taken against the Communist writers Pavel Kohout, Ivan Klima, Antonin Liehm, and Ludovik Vaculik. All those who took part in the debate agreed that this action had been an administrative measure not in accordance with the usual practice. The September plenary session had made its decision on the basis of erroneous, distorted information which it had received about the Fourth Writers Congress.

"Having taken all the circumstances of the case into account, the April plenary session has revoked the expulsion from the Party of the writers Ivan Klima, Antonin Liehm, and Ludovik Vaculik, as well as the reprimand and caution given Comrade Pavel Kohout. It has further been decided to drop the disciplinary proceedings against Comrade Milan Kundera. The April plenum instructed the Party organization of the Writers Union to evaluate the preparations for the Fourth Writers Congress, the work of the Party groups, as well as the individual speeches made at the Congress. It also recommended a review of the resolution adopted on the withdrawal of Comrade Jan Prochazka from the function of candidate of the Central Committee of the Communist Party of Czechoslovakia."

This meant in fact that I had been asked to preside over the tribunal that was to try my own case. Our Party organization naturally refused to go along with this, for it had "evaluated" the Congress shortly after the pogrom and had come to quite unambiguous conclusions. It made only one demand, that the remedy had to be in keeping with the extent of the damage.

We conveyed this demand by telephone to the Central Control and Supervisory Commission. This body must have conferred very briefly, for almost immediately afterward they called us back.

"We're sending you their Party cards and you will simply return them," the man said, full of optimism.

"But what if they refuse to accept them?" I asked.

There was profound silence at the other end of the line.

"Quite apart from the fact," I added, "that since we did not expel ourselves, I don't see why we should readmit ourselves to the Party."

Then I passed on our committee's proposal.

"We'll call a meeting of all Communist writers living in Prague. You can give your explanation to them, the punished comrades can state their views, and then we'll see."

"What if they refuse to accept?"

"Then you can at least take the Party cards back with you."

It was May, the month of love, and mutual relationships were frank and open.

Liehm was in Japan, but Vaculik and Klima said they would come. They did not adopt any standpoint. Today's meeting was therefore attended with as much interest and anticipation as if it were the first night of a new play with an all-star cast.

I could not help recalling a similar meeting, held not quite seven months ago only a little distance away, in the People's House in Hybernska Street, where we had been invited for our punishment in public. It was on 6 October last year, and I arrived there half an hour late, having returned from the Hamburg première of my adaptation of Schweik at three o'clock that morning. Comrade Jiri Hendrych was already standing on the platform. On behalf of the Central Committee of the Party as well as that of Antonin Novotny personally he read us the riot act at his usual speed of six words a minute. The only vacant seats were right up in front, quite understandable under the circumstances. I took one and sat down.

Comrade Hendrych saw me and his round face turned pale. Putting on his jacket, which had been draped over the back of his chair, he left the room, exclaiming as he went: "You've buggered up everything!"

No, that's not true . . . this happened three months earlier, at the writers congress. This time he stayed put because he had things well in hand. It was the audience who was surprised to see me, since there had been rumors in Prague for several days now that, like Ladislav Mnacko, I had decided to stay abroad. P_____ was among those on the platform, taking some notes. When he raised his head and caught sight of me, he nodded, looking pleased.

I had come just in time to hear that I, too, had been in danger of being expelled from the Party, but that the leadership, including

Leader No. 1, had decided to take into account my activity with the Youth Union and especially the positive character of my exchange of views in Hamburg with Gunter Grass, which was published in Die Zeit. I was to be given a last opportunity, my punishment a mere reprimand and caution. The harsh verdicts delivered, there was an intermission to give us time to examine our respective consciences before the discussion started.

P_____ was obviously waiting until I had greeted my friends and fellow culprits, for he came up to me only just before the beginning of the second round and gave me a vigorous handshake.

"Glad to see you. People were saying that you wouldn't be back."

"Just wishful thinking. Don't worry, I won't give anyone that pleasure."

"I wouldn't have been very pleased. You'd have made a lot of trouble for me if you had stayed away."

"I know. When I had that business at the border I was already beginning to think that you were an old pig. But then you behaved like a real friend."

"Well, our first report had seemed to indicate that you had committed a criminal offense."

"You of all people shouldn't have believed that. You should have trusted me."

"That's exactly what I did."

"True. Thanks once again."

"Not at all. I congratulate you."

"What on?"

"That you haven't been tossed out of the Party. It was a tough job to talk them out of it."

"I can well imagine."

"I hope you're not going to be foolish ..."

He went back to his place on the platform, walking like a very tired man. Suddenly I felt terribly sorry for him. It was pure chance that I was not sitting in his chair and he down here among the "rebels."

Then I asked to be allowed to read them my six-page letter addressed to the Central Committee of the Party.

"... It is a gross distortion of the truth to say that the speeches made at the writers congress by Comrades Klima, Vaculik, Liehm, Kundera, Kosik, and myself, as well as by others, were aimed against the Party. The truth is that criticism by these and many other Communists has for some years now been leveled—as is the custom in any normal political organization—against certain comrades who represent certain tendencies harmful, in the opinion of many, to the Party. Neither at the Congress, nor at any time before it, was the Party as such criticized, but only the methods by which its cultural policy was being conducted, the letter as well as the implementation of the Press laws, and other shortcomings for which not the Party but certain individuals are responsible. They are now again, as so often before, trying to cover up the consequences of their own lack of qualifications and talent by means of increased pseudo-revolutionary fervor, thus exacerbating the existing crisis whose objective analysis would show them in an unfavorable light. . . .

"I have never known a writer who would claim to be infallible. Many of us—myself included—were the troubadours of schematism in the early years of the revolution. Comrades Novotny, Hendrych, and others like to remind us of this whenever they wish to put our present standpoint in doubt. They, however, never bother to mention that in those years the Party as a whole implicitly trusted the leadership. I do not even mention the fact that in spite of this there is in the majority of our lives a dividing line showing where we lost this unquestioning faith, a summing up of our own mistakes, private and public. In the life of the comrades who continually rebuke us in the most severe terms such a dividing line is unfortunately missing. . . .

"If I take into account all the circumstances, I cannot consider the reprimand and caution a generous gesture but must see it for what it is: an attempt to intimidate me, an affront to my honor as a Party member. I demand that the Central Committee enable me and the other accused comrades, some of whom have already been expelled, to state our case directly and without any intermediaries, and that it once more and objectively judge our thoughts and actions. It will then surely see that the harsh measures taken against us concern not simply a small number of people and one literary magazine but, in their consequences, Czech and Slovak culture as a whole, our whole nation, our allies abroad; and that the motives behind them were due to nothing but the fear that forces capable of overcoming the present patriarchal system might prevail in the

Party and replace that system with another, which would be consistent with the standards and the requirements of both our Party and our state. . . .

"This is the year 1967. In the knowledge of all that it implies, comrades, do not allow people to be again unjustly eliminated. Remember that it is only a short step from eliminating them from a list of candidates to eliminating them from our culture—and even from life."

Jiri Hendrych was inscrutable, P_____ visibly unhappy. It seemed unlikely that we two could ever understand one another again.

Now it was April 1968, and we were holding our meeting on the premises of the Marx-Leninist Institute in Celetna Street. I went to the point at once, asking Comrade Hlina, a member of the Party's Central Control and Supervisory Commission, to speak to us. He was evidently uncertain, but he said he was glad that he had been entrusted with this particular task, as he had not been present at the meeting in autumn at which the decision to punish the writers had been taken.

"The decision was influenced by the complicated international situation"—as if the international situation were ever anything but complicated—"which led to erroneous administrative and personnel measures in assessing your Congress. A negative role was likewise played by Comrade Novotny's assertion that the Congress was organized from abroad.

"Now it is quite obvious that, in the spirit of democratic centralism, it was not the Central Committee which should have dealt with this matter but the various Party organizations of which the comrades concerned were members. . . .

"The Central Control and Supervisory Committee erred by not recognizing in time the real causes of the controversy and by recommending the highest Party penalties instead of encouraging a well-informed exchange of opinions."

In conclusion Comrade Hlina expressed the Commission's apologies for the injustice it had committed, asking the comrades concerned to accept the Party cards which had been wrongfully taken from them and which he was now returning.

Being the nearest to the microphone, I expressed my satisfaction about the fact that the Central Control and Supervisory Commission was really best qualified to carry out this rehabilitation, if its members alternately can rectify wrongs in which they happen to have played no part. It was one more argument in favor of an extraordinary Party Congress, which would elect a new Party leadership—including a new Central Control and Supervisory Commission.

Jan Prochazka explained why he had decided to withdraw from his post as a candidate of the Central Committee.

"Several times I did my best to speak to Antonin Novotny with absolute frankness. I told him that a continuation of the present policy would lead the nation either into civil war or some other catastrophe. . . .

"Shortly before our Congress the Party's ideological department divided people into a number of categories: there were people they promised things to, people they threatened, and people they begged not to attend the Congress, or at least to refrain from making speeches there. One writer was offered a trip round the world, another was shown the stick. At that time the Central Committee presidium empowered Jiri Hendrych to reprimand me for very serious mistakes. . . . The day before I had co-signed a letter criticizing our policy toward Israel. Comrade Hendrych shouted at me that I was a fool and did not understand politics, that I ought to stick to literature. First of all, I was to write a letter of explanation to the presidium, on the basis of which they would decide on my future. I wrote something like this: Comrade Hendrych, following our talk I have the impression that politics is something to be feared and even better avoided. Perhaps it will be best if I do not become a member of the Central Committee, so that we do not compromise one another with our divergent standpoints."

Prochazka now expressed his willingness to work in the Central Committee, in which a different atmosphere seemed to prevail these days.

Ludovik Vaculik came to the microphone, his glasses and mop of hair giving him the appearance of a harmless piano tuner.

"This new resolution in fact only says that some kind of procedural error had been made, that what happened wasn't nice or correct. Nothing is said about fundamental issues, about the views I expressed at the Writers Congress. My first reaction was that one ought to refuse to be treated as a parcel posted one day to one address, only to be sent back again by the same people.

Whether one belongs to a community or not does not thus depend on the individual but on those who say yes one day and no the next. Yet, however much I wanted to refuse this, I could not because that would be to adopt a supercilious attitude to the people whose welfare concerns me.

"I'll gladly be a member of a Communist Party which will renew its authority by acting above all on a moral plane in conditions where—and you can understand this metaphorically or take it literally, as you wish—the Party has been separated from the state.

"Otherwise I have not changed my opinions one iota, nor will I change them even if the said Post Office decides to send me back again."

Applause and a feeling of relief that Vaculik, who so determinedly rejects all machinations, had taken the same decision as so many others. Ivan Klima also joined in.

"Finally I must say that this half year I have spent 'being punished' has on the whole been very encouraging because it has shown me true human solidarity, especially in this plenum, often in the case of people with whom my relations have not been too friendly. In our world this is immensely valuable. Together with what is happening in our society as a whole it gives me renewed hope. And so, although I had decided to let everything slide, I have again allowed myself to be drawn into the fray and I'll continue to strive for the same things I tried to achieve earlier."

All of us felt moved now, and it was suddenly clear to us that everything would be spoiled if the Party cards were returned by those who had been instrumental in confiscating them. So we went up to take them ourselves and the writer Heda Volanska immediately handed them over to our friends.

One of the speakers in the discussion on the present situation was one of the secretaries of the Party's Central Committee, Dr. Cestmir Cisar, who had at last returned from Rumania—where he had been sent by the aforementioned Post Office, with Antonin the Great himself playing postmaster.

"Our experiment arouses misgivings on the part of certain Communist Parties. It would be wrong to dramatize them. What we must do is see to it that the Party's Action Program is consistently put into practice and thus make our version of socialist democracy a historical reality. That will be our greatest triumph which will eliminate the question marks that hang over our path. . . .

"The relationship between Party and state will always remain a problem. Even on the basis of democratic elections the Communists will still remain in power. It is therefore necessary to create safeguards against its misuse, with the Communists subject to the same democratic control as all the other citizens. This problem can be solved if the Party itself recalls those of its functionaries who have failed in their duty, and if it does this before it is forced to do so by public pressure. That has been conspicuously lacking hitherto.

"The process of democratization cannot be carried out without far-reaching changes in personnel all the way down from the Central Committee to the individual works councils. A radical restriction of the Party apparatus will also be necessary, as it is no longer intended to serve as a watchdog."

Hearing this sentence I suddenly realized that I had not seen P_____ today. I asked a woman from the Prague regional committee about him. "Didn't you know?" she said in surprise. "He was recalled from his post yesterday."

"What is he going to do?"

"Oh, he speaks several languages. I guess they'll send him abroad somewhere now that so many diplomatic posts will be available."

◻

1 V 50 / Moscow

I picked up the axe and chopped the mahogany table into small splinters. I worked hard at it. To warm myself. Also to stop myself thinking about the happy times when we sat around it. Then I lit the small round stove, using the splinters for firewood, and watched the flickering flames, thinking that here was the last vestige of my childhood, my youth, my brief twenty-two years.

She opened her eyes.

"Sleep," I told her, annoyed that my own voice, hoarse from the frost, was incapable of expressing affection. I could not even caress her, as my hands were covered with ugly sores. All that remained were my eyes, which she could not see because she had secretly swapped her glasses for a dozen eggs.

"Go back to sleep, it'll be warm here soon."

She fell asleep as obediently as if she were my child. I picked

Father up and carried him into the passageway, strapping him to the sleigh with the same strap which had kept me secure when I was a child. I took him along Zykmund Wintr Street, where he used to take me for walks, up to the Castle and across Hradcany Square, where he used to lift me up in his arms so that I would get a better view of the fireworks on 28 October, our Independence Day. Now those hands of his were thin and whiter than his hair. I stopped and wanted to give him my gloves. My fingers let me down.

"Sorry," I said.

I put my gloves on again to continue our journey. I felt like crying, but the severe frost did not allow the tears to seep out. More and more sleighs came out of the houses, as if everyone wanted to show off everything they ever had.

In the Petrin Park, where I had built my first sand castles, soldiers were digging long, deep trenches. The hard, frozen soil broke spades as well as people. I waited in a fast-moving queue. Two men stood at its head, taking the bodies and placing them adroitly on the bottom of the pit. I wanted to lay Father down myself.

"Don't hold things up," one of the men said wearily. "The live ones are freezing."

They laid Father next to a woman with a child. They gave me back the scarf covering his face.

"Leave it there!" I almost shouted.

I could feel the ice-cold earth on my own face. They shrugged their shoulders. I asked them to tell me the number of his grave, and they each said something else. I set my watch with one hand pointing to the observation tower and the other to the church of St. Nicholas so that I should remember which grave it was.

On my way back I collected the bread ration for Mother and myself. They gave seventy-five grams of bran bread. I still had four lumps of sugar, so I would make some tasty sweet water for her to go with the bread. As soon as my hands warmed a little I would feed her and we would talk about pleasant things: how one day we would light the lamp and have tea in a restaurant.

The fire was still blazing in the stove, but she was dead. I ate both pieces of bread—the last of her many gifts. The first had been my life. What was I to do with it now? As evening fell, hundreds of airplanes swam in the sky above Prague like so many monstrous fishes. I felt like going out and throwing it to them. . . .

A bad dream, you think? No, that is a story which I tried to imagine in the context of my own life to savor its full impact. No doubt it sounds like the figment of a diseased imagination. Yet its living hero was standing right next to me a mere hour ago, in the midst of the dancing multitude in Red Square.

"And where *did* you go?" I asked him.

"Up on the roof. There was an air raid on. That night incendiaries rained down on the city and I put them out with my coat. Next morning the Home Guard was called up; the Germans had launched their offensive. Our neighbors buried my mother. They died before I returned, so I don't even know where her grave is."

In Leningrad alone a million people perished. But those who remained did not surrender. What words can express the suffering and the glory of this land? What gave rise to the mighty power that threw the most formidable army in the world back from the outskirts of Moscow, back from the graves of Leningrad and the ruins of Stalingrad and turned it into dust? You can read about it a hundred times and yet you will not come to understand it until a contemporary of yours, who crossed half of Europe on foot only to be brought down in Prague by the last grenade of the war, looks up above the Kremlin walls and says with great emotion:

"Stalin. That night he became my father. And my homeland my mother."

Does that sound pathetic to our ears? Maybe, but it is the truth. What was he to do, to whom was he to cling when death had shorn him of everything, like a stripped tree? Whom was he to think of as he fell asleep after a day's fighting, for whom was he to go into battle again in the morning? No wonder that everything he had lost and everything he could still hope for was personified for him by the man who led that great struggle as he had earlier led the struggle for bread and steel.

I confess that when I drove into Moscow for the first time from the Vnukovo airport I was staggered by the log cabins which I could see all the way from the interminable outskirts right into the center of the city. The postwar austerity of Czechoslovakia was luxury compared to the poverty of Moscow. The shop windows, the clothes of the people in the streets, even the furnishings of my hotel room could not compete with the smallest Czech provincial town. When I was asked to write my first article for a Prague paper I was desperate. But it only took a few weeks for me to understand Russia and to fall in love.

How old was the revolution that had set out to transform a backward Tsardom into a modern socialist state? Next autumn it would be thirty-three. The age of Christ. Since the civil war one Calvary after another, with blows raining down on face and back.

Now I understood why the Party had sent me out here on a diplomatic assignment. The poet who perhaps resided in me had been posed a question: what kind of eyes have you got? Will you join this country's enemies in derisively describing the primitive Russian shoes which it hadn't time to exchange for better ones, or will you instead discover the miracles it had managed to achieve wearing them?

It would soon be five years since the Liberation, but I still vividly recalled my gallop through newly liberated Prague. Somewhere on an operating table in my vicinity lay a boy from Leningrad just as old as I. They were amputating his leg. How many such people did I meet daily in the streets of this teeming city? No, no one need fear for my eyes. They know how to look and they can see under people's coats and behind walls where human hearts are beating.

I do not deny that I sometimes feel miserable here. I am no diplomat. It goes against my grain to speak in formal tones to people I would like to embrace. And I cannot resign myself to the fact that I am not allowed to visit them in their homes; they are still on the defensive against spies and traitors. I miss Prague. And I miss you. But I know I am serving a good and great cause, even though I am merely organizing an exchange of books and songs.

Midnight is descending on Gorky Avenue, and in a few seconds it will bring the Kremlin bells to life ... I have my window open ... Now! In Prague it is only ten, in Prague it is still the first of May, Petrin is full of lovers ... and there are two thousand kilometers between us.

I did not even wait for the changing of the guard outside Lenin's mausoleum because I wanted to write you as soon as I could about this whole day, and above all about the greatest experience of my life. But before that, the woman receptionist at the hotel gave me my mail. May Day greetings from Father. The usual crop of anxious advice from Mother, the sort she has been giving me since my elementary-school days, poor thing. And a letter from you—I opened it and the room was dressed in mourning.

Perhaps that is why I started with that sad story, to remind myself of the times we are living in.

"I feel sad," you wrote, "because I am all alone and I'm afraid that there's going to be another war. . . ."

I'd like to embrace you and whisper with you all night, as I did before my departure. I whispered words of affection then. Tonight they would be words of reassurance. Because today I at last saw Him in person!

He was standing on the gallery over the marble tomb which is the last resting place of his great teacher. It struck me for the first time that he was now already sixteen years older than Lenin, even though he had been born ten years later . . . it is only in our thoughts that the dead age with us; in actual fact our fathers become our brothers, sometimes even our sons! Thus the pupil who was standing there in his Army greatcoat and with raised palm acknowledging the love of hundreds of thousands had outlived his master by a full quarter-century of thought and struggle. I was oblivious of the music and the cheers. At a distance of a few dozen meters for several hours I followed his every movement, his every gesture, every hint of a smile so as to engrave them forever in my memory.

Now I knew for certain that he was no legend, no dream. He really did exist, a man of flesh and blood, standing on the bridge of a ship that was taking us into the promised age. We, who found safety on its deck in 1945, had sailed on a different ship before that, built out of blood and sweat by our fathers so that they should never again have to slave on foreign galleys. On its mast they had raised that lyrical red-white-and-blue flag of national hope and they believed in a safe passage, with their ship protected by the cruisers of the great powers. Then came Munich— and the proud fleet quietly steamed aside to allow the torpedo marked Hitler to hit us amidships.

That catastrophe will never be repeated! Maybe back there at home, on the very edge of the big deck, it seems to you that the enemy is in sight and getting ready to fire. Don't be afraid. We are no longer a small crew on a stormy sea. Together with the Soviet Union, with China and the other nations which have run up the flag of socialism, we are a thousand million. We are the greatest aircraft carrier in the world—and today I greeted its captain, for you as well as for myself.

He will never lead us into a war of conquest. But he will not hesitate to give the order for battle stations should anyone threaten us. Because where once Columbus' sailor cried out *Land ahoy!* we and our children will shout *Communism ahoy!*

On this boat no one must ever feel sad, my dear. On a boat such as ours no one is alone. What does it matter that we cannot kiss each other tonight? We have the good fortune of being among the first few on our planet to experience a relationship people have not known hitherto. It is formed by our love and our *Weltanschauung*. It is the bond of lovers who are at the same time comrades in arms. How much richer are we than those who stifle their emotions in a bourgeois corset of tears and jealousy.

This is our dress rehearsal. I am working and studying to be better able to write wonderful true stories about the life of my times. You must work and study so that you can give them new life on stage. Nothing less, but also nothing more difficult is implied by those two magic words, *socialist realism*, which have become our banner. Just as Stalin concentrated in himself the revolutionary experience and wisdom of millions of people, may the characters of our dramas personify their work, their hope, and their love. The classics of Marxism knew what they were talking about when they said that fairy tales were the purest source of realism. They are no less literature because they always allow Good to triumph over Evil. On the contrary. They became the water of life which gave people new faith. Today Faith has taken root in half the world, but that is one more reason why art must nurture its frail shoots. Let us oppose the decadent heroes of the West with the hero of a modern fairy tale that is becoming reality in our part of the world.

And all this emerges into a protest and a belief. My protest against sorrow, fear, and loneliness. My creed and—my confession on love.

It is the first of May, the time of love....

Those unforgettable verses of Karel Hynek Macha's!

The first of May, the time of strife!

That prophetic cry of Jan Neruda's from the gloom of the nineteenth century!

How should I call my First of May, I, their as-yet-unknown successor? — — —

A time of Love and Strife!

A time of strife for a better world into which our son will be born, conceived in a time of love.

Under the windows of the National Hotel there still surges a merry throng of people who have known how to bury sorrows, fears, and loneliness far more terrible than any experienced by you or me. They are disappearing around the bend of Gorky Avenue, but that is not the last of them; I am sure the crowd continues all the way to where the crescent moon is slowly sailing, the crescent moon that always reminds me of your monogram on a handkerchief.

It seems to me that if I leaned out of the window and gave the nearest person your name with the request that he pass it on, it would soon make its way to you. Let me try.

C____

___

Thursday, 22 August 1968 / Rome
(Continued)

I had not had time to rebuke the receptionist when his Skoda pulled in at the curb. It was too late now to find another hotel, so I left it for the next day. We returned to the table. The Canadian Czech had forgotten in his excitement to pay the bill, and we just carried on where he and I had left off. It was now almost six. The sun had ceased firing at last, but whisky and ice was still the best thing to drink.

The news he brought was meager enough. Among the first

buildings to be occupied in Prague were the Academy of Sciences and the Writers Union. Nothing more released on that subject. The Embassy had got hold of the note sent by our Ministry of Foreign Affairs to the governments of the five socialist countries, which repeated that the occupation contravened the UN Charter as well as the principles of the Warsaw Pact and demanded the release of all our interned politicians. His last news eclipsed everything else. The impossible had become a fact: since morning the Fourteenth Extraordinary Congress of the Party had been in session in one of Prague's factories, attended by over eighty per cent of the legally elected delegates. A communiqué was expected late tonight.

There was nothing to do but wait. We could now resume yesterday's Socratic dialogue. From the very start he was trying hard to keep it friendly:

I didn't mean to imply that it was your fault they invaded us. But surely we can't be naïve enough to believe that it is some misunderstanding that will be explained away tomorrow. The consequences of what has happened can hardly be foreseen, and they will last for years. Not only in our country, where they will again awaken the trauma of Munich and give rise to a reactionary nationalism which will identify the present power politics of the Soviet Union with socialism as such. The entire revolutionary movement will be equally hard hit. The Communist parties of the West base their existence on the theory that the center fully respects specific national conditions. What are they to say now? The right wing is jubilant.

I   Are these supposed to be arguments *against* me?

He   Those are arguments against political blindness. If the Soviets took this appalling risk nevertheless, the second alternative must have seemed even more catastrophic to them.

I   I don't much care for telling the future from tea leaves. Don't be offended, but it reminds me too much of Schweik's dialogue with the detective Brettschneider about His Imperial Majesty's marvelous strategy.

He   Marxist knowledge is based on analysis. If you claim to be Marxists, try and act like them more than we who, according to you, have discredited Marxism ... The chief difference between the socialist revolution and all previous ones lies in its international character. The bourgeoisie was able to triumph in a single country. It was in fact to its advantage. Its idea and modern organization give it strength, and it could then expand further.

I   But socialism also triumphed first of all in one country. One of the first ideas it had to discard for the sake of its very existence was the theory of a permanent revolution. Or are you perhaps at your time of life going to start defending Trotsky? Surely that's more my province. . . .

He   Truth becomes truth only in relation to objective conditions. Trotsky's truth was premature and that is why it became a dangerous lie. But ever since the end of the Second World War, when socialism spread to a large number of countries, its major threat came from its unequal development. While Czechoslovakia and the German Democratic Republic on the one hand entered the community of socialist nations with an advanced culture and a high standard of living, a country like China could only contribute illiteracy and famine; the Soviet Union and the other People's Democracies were somewhat in between these two extremes. With time these disparities increased still further, the poles grew farther apart. While some had to don uniforms and fight for the revolution, we decided to lift censorship and include the rights of minorities in our Party statutes. The scales became overweighted and were in danger of breaking down. That is why the center took action by reducing the load on one side.

I   This explanation will come in handy for all who have been saying these past twenty-three years that Czechoslovakia needed socialism about as much as a farmer needs lice.

He   The important thing is that socialism needed Czechoslovakia. The mistake you keep making is that you judge historical developments by the criteria of human life.

I   If I remember correctly, we promised our children that they would live in Communism. We even intended to enjoy it ourselves as old-age pensioners.

He   That, of course, is our greatest error, or rather the error of our teachers and leaders. We countered the illusions of our enemies by illusions of our own making. Instead of teaching them the ABC of revolution we told the masses fairy tales, describing five-year plans as some sort of express elevators that would take them straight into a paradise resembling Breughel's *Feast*. In this the politicians and the artists were equally guilty. One cold war and a number of homemade political-economic blunders were enough for the feast not to materialize. And at once people started to grit their teeth and complain about why should they cut pieces off their own small cake to give to some niggers. Last January the process culminated. At a time when China was holding the Soviet Union's living standards and political practices up as proof of its bourgeois treason, we solemnly launched our process of democratization. Don't you think it was short-sighted, to say the least?

I   I quite see that you can hardly be expected to jump for joy when January is mentioned. Your case made me ask myself whether people who in time might have changed their views had not unnecessarily been forced into opposition. But however that may be you should not lose your ability to think straight. January was to all intents and purposes the last opportunity to save the Party's prestige.

He   I am neither a little kid nor Antonin Novotny to compensate an inferiority complex by means of instinctive hatred. I would even go so far as to say that January was inevitable. It snatched the blinkers from our eyes and allowed us to see things in their true light. It revealed a split that had in fact started way back in 1956.

I   You mean the Twentieth Congress of the Soviet Communist Party?

He   Yes, that's exactly what I mean. I hope you won't suspect me of trying to defend Stalinist distortions. But they should have been eliminated differently! Khrushchev behaved like a doctor who tells a newspaper reporter that his entire clinic is suffering from cancer. Communists the world over were in a state of collapse. The more sensitive among them, especially the intellectuals, panicky, started to express doubts about the basic principles of revolutionary theory. Whole sectors of the front were now undefended, and naturally counterrevolution took advantage of this. One extreme begets another. There followed a tightening of the screws, which immediately provoked a new reaction. Since Khrushchev's speech socialism has been in a state of permanent crisis. Hungary represented its visible excess. Our January was less obvious, but for many it was even more suspicious.

I   Are you trying to defend the nonsensical propaganda from the German Democratic Republic about our insidious counterrevolution?

He   In the first place I'm not defending anything but merely stating facts. And secondly, if you want socialism in Czechoslovakia to be based on our very own national traditions, you ought to admit that socialism made in the GDR is strangely enough quite in keeping with their particular traditions. Unfortunately we know them better in their earlier version and as a result have a natural tendency to refute anything that comes from that quarter... and at the same time some people forget that the West Germans come from one and the same family. However, the standpoint of the Workers Party of the German Democratic Republic as regards our democratization process is the same as that adopted by a number of other Communist parties...

I   In particular those which have scarcely thirteen members.

He   The Cuban party is certainly not one of them, and it enjoys the confidence of the entire Latin American revolutionary movement...

I   While the biggest and best-organized Communist Party of Western Europe saw in the Prague Spring the first practical attempt to implement the testament of Palmiro Togliatti.

He   Don't delude yourself. I have just spent several hours talking to the leading representatives of the Secretariat of the Italian Communist Party. It's the old paradox all over again of dissidents being side-tracked into the diplomatic service, so that under these present circumstances they become devil's advocates. I assure you that I adhered faithfully to the latest statement of the presidium of our Central Committee; if anything, I overdid it because I'm a Czech Communist just like you. They were frank with me and told me that a large number of their organizations were critical of Longo's attitude because they too are not sure what it is we are really trying to do. Their own position in a capitalist country and their proletarian instincts make them see the Soviet intervention as a desperate attempt to prevent the disintegration of the socialist system. You see, the talkative man who is now spending his retirement fishing on his dacha near Moscow released a terrible genie out of the bottle. Having been thrown out of the window, Stalinism has returned by the door, holding Chairman Mao's little red book. If the Soviet leadership is successfully to withstand the attack from the left—not only for their own sake but also for that of the other European parties—it had to avert an assault by the right wing. Only a rank amateur cannot see that the occupation of Czechoslovakia at the same time resolves yet another problem. Hasn't it occurred to you that it was an operation for which something like a third of the forces actually used would have been ample?

I   I couldn't say. I'm only a captain in the reserves.

He   As long as they didn't mean to provoke armed resistance themselves—and they obviously didn't because they refrained from doing so—they knew there was no danger of such a thing. Our entire defensive system is aimed at the West. In that case, what was the reason? Maybe because of what they have already achieved. The West will now no doubt feel obliged to continue the existence of NATO. After all NATO would not have lasted much longer. That would at once cast doubt on the necessity for the continued existence of the Warsaw Pact, which had been expressly created as a counterweight to NATO. Have you any idea of the situation that would develop in Hungary, Poland, and the German Democratic Republic, where socialism has not taken such firm root as in our country and where anti-Soviet, and even anti-Russian, sentiments still play a large part?

I	Are you trying to tell me that sincere socialists and friends have been sacrificed for the sake of insincere ones?
He	For the sake of a balance of power that would once more have changed in favor of the imperialists.
I	But that's horrible!
He	Maybe, but it's as logical as free fall. This is not meant as an excuse, simply by way of explanation. Unless we understand this, we cannot possibly understand what has happened to us. And understand it we must or we'll perish. The USSR needed a basis on the strength of which it could refute Chinese accusations of revisionism and once more try to resolve their disagreements.
I	Don't be naïve! Even if the Soviets were to revoke the entire Twentieth Congress and send them Nikita Khrushchev in a crate, the Chinese would merely say: "Okay—now fall in line! You have shown how unreliable you are. From now on the center of the movement is in Peking."
He	I thought you said you didn't care for prophecies made from tea leaves. However, since you have taken the argument this far I can only agree with you. I'm very much afraid that socialism of the European type simply isn't capable of leading a real revolution of the starving masses in Asia, Africa, and South America. The proletariat in its classical form now exists in Europe only sporadically. The class consciousness of the working people is thawing in the soft climate of the consumer society. Just take a trip from Palermo to Milan and you will see what I mean. And as for the intelligentsia ... the intellectuals tend more and more to abandon revolutionary attitudes as soon as they first come into conflict with their conscience, which functions on bourgeois humanist lines. Just think of those three old friends who once swore to devote their lives and talents to the propagation of Communism. In the end only one has been left.
I	After all that has happened, you still think that the other two were traitors?
He	I think that only one of the two had the guts to go whole hog and declare his opposition openly.

I	You astonish me. Do you really consider it an aggravating circumstance that the other has remained a Communist?
He	Remained in the Party, you mean to say. You and thousands of other intellectuals have objectively made a political factor out of your private trauma. Instead of adapting yourselves to fit the revolution you have tried to adapt the revolution to fit you. If I tell you to your face that this has led to a revision of Marxism, then I'm not just quoting the Moscow *Pravda* but simply calling a spade a spade. There can be no socialism with a human face in a world full of wolves.
I	I have heard something like this once before today.
He	Well, it's about time you started believing it. It's the most dangerous of all illusions, which in our country has been drowned several times in blood. That is why it was doomed from the outset. It may be cruel, but that's how it is— revolution cannot be cheated, it has to be carried through to the bitter end.
I	You talk like a Maoist.
He	No, I'm only a tired middle-aged man suffering from a guilt complex. Although I *knew*, although I was really capable of sacrificing my life to the ideals of our youth, I have, when you come to think of it, finished up worse than you. I'm a victim of the same sentimentality I find in you. The difference is *I* was in the Party apparatus, which means I was co-responsible for permitting its liberalization. The liberalization manifested itself already in the choice of so incapable an amateur as Novotny for the post of First Secretary. We did not want to be tough with you, but on the other hand we did not know how to be anything else. That is why you were able to become a political force. And that is why we are drinking to the last hours of the Party. With your lips it offered the nation something it could never fulfil. It has lost, and the price it will have to pay is the loss of confidence. It is quitting a stage on which there is no other alternative. You and I both are responsible for the catastrophe which will follow. We can watch it through a telescope as if it were some eruption on the sun, and we can sing with Dante: *Lasciate ogni speranza voi ch'entrate!*

She called me at half past nine in the evening. I thought it was
C——— calling and hurriedly snatched up the receiver.

"I must speak with you," she said. "Can I see you for a while?"

I had met her twice in the past few years, on both occasions
with her senile gentleman. He must have been forty at the very least.
We both averted our eyes. Later Peter told me that her parents
had thrown her out and she was living in the student hostel. That
was all I knew about her.

Mother was asleep already. Since she became manageress of an
industrial canteen she has had to get up at five. Father was away
on business, something to do with the Poznan Trade Fair.

I waited for her in the park and then led her to my room in
silence.

"You have a huge flat . . ."

"Yes, we exchanged it because we had certain plans at the
time."

"Plans!"

She laughed harshly. I had expected her to be different, but I
had not anticipated quite how different. Despite my disillusion, I
often recalled her as she was in 1944. The wartime summer of
our radio ensemble in South Bohemia. A round, girlish face with
merry eyes, framed with short pigtails.

Now she wore her hair long, right down to her shoulders; she
had matured into a woman, and she was perhaps a trifle taller
than I. But the greatest change was in her eyes. Looking at them
I thought they had seen more than they had been able to grasp.

"I've heard you're getting divorced."

That hurt. But I did not want to play the usual comedy, not
with her.

"Yes, I've heard something to that effect too. Maybe she'll
change her mind yet, though.

"I could have sworn that you two would make a go of it."

"I guess we should have lived on our own and not with my
parents."

"But your mother is such a dear."

"Provided no one makes any claim on me."

"Funny, isn't it, that the woman always has to pay."

"What about you?"

"I'd like something to drink."

"Coffee?"

She shook her head, almost surprised that I could ask such a stupid question. For the first time I felt younger than she. Suddenly it occurred to me: it's exactly seven years since that night we spent together during the Prague Rising! Was that why she had come?

"I'll go and buy something."

"No, please don't. I'm going on trial tomorrow."

"What?"

"I'm going to be tried with a group of other people for subversive activity."

I thought she must have gone out of her mind.

"You think I'm crazy? Well, maybe I was at that . . . I sheltered Slavek."

"Slavek?! But he's in the West."

"He was arrested at the beginning of March."

I opened my mouth in surprise, but she began to speak at once, quickly and matter-of-factly, as if rehearsing a stage rôle. He waited for her outside her school department one evening, last February. She could not recognize him at first; it was dark in the street and he was wearing glasses and a police uniform. He told her he had returned home, received an amnesty, and had to join up in Moravia. Now he was in Prague on leave; his parents had moved out of the city and he had nowhere to sleep. He asked her to help him out.

"I still had the keys of our weekend cottage. It's empty in winter."

"How could you swallow his story? Don't you know that people are not called up for the police?"

"I thought maybe it was a kind of punishment."

"For God's sake, didn't it occur to you that he could only have come as a spy or saboteur? Haven't you read about the assassination at Babice and Revnicov?"

"He said he was very tired and wanted to rest."

Was she really so naïve or was she such a good actress?

"He spent a week at the cottage, then he said thank you and went away."

"Did you report it?"

"No."

"Why didn't you mention it to someone—me, for instance?"

"I was afraid of all Communists."

I had half a mind to get up and ask her to leave the house. But before I could move she burst into tears. I tried to soothe her. Then I started asking questions, but it was difficult to get anything out of her. She had been picked up at five in the morning and taken away, blindfolded, in a car.

"Is that a fact?"

It was. She had been interrogated all day, until midnight. They treated her decently. They wanted to know about the Academy and the theater; they gave her lunch, cigarettes, even some wine! That night they took her home and kissed her hand in front of her friends, who had already given her up.

"You can thank your lucky stars it was our chaps who interrogated you. Anywhere else in the world today things would have been far worse for you. Why are you still crying?"

They had come again, telling her she was to testify that Slavek had been preparing a political assassination.

"What? Slavek meant to kill Klement Gottwald?"

"That's more than I know."

"Well, what was it all about, then?"

"They said he had confessed that he had told me about it. I swore it wasn't true. They insisted. Today I was there for the third time. Think it over, they said. Either you go to court as a witness—or as one of the defendants! In that case the charge will be accessory before the fact, and that means from five to ten years in jail."

"Rubbish!" I cried. "They can't give you a choice like that twelve hours before the trial! If they meant to put you on trial tomorrow, they would have arrested you long before this."

"They showed me the indictment."

I could not believe my ears.

"And what did you do?"

"What could I do? You don't expect me to perjure myself, do you?"

I gave her a sleeping pill and put her to bed on my sofa. Then I went to see Peter. We had not met since we had both married. As in former times I threw small stones at his window. He was busy writing a propaganda brochure on the establishment of co-operative farms.

"This is my poetry now."

He never said it out loud, but I had the impression that he missed his work on the radio. I went straight to the point. His reply staggered me.

"I know all about it. They questioned me too and had me sign a statement."

"Why didn't they call me?"

"You know how busy they are these days. I told them everything that I thought could be counted in his favor. Unfortunately it seems to have had just the opposite effect."

"Yes, all right. But what about her?"

He knew nothing about the way the police had treated A_____. When I told him he was angry.

"That's unheard of! In the morning you and I are going to see the prosecutor."

Though we spoke as quietly as we could we woke his wife.

"What's the matter?" she asked.

"He has heard about Slavek."

"I keep telling you that you're terribly credulous. Like a couple of children."

She herself looked like a child, small and frail, almost transparent. I did not say any more about A_____.

Before I fell asleep next to her I stared a long time at her face. In sleep it had regained its former expression, free from deceit and incapable of betrayal. The old offense suddenly faded into insignificance. I was moved; I admired her. I would never have expected her actions.

Perhaps it was my gaze that woke her. Her eyes were anxious.

"Come on," I said.

We got dressed and went to Peter's place. Then a taxi took us all the way to the gates of the Pankrac prison. Peter rang the bell and produced his pass.

"I am from the Secretariat of the Central Committee of the

Party. These are my comrades. We have to see the prisoner from cell 1944!"

They led us down an endless corridor. Every few meters a barred door, each of which they opened with a different key. Behind the doors of the cells, depressing silence.

We reached the last one. It was empty. A____ clapped her hands.

"Oh, you've let him go!"

I notice the warden's eye fixed on an electric clock on the wall, a long, thin hand running swiftly round its face.

"He'll be executed in five seconds. Now!"

Suddenly, the whole prison seemed filled with a shrill clanging as a large number of bells started ringing all at once. My head ached. I turned off the alarm.

Still drowsy from the sleeping pill, A____ came only slowly out of her sleep. Mother had been gone a long time. We drank our tea in the hall. I told A____ about my talk with Peter and I succeeded in calming her a little.

At my suggestion she left the house ahead of me, walking directly under the caretaker's window. I did not want us to be seen together. C____ still belongs to my life and to this flat.

We parted company in the big square in front of the courthouse. I had nothing I could give her for luck, but I wrenched off one of my buttons; somehow this vaguely seemed a connection with her in my mind. Her eyes misted over, and she gave me a fleeting kiss.

"Please don't be angry with me for what I did to you ... I'm just a stupid girl."

She stopped in the doorway to wave to me. I did not think she even saw me. My heart contracted as I realized what must be going through her head. She must be thinking that it may be many months before she sees this square, the shops, parks, and bars again.

The prosecutor was not much older than we were. I felt admiration for him. Such people now had to carry the brunt of the struggle against the agents of Tito's revisionism and Western capital who had managed to penetrate the highest ranks of the Party.

I discovered that he had read my poems. That turned out to

carry more weight with him than Peter's special pass. Unexpectedly, he began to recite:

Genuine love has the greatest strength.
It gives us work and friends and love again,
But it comes neither at once nor for only a night,
For it remains true, decades, forever, through all human flux.

I again tortured myself with the question why this stanza had convinced so many people and yet never the one person it was meant for.

"I ought really to put you on the stand," the prosecutor said, laughing. "It's your fault that I got married."

Then he asked if we wished to be present at the trial. "But of course it's a relatively trivial case. Why don't you come when we're trying Slansky? Now *that's* going to be the real show."

We explained that it was this relatively unimportant case we were interested in. I gave him a brief summary.

"That, as I see it, is sabotage of revolutionary justice," I concluded. "Such interrogators in fact serve the enemy, and I can't help asking whether they don't do it on purpose!"

"You're making a very serious accusation," he said. "I'll certainly look into it. But the fact remains I have to put your lady friend on trial."

"Look, we've known her for eight years," said Peter. "If she *is* guilty of anything, then it can only be her bloody stupidity."

The prosecutor leafed through his papers.

"All right, I'll tell you what. My deputy is actually handling this case, but I'll interrogate her personally. You can depend on it, comrades, that she'll tell me everything."

As we were about to leave I plucked up my courage to ask:

"And what about him?"

"He is likely to be sentenced to life imprisonment. Unless of course more comes to light than we know already."

I was rendered speechless, and Peter was no doubt thinking the same thing. What must it be like to be told that for me the woods will no longer smell of pine and lichen, the rivers will cease to flow, and the city lights as well as the stars will be extinguished—for a whole lifetime?

Slavek entered the courtroom behind two elderly men, the third of a group of twelve men, boys, and women. A_____ brought up the rear. The courtroom was half empty. I thought he had caught sight of us.

IT IS TO YOU THAT I'M WRITING MY LAST LETTER!

Flanked by two tall uniformed policemen he looked lost. He was much thinner than I had known him. And he looked much older.

The two elderly men were former Army officers who had founded a subversive organization serving American intelligence. And Slavek had acted as their courier.

"So you and your mistress arrived at the refugee camp in Regensburg," said the judge, reading from the indictment. "Her family was already there?"

"Yes, they were waiting for us."

"Did they also live in the camp?"

"No."

"Where *did* they live?"

"In a hotel."

"Did you live in this hotel with them?"

"No."

"Where, then?"

"In the camp."

"And your mistress was with you?"

"No. She stayed with them."

"Why was that?"

"We weren't married. They didn't want their daughters to create a bad impression."

"They could scarcely have created a worse one. Her sister had sold herself already in Prague."

I felt the blood rushing to my face.

Now Slavek was testifying how Ofinka's parents had sent him— did I hear right?—back to Prague to visit an aunt who was to give him the family jewels. They were to grace the wedding when he married Ofinka.

"Did you bring the jewels?"

"No."

"Why not?"

"Because I didn't find any aunt."

"What did you think of that?"

"I didn't know what to think."

"And what do you think now?"

"That she never existed."

"In that case why did they send you to her?"

Silence. His head was bowed, his back bent. His voice grew quieter until it faded completely. Was he ashamed to speak in front of us? The prosecutor also seemed to have us in mind.

"I must ask the defendant to speak up."

"I guess they didn't want me to come back."

"What gave you that idea?"

"A day after my departure they left Regensburg."

"Where did they go?"

"To America."

Peter and I stared at each other uncomprehendingly. Surely not even the most primitive of propagandists would have thought up something like this.

"You had the doubtful good fortune of getting across the border once more. How did you feel?"

They had left him neither a message nor money. For two months he went on believing that sooner or later they would write. Then he reached the end of his tether. As if they knew exactly how badly off he was, the men from the CIA came to see him just at the right time. They gave him money, clothes, a flat, and offered him a future.

"You mean a future in a Czechoslovakia liberated from the Communists?"

"Yes."

"May I ask what post you had in mind?"

"None. All I wanted was to be an actor."

Laughter in court.

"And what theater would you have wanted to act in if you had the choice?"

"The National."

Again people laughed. Except Peter and me.

"Well, you'd have been the first actor who had shot his way into the National Theater," the prosecutor told him, as if speaking our thoughts.

Slavek had made four more trips to and from Czechoslovakia. Next month it would be five years since we left school. I still saw him as he used to stand, a neat, well-behaved boy, in front of the blackboard. I still saw his undernourished body in the gym—"What, you want to be an actor?" a teacher had taunted him. "Why, you'd faint on stage in the middle of a monologue!"

Twelve times he had crossed the frontier that was guarded with increasing vigilance, having to leap over obstacles, ford a river, crawl long distances on his belly to do it. His last mission was to go to Prague and await further orders, equipped with a Czech police uniform and false papers. And a service revolver.

BUT I'M NOT LEAVING TO FIGHT AGAINST YOU!

"What orders did you get in Prague?"

"To go to the Klement Gottwald Steel Works and find out how sabotage operations could be carried out there."

"Weren't you there on a work brigade?"

"Yes."

"So that you now wanted to destroy what you had earlier helped to build."

"No, I didn't go."

"Where *did* you go?"

"To a weekend cottage in the country."

The few spectators laughed once more. Sitting in the last row among the accused, A____ hid her head below her shoulders. My first, long-lost love, I do not envy you. . . .

"That makes you the first holiday-maker in the service of the CIA!"

He had had enough. The whole business seemed absurd. After a week he returned to Prague and reported some fictitious names and addresses. On his way home from his meeting he was arrested.

"Tell me . . ."

It came suddenly, like the crack of a whip.

". . . didn't you intend to assassinate the President of the Republic and Chairman of the Communist Party, Comrade Klement Gottwald?"

"No!"

"Are you quite sure you didn't?"

"Yes!"

My dream of the night before surfaced again, and I felt a chill run down my spine.

He suddenly raised his voice, stuttered so agitatedly.

"Your Honor, I was concerned from the start only with the Klement Gottwald Steel Works, never Comrade Gottwald—"

"The accused," exclaimed the prosecutor, "has forfeited the right to call anyone in this country comrade!"

The court adjourned for lunch. Peter and I ate at a buffet on the other side of the square. Having no meat coupons, we ordered potato pancakes and beer, eating and drinking in silence. On our way back to the courthouse Peter said:

"How could he ruin his life like this? It's so futile, so pointless."

A_____'s turn came at about five that afternoon. Nobody would have guessed that this girl in the dock had four years of training at the Academy of Drama behind her, she could scarcely control her voice. After she had repeated what she had told me the night before, the prosecutor asked:

"Did the accused confide his intentions to you?"

"No, he didn't."

"Did he tell you he meant to carry out an assassination?"

"No!"

"That he meant to kill Comrade Klement Gottwald?"

"He didn't tell me anything."

"Did anyone come to see him or did he go anywhere during that week?"

"No."

I had the feeling that the prosecutor gave a friendly look in our direction when he said:

"He didn't tell you anything, didn't leave the place? Can you enlighten us as to what the two of you did in that cottage all week?"

She remained silent, and I felt myself blush in her stead.

"Did you have sexual intercourse with the defendant?"

After a pause she nodded almost imperceptibly.

"I can't hear you."

"Yes . . ."

"Louder!"

"Yes."

"Had you cohabited before this time?"

"No . . ."

"Never until you went to the cottage with him?"

"That's right."

"As you did not have time to talk, I take it that you and he went to bed immediately on arrival?"

"Yes."

"Are you always so quick about it?"

I glanced appalled at Peter. He was sitting there unmoving, biting his lips.

"Let me put it another way: was the defendant the first man you had ever had sexual intercourse with?"

She shook her head.

"Answer me!"

"No."

"Would it be right to say that you had had sexual relations with more than one man before him?"

"Yes."

"Did you sleep with the accused all that week?"

"Yes."

"Every night?"

"Yes."

"And sometimes during the day as well?"

I fully expected her to break down. But his voice held her like a lifeguard's rope.

"Even during the day?"

"Yes."

"That would explain why you two didn't find time for conversation. And one other thing. Perhaps the accused would tell the court whether she has had sexual intercourse with anyone else since the defendant was arrested."

"Yes."

He turned with a smile to the judge.

"Your Honor, I think this particular case should go before a different court."

I was still dazed as we stood outside in the corridor, awaiting the verdict. Peter was thinking aloud.

"I suppose he's now telling the judge he doesn't insist on the eighteen months originally demanded by the prosecution and that all this was intended as a lesson she would not easily forget."

The court rose. In the silence I could hear my own heart beating. The two resident agents received life sentences, Slavek was sentenced to twelve years, the others to imprisonment ranging from five to twelve. She was acquitted.

As they led Slavek away he turned once more to look at us. He was pale, he shook his head as though he were astounded, and there was a terrified look in his eyes. THE FUTURE WILL DECIDE WHICH OF US WAS RIGHT.

Now it had decided. But we'll be waiting when you come out. I promise! The revolution must defend itself but it isn't vindictive. Just grit your teeth and bear it.

How old will we be when he is released?

Peter hurried to the Central Committee. I waited for A_____. I wanted to congratulate her and did not want her to be alone today.

"Let's go and treat ourselves to a three-star dinner. You can eat without coupons at the Alcron. We two have an anniversary today."

She did not even ask what it was.

"I don't know how I'll be able to face people these next ten years."

"Why??"

"Because I'd rather be a spy than a whore, that's why!"

Now it is almost dawn. I don't feel like sleeping. I am hurt not by lack of thanks but lack of understanding. So many still don't understand. And as a result they suffer in an era intended to make people happy.

Happiness? Yes and no.

Why, does our room shout its emptiness? And you? Whom are you with at this moment? When will you realize that you can only find love here, where you deserted it?

◧

30 May 1968 / Saarbrucken
(From the diary of the writer PK)

I was on top of the world. For two hours I had been pulling a wire fence in front of the camera to create the illusion of a train in motion. At last my heroine, Lida Matysova, fell convincingly off the train. Such a love is hazardous. It appeared to me wonderful to have survived mine with health intact. I said "See you all day after tomorrow" in two languages, collected the mail my friends wanted me to take to Prague, and drove off. The world again seemed such a marvelous place. I sang to myself as I drove.

My clutch started acting up before I had reached Frankfurt, but even that could not spoil my mood.

The frontier post at R____ greeted me at three in the morning like a long-lost brother. The unpleasantness last year, when they had forced my involuntary striptease, seemed to all of us like a comic incident from our childhood. They told me that the Czechoslovak process of regeneration had been making successful progress while I was away.

By the time I got to Pilsen the only gear I could use was fourth, yet I hurtled on, aware that this was a time of miracles. Prague welcomed me like a sleeping virgin—gentle and passive. I left the Renault in the new service station in Motol, the incorruptible chief mechanic this time agreeing to take it for repairs. He even provided a car to take me home. That was the first positive gain my political activity had brought me.

It was too late to go to bed, too early to go out and see people. I sorted my mail. Among all the letters that had accumulated while I had been away I discovered a black-bordered announcement that one of my former friends had died. The funeral was in the Motol crematorium at five. Well, I had to go there anyway to fetch my car.

As I left the house an official Tatra drove by with Dubcek inside, followed immediately by the Minister of National Defense. From the nearby cloister, promoted to a kind of Hilton for high Party dignitaries, came a long procession of men, some cheerful, others sour. I realized that a Central Committee meeting was about to begin at the Castle.

I knew I would not have time to go home and change, so I had to put on a black suit and wear it all day. Over lunch I told Z____ it was in her honor, unsure whether she would understand my real motives.

I all but forgot the funeral as I talked to people, listened to a mass of information and engaged in discussions on the political situation. I was amused by a letter that had been received by the Writers Union in response to our query about whether it was not time to shed light on an old incident.

"HEAD OF THE STATE SECURITY ADMINISTRATION
to the Committee of the Writers Union Communist Party
Organization
Ref.: N/Ka-43 /1-1968
"Dear Comrades, first of all allow me to apologize on my own
behalf and on behalf of the passport officials at R_____, and in particular Chief Passport Officer B_____, to the writer Comrade PK
for what was a regrettable action on our part against his person,
this said action having taken place in August of last year on his
journey to the German Federal Republic.

"It has also been stated on this subject, but only by persons outside our service, that Comrade PK was trying to smuggle out undesirable printed matter and correspondence. On both these counts
I confirm that such allegations have no foundation in fact. Comrade PK only had with him some Czech daily newspapers which,
as he explained at the time, he had not had time to read during his
sojourn at home and had therefore taken with him on his trip. This
explanation should have satisfied the passport officials concerned
and there was no reason for any suspicion. As regards his personal
correspondence, this is his own private concern and it was no
business of ours to interfere or express certain suspicions.

"In the course of the interrogation carried out at the frontier
post at R_____, a statement was taken down to the effect that
Comrade PK had failed to register certain sums of our and foreign
currency and by so doing had committed a currency offense. Comrade PK explained this at the time, convincingly in my view, but
it was only when the whole matter was subsequently investigated
in Prague that it was discovered that the accusations leveled against
him in this respect, too, were without foundation.

"In conclusion I would like to assure you, dear Comrades, that I
have already taken steps to prevent a repetition of this incident in
the future. Lieut. Colonel J. B., Deputy Chief of the State Security
Administration."

It was gratifying to see how, in this remarkable spring, even the
State Security was beginning to learn manners. It was a pity,
though, that it was still incapable of admitting what it was they had
wanted to find on me. Another reason to talk to P_____.

At three in the afternoon I remembered the funeral and my car.
Taxis seemed to be an extinct species. I therefore ran through the

crowd to the nearest streetcar stop. That was how I came to bump into her.

The fantastic thing was that I had thought of her only a few moments earlier. But perhaps that is because when there is a funeral one automatically rummages in the drawers of one's relationships. She spoke first; I almost did not recognize her. She looked better than in the old days. The long-legged youngster at her side, doing her best to look grown-up, could easily have been her younger sister. I told her so.

"Well, that's some consolation, anyway," she said. "When I saw you sitting in the first row at the theater the other night with that bunny of yours I felt as if I were eighty."

"That bunny is twenty-six," I pointed out.

"Shut up, I'll start having an inferiority complex again."

It was a clear day and from nearby Wenceslas Square we could hear the lyrical roar of pneumatic drills building the pedestrian subway. The young lady had discreetly retired to examine the sausage and salami in a shop window. We gossiped at high speed about everything and nothing.

"I went for a walk at Vysehrad a few days ago and I stopped to look at Father's grave."

"Your father's buried at Vysehrad?"

"No, of course not. I mean your father."

She did not mention Mother. Women do not forgive other women even when they are dead. I was moved, nevertheless.

"I wondered," she went on, "what he would have thought if he had lived to see all this."

"Perhaps he would have turned conservative for a change," I said. "He was always a nonconformist!"

I was pleased to see that I was again able to speak about him so calmly. Time seems to disarm death. Graves lose their tragic effect and you begin to imagine that you can call that old phone number or write to that familiar address at any time. Is it because you are drawing nearer to them?

"You know, your father was the only Communist I never stopped trusting," she said.

"Thanks for the compliment," I replied, laughing.

"Well, it may please you to know that I have started to trust you again."

The daughter, guarding the interests of her father, had evidently decided that we had been talking long enough, for she came strolling back to us looking bored. We parted cordially, the silence of many years wiped out like so many other phantoms.

Had her words given me pleasure? Hard to say. One of several commandments I had given myself in 1956 went like this:

"Thou shalt not form any opinion of thyself on the basis of other people's praise or detraction, neither from the left nor from the right, for thy kingdom and thy power and thy glory dwell solely within thine own self. Amen."

But I was immensely grateful to her. She had thrown me, unintentionally perhaps, off the track on which P——— had remained to this day.

In the tram I felt like a yokel; the extensive rebuilding in the center of Prague had thrown the streetcar lines into confusion. I kept asking the way and the conductors replied disdainfully, thinking from my fine clothes I was a demoted politician who had just been deprived of his official car.

There were still far too few demoted politicians though, worse luck, to make any difference to municipal transport. All the recent analyses were unanimous in showing that the delay was sowing seeds of evil. A number of leading hardliners had dug their heels in. Not deeming it necessary to say a single word about their part in the distortions, they again began to identify themselves with the Party and, using a Stalinist tactic, to inflate the bubble of an anti-socialist conspiracy. Apart from the press, radio, and television, they accused the recently formed organizations of non-Communists and former political prisoners sentenced in the trials of the fifties.

I naturally gave a lot of thought to them too. Only our conclusions were so divergent. It was my conviction that the defensive communal instinct of the non-Party people would correspond to the results of the Party's own democratization process. After the A uttered in January, which had merely given rise to hope, it was necessary to say B—only then would people really gain confidence. The anxious appeals of the Party leaders for unity within the Party thus carried with them a certain danger under the present circumstances. In the morning I had collected the last issue but one of Literární listy, which had printed my front-page article on this very subject:

"It is time we realized that unity is a concept open to a number of different interpretations. If we just take the unity of the Party before and after February 1948 we shall see that it had a completely different character.

"Party unity before February was a moral one. The members of the Party had voluntarily accepted its revolutionary program because it had contained a humanitarian message. This program they fulfilled and supervised. The unity of the fifties was immoral. The members of the Party had allowed themselves to be degraded to privates trusting in the infallibility of their generals. The generals dehumanized the revolution and the guilt was shared by the privates.

"Some of the Party's members wanted to put matters right, taking the essential steps. At that moment the Party's unity ceased to exist.

"The disunity that arose can roughly be compared to the guilt shared and the differences of opinion between Antonin Novotny and Ludovik Vaculik. As long as both these men must remain in one and the same Party, that disunity again becomes moral.

"Two parties in one cannot exist for long. A Party of two parties cannot hope to gain the nation's confidence. That is why an extraordinary congress must unavoidably be held. Then the Communist Party will either have to purge or divide itself.

"'Only in this way can one create a Party with a new moral unity."

How true this was became abundantly clear in what was an almost absurd fashion by the fact that at the April plenary session of the Central Committee one of those who spoke up in favor of the process of democratization was none other than Antonin Novotny himself!

All my discussions made me feel that the anti-Novotnyite coalition was now falling apart permanently. That, of course, was all to the good, since by now it embraced a very weird assortment of people. Less good was the considerable shift of forces that took place at the same time. Now it was no longer merely the Stalinists who were scared of the extraordinary Party Congress but, unfortunately, also many of the centrists who had played a not negligible part in paving the way to the introduction of this year's January reforms. No doubt they had had second thoughts because they were unable to shed their skins and to imagine different methods of running the country than those used for so many years. But perhaps— no, not perhaps, certainly—it was also partly our own fault. Perhaps we had stressed too much that they would never be worthy of the rôles they so badly wanted to play.

Even the best of theaters must occasionally use ordinary, run-of-the-mill actors. An actor who is constantly reminded how average he is will then be capable of throwing away a scene he might otherwise have carried off quite well. His own minimal risks are amply compensated by the knowledge which is the best cure for an inferiority complex: the knowledge that as he does so, the great actor who is in the scene with him will also not give his best performance.

Maybe that is one of the reasons why Alois Indra spoke in Ostrava criticizing the journalists in terms unparalleled since the aftermath of the Fourth Writers Congress last year.

Let it be said at once that this had its positive aspect as well. In response to Indra's attack Committees for the Defense of the Free Press were formed in the biggest Ostrava mines and factories. When one realizes that from January to this day the workers had chiefly been making wage claims—roughly totaling some twenty thousand million crowns—this will be seen to be a very important development indeed: after a great many years the working class had for the first time put forward a political demand.

The Regional Party Committee in Ostrava and the newly elected and strongly progressive Municipal Committees in Prague and Brno came up almost simultaneously with a suggestion that was best formulated by Zdenek Hejzlar in his article "A Czech Initiative." If the Party leadership, after due deliberation, abided by its decision not to hold the Party Congress sooner than next year in spite of the opinion of a majority of Communists that it should be earlier, then they should at once form a new top body of Czech Communists—possibly from among the delegates elected for the Congress by the regional Party organizations—which would correspond to a similar body that existed in Slovakia. This would contribute to the forthcoming federalization of the country, and would give rise to a trustworthy organ capable of doing some of the work of the discredited Central Committee until such a time as the Congress was able to meet.

This suggestion was fully in keeping with the requirements of the day and the principles of the Party's Action Program. It could not be simply thrown under the table or passed over in silence.

Alexander Dubcek was said to have attempted one more compromise in his own typical way. He asked several members of the Central Committee to resign of their own accord and thus help lessen the pressure for an extraordinary congress or special measures to deal with the situation within the Party. In his admirable enthusiasm he seemed still to believe that these people really had the interests of the Party at heart. Naturally, with but one exception, they all refused to resign. Why should anyone voluntarily quit the shop if he can stay on and continue to cover up his deficit?

And so the question was still there, baring its teeth at us, as before.

In the streets I noticed that the most widely used accessory in Prague nowadays was a transistor radio. After fasting for many years the population could not have enough information. I had to change trams at the Angel, and standing at the tram stop I heard the end of the news from several different sources.

According to the Czechoslovak News Agency a Warsaw Pact Army group led by General Kazakov arrived in Czechoslovakia today to take part in allied staff maneuvers. No doubt they picked this very day in honor of the plenary session of the Central Committee. I found it incredible that no one should explain to our allies how delighted people are when their guests come to lunch even though they have received their telegram saying that the house is being redecorated. I could not help recalling a recent courtesy visit paid to the offices of the Writers Union by several members of the Soviet Embassy staff. Their apprehensions, impressions, and advice made you think they were carrying out their duties in some strange, unknown land and had only stopped for the night. After they left we asked ourselves, horrified, what kind of information and recommendations they were likely to send to their government and what political decisions could be taken.

One of these had just materialized: a small brotherly demonstration of force. This whole policy began to strike me as the behavior of an insanely jealous man who after twenty years of faithful wedlock orders his wife to wear a chastity belt.

I still had some time to spare, so *I* made several telephone calls from the Renault service center. P____ again did not reply. But S____ at last came to the phone.

"Yes, I know," he told me. "I read it in the papers."

"Didn't you get the announcement?"

"No, I didn't. It would hardly be the thing for me to go to the funeral anyway."

"How did it happen?"

"On Friday afternoon he left his office as usual. Hanged himself on the central-heating pipes in the garage. She found him there lunchtime Saturday."

I had thought as much. His death was one of a series of suicides that started in March. Unfortunately even the Prague Spring was not to be without its graves. Some of the tragic actors of the fifties had decided to settle their accounts themselves.

"I really ought to be grateful to him," I said. "It was at the trial that it occurred to me for the first time that not only in the state of Denmark is something rotten."

"Trouble is," commented S____, "that in the past the law of social development decreed that one generation made a mess of things and a second took over to clean up. We have managed to do the whole thing ourselves. Our children will gain the impression that they must have had at least two fathers apiece."

That reminded me I had to call yet another number. Instead of the soft alto voice I heard a gruff, unfamiliar bass. I put the receiver down and tried again. I got the bass once more. A burglar must have broken in or something. I asked curtly who it was I was speaking to.

"Hi, Dad," said the bass. "Mother's out."

"Hi," I replied. "Have you got a cold?"

"No," he said. "My voice is changing. Hormones, you know."

"Ah," I said, "hormones. I know. All right, if it's changing, it's changing."

"It's wonderful that you're back," he said. "Coming to see us tonight?"

"No," I said. "I have to return to Germany."

"I see," he said. "Oh, by the way, your article in the literary rag was great!"

"Fine," I said. "Did you understand it?"

"Sure I did," he said. "They're all a bunch of fools."

"I see," I said. "Well, in that case maybe you ought to read it once more."

"Sure," he said. "Well, have a good time. And please bring me a Paul Klee and those vampire fangs. I want to scare the girls with them."

"Sure," I said, "I'll bring all that. Love to everybody. Ciao."

I hung up my own life and set off for someone else's death. I could no longer recall his face, but I tried to imagine what the last years, months, and days must have meant to a man around whose neck the noose of conscience slowly knotted tighter. When was it that he realized that his service to the Party had become a crime? Face to face with nonexistence I felt a certain respect for what he had done. Though it could not restore his honor, it preserved at least a certain human dignity.

Only a handful of mourners at the crematorium. Judging by certain signs, I would have said they were his colleagues. Perhaps even a few old friends from the State Security? Whoever they were, they did not look too kindly upon me.

When had I seen her last? In some bar, I thought. . . . No, that night when she had told me about her married life with the man who was now dead and about to be cremated. It was so dreadful a story that I scarcely found the courage to write it down. Here she was, weeping loudly, holding a boy of about five by the hand. For the first time in years I did not have the impression that she was merely play-acting.

After the ceremony, I thought she wanted to speak with me, so I waited until I was last in the line of those offering condolences. Still weeping, she whispered only one sentence:

"Why did you have to hound him to death?"

The night was clear, my car in perfect order. At the border post in R____ the officer on duty at midnight was the sympathetic lieutenant who kept winking encouragingly at me during my contretemps with the frontier guards last year. As a reward I showed him the letter of apology I had received from the high-ups in Prague.

"Well, I'll be damned," he said. "So they've put the blame on us again, have they?"

I was seized by the nostalgia I always experience as soon as I

cross the border. I had to smile once more at the thought that anyone could have supposed I would emigrate.

There were no hitchhikers out at this time of night, but even
so it seemed that the car was full of human destinies—those of my
loves, my friends and acquaintances, people among whom I lived
my life. I kept the car at a steady 150 kilometers an hour on the
Autobahn to give that life a regular rhythm, at least for a short
while.

I covered the seven hundred kilometers in my usual nine hours.
I passed the Am Staden Hotel and made straight for Hallberg.
Several dozen French cars were waiting at the service station; the
general strike in France had swallowed up all the gas between
the Bay of Biscay and the Saar.

In front of the studio I met a young stagehand. He wore a
beard and was an enthusiastic member of the non-Parliamentary
opposition. Proudly he informed me that the demonstration
against the emergency powers had gone off without a hitch.

"But the old fascists have passed the laws nevertheless," he said
angrily. "I guess we'll have to show them what's what just as they
did in France and in your country."

I was pleased to meet my own youth, in West Germany of
all places.

I came onto the set just before the first take. My heroine Lida
Matysova was embracing Petrus for a change. This story in which
people committed suicide for love struck me as something from
another century.

Mr. Belka, the director, was reading the newspaper near the
monitor.

"Hello," he beamed. "That's fine!"

"What's fine?"

"You've done it."

"What have I done?"

"The thing in Prague."

"What thing in Prague?"

That was the way I learned that Antonin Novotny had been
recalled from the Central Committee and that Alexander Dubcek
had unexpectedly proposed that the extraordinary congress of the
Communist Party of Czechoslovakia should be held in September.

The shirt washed a hundred times, its khaki color bleached like the grass in August, stiff, unyielding pants which seemed to me lined with sandpaper, the belt smelling pungently of new leather, heavy calf-length jackboots fastened with straps, bleary eyes, sunken cheeks, frost-swollen hands covered with purple scratches—is this me?

Streets draped with limply hanging black flags, silent streetcars, row upon row of tired faces, the radio endlessly repeating the Prague signal, the depressing funeral music coming over the street loudspeaker system—is this my city?

A faint scent of perfume, the sound of someone's soft breathing, an open chest of drawers inside which strange little piles of blue and pink wool have been carefully stacked—is this my room?

Is this the same planet, the same continent, the same century as the one I lived in until the fourth of March?

That day I had carried a heavy machine gun on my back, refusing to let anyone relieve me; we each clung to our burden as if it would help to lift the load off our hearts. We went to bed, but ours was not the healthy sleep of tired men, it was more like the last rest before battle, before a court martial. When the duty non-com switched on the lights he did not have to say anything to wake us, even though it was still a full hour to reveille. No one gave any order, yet the whole regiment fell in, waiting for a liberating word. But the officers were just as silent as we were. The regimental band came marching out of the darkness, though no one had summoned it, and they struck up the "March of the Fallen Revolutionaries" in the chill of early morning.

> Though all our hearts are filled with sorrow
> Our world will not fall apart.
> Stalin's dead, yet new faith we'll borrow;
> He will remain in every heart.

I wrote verses for several nights, I did not count them; I did not count the days, I went on sentry duty, I ate, slept, wrote. All our thoughts, all our hope was now directed toward Klement Gottwald.

He died nine days after Stalin, as if he refused to go on living without him.

That day we threw live grenades, cold as death. Again and again I was tempted to hold one a few seconds longer in my hand ...in the hand he once shook. I felt as though a whole era were ending, and as though we were to end with it.

That evening we boarded the same train that had brought us, depressed and with heads clipped, to Karlovy Vary the previous October, to begin our national service. Although I had intended to be a good soldier, I started counting the days as soon as I arrived. Now I was returning home, but I was oblivious of my surroundings. Until this afternoon. One o'clock, to be exact. It was with that hour in mind that we had rehearsed the funeral march for a whole week, back and forth, back and forth, across the concrete runways of Ruzyne Airport, so that our bayonets should merge into one. Now the hour was here. The hour of the last march past.

Somewhere on the other side of Prague a siren wailed, then a second and a third. Their mighty chorale spread out over the city just as it had five years ago, in February 1948. Then it had announced a victory. Today it was lamenting a death.

I stood lost among the correctly dressed formations on Letna Plain. Like me, the whole country had stopped still. Silent were the machines and the typewriters, the trains halted in the fields. Only the wind blew and time passed, water flowed in the rivers and blood in people's veins. And with it came fear to fill their hearts.

WHAT WILL THE FUTURE BRING?

There is bloodshed in Korea and Vietnam, Germany is building the *Bundeswehr*, new concentration camps are springing up in Europe, in an American death cell Ethel and Julius Rosenberg are waiting for the sound of keys in the locks of their doors. Stalin is dead, we have just buried Klement Gottwald and have been given passes to go on leave. For the first time in my Army days I saw soldiers hesitate before dispersing.

WHAT WILL THE FUTURE BRING?

I am sitting in a room left from some other century, looking at the strange objects made of soft wool and listening to D____ swim silently in a dream.

She had rung my bell an hour after my return from the court where I had obtained my divorce. I had not seen her since that sad summer, when I had in various ways—finally in vain—tried to forget my sorrow and despair. She had come to tell me in a subdued voice that she was expecting my child and that she would get rid of it.

Heavens! Whenever I had a girl, whenever I really felt passion, I always had a child in mind. I knew by now how shortlived love could be, but I wanted a child. I had been working to give it a wonderful future, a homeland in which the most exalted dreams of mankind would come true. I asked her to marry me. A week later I joined my regiment.

WHAT WILL THE FUTURE BRING?

Both their lives had formed part of the Party's history, they knew it like a gardener knows his flowerbeds, they knew from which shoot a beautiful unknown rose would grow and they unerringly detected all dangerous weeds. Who else but these two could have transformed a million small energies into the high tension of revolution! Who else but they could have unmasked Judases in the very top echelons of the Party—Judases who only three months ago had been justly punished for their crimes! Streams of tears fell today in front of thousands of catafalques in schools and factories and Army barracks. How many of these were crocodile tears?

The yet undiscovered wreckers would tonight be dancing with joy at our misfortune, counting the last hours of the Party. How were we, our captains gone, to plot our course in the starless night and avoid the Scylla of treason as well as the Charybdis of our fatigue and our own mistakes? In a Europe in which normal roads have been cut, a Europe of trenches, obstacles, and minefields, a Europe that was becoming a battlefield even before it had concluded peace.

We are an army that has lost both its highest commanders the night before it goes into battle.

WHAT WILL THE FUTURE BRING?

We had admired and loved Stalin and Klement Gottwald so much that we never thought of their death, never thought them mortal. Now we were shocked to the core. At times it seems to us the end of everything.

D—— sleeps with reddened eyes.

"I don't know how to put it," she had said that evening. "I just feel that he will be born into a world that's ... less good, I feel as if he—"

"Yes," I finished the sentence for her, "a posthumous child."

I sit on the edge of the sofa, lean in my stiff uniform smelling of mothballs. I will have to go shortly. I have to and I want to. I put my hand on her large belly, silhouetted in the glow from the street lamp. Just the same shape as the mountain of Rip, where the Czech nation began its existence. A helmet of clay, as the poet Jaroslav Seifert called it. I put my hand on the helmet of life.

I can hear you. I don't know who you are or what your name is, I don't know where you come from and why. But if you have decided to enter my home, it is yours with all that is in it, love, disappointment, defeats, poetry ... and this Night of the Great Deceased.

When you grow up you will learn their names, you will hear and read about their heroic lives. They lived in difficult times, but times that were also glorious and great. Times in which the nations of the world threw off their chains and the earth trembled as they marched. Times in which the old, rotten world had tried, like a Pharaoh, to drag us into its own grave. It was a time of life-and-death struggle.

When you grow older you will begin to discover Stalin and get to know him better, as we who were born after 1924 had discovered Vladimir Ilyich Lenin and had learned to know him better. When you grow older you will admire the wisdom of Klement Gottwald, who triumphed for us in February 1948 without a shot being fired. When you grow older I'll tell you all about them in the midst of a beautiful spring in which all men will be brothers.

Sleep in peace, my little one. To make sure that spring comes, to make sure the frost does not kill it, I now have to leave and again throw live grenades which inspire fear. And so that I shall not be afraid I sing as I march:

> We haven't been young for quite some time,
> We haven't been unprotected sheep,
> If Stalin is dead, then let us be Stalin,
> If Gottwald is dead, our life shall be his.

The Italian girl rose from the couch and switched on the tape recorder. It played the theme song of *Dr. Zhivago*, Lara's song, warm and luscious. The girl slowly unbuttoned her velvet jacket which had nothing underneath. I had to admit she was magnificent. She looked at me with a peculiar kind of smile, produced only by the lips, with no assistance from the eyes. She walked up to me. I remained seated. She knelt at my side, took my hand between hers and laid it gently on the zip of her narrow trousers. I shook my head, extricated my hand, and picked up my cigarette. The smile was still there on her face, but it had turned into a mask. I distinctly heard her contemptuous hiss. She now turned her head toward him. Her profile disclosed that she could not be more than eighteen. He surprised me, inclining his head a little as if to say he was sorry and lowered the zip right down the trouser leg. The girl rose to her feet as he did so, to remain standing there completely naked. There was some applause and she acknowledged it with a dazzling smile. Then she threw me a last glance, like a dagger.

The lights went up. The waiters came round for new orders. I again ordered 7-Up, even though it was as expensive here as the Scotch with which a while ago they had toasted each other, having decided to put their relationship on a first-name basis. He was charm itself. Overdoing it a little, I thought. I had never seen him quite like this before. I drank soft drinks to show her I wanted to go home, but I only succeeded in producing the opposite effect. She started needling me.

"A gentleman should always stick to the rules of the game," she said.

"You know I can't stand striptease."

"But I thought you were *both* in the Youth Union?"

"Well, I guess it's left more of an impression on me, that's all."

"I can't say I'm mad about it," he said, "but on the other hand it doesn't offend me either. When all's said and done, it

151

is a return to the folklore of ancient Rome. What is it you mind so much about it?"

"I don't know. Maybe that they play-act so much."

"What a strange thing to say," she said, "considering that you're a playwright who cries every time The Clown is eaten by the tigers although you know damn well it's only Mr. Brodsky."

"So it must be something else," I snapped. "Perhaps that they're so impersonal. An actor on stage transforms himself. A naked woman showing herself to an audience has no meaning. She's as grotesque as a concert piano with an amplifier instead of chords, as absurd as our army that twice in this century cost so much energy and money only to serve the nation best by not fighting."

"Kindly notice," she told him, as if showing off a trained monkey, "how he can get to Communism in three sentences even if the subject under discussion is striptease. Was he always such a hypocrite?"

She was deliberately trying to provoke me. I had a good mind to remind her of a certain party at which she had persuaded the small gathering to play for pledges and "to take everything off" only to slap the face of a credulous friend who took her suggestion seriously. I also wanted to recall how throughout our first year together she would not let me so much as switch on the radio when we made love because it gave off a little light. But all I said was:

"I just want to remain an amateur in these things. I have never yet found it necessary to pay women for getting undressed."

"I suppose you paid much more, but in a different way?"

That was asking for a return shot which might easily have hit her. It even seemed that she wanted it in order to have a pretext for starting a second round. But since we had left Perugia the situation had changed, and I had changed with it. I did not find it difficult to stay calm.

"I have a splitting headache," I said in the friendliest manner I was capable of. "Must be the heat. Would you two mind very much if I went home without you?"

She responded exactly as I had expected her to: as if she belonged to him.

"Not in the least. I'm sure we'll enjoy ourselves on our own.

You can tell us later whether we have already become a Soviet republic."

He did not comment. As he got to his feet and held out his hand to me I realized that he was tipsy. He shook my hand as if we were meeting either for the first time or the last.

I walked home past the monstrous statue of King Victor Emmanuel, and under the balcony on which the greatest actor of Italian Fascism used to give the performances that held his audiences breathless. Via del Corso was usually quiet, like all the streets of Europe that summer—with the exception of ours. My irritation slowly receded. Perhaps the cooler air had something to do with it, it was now quite bearable and I no longer perspired all the time. My brain, which three words had struck like so many stones in Perugia, suddenly started functioning again, coolly and rationally.

As always in time of crisis, all the complexities of our relationship had given way before the instinct of self-preservation. We had again clung to one another because that was the only thing to do when the flood threatened to wash us away. Then the wave had receded and here we were, stunned and hurt but still alive. The laws of life had reasserted themselves. The armistice was over and our quarrel was with us once more, as insoluble as ever. While I was drowning under the waters that had inundated my city, she took out her bathing suit and was waiting to go for a swim. . . .

A sudden commotion shattered the silence of the street. A procession of young Italians carrying tattered banners with the words ABASSO BREZHNEV—VIVA DUBCEK! was approaching from the Piazza di Spania, accompanied by mounted police. I recalled a song that had once long ago been carried to Bohemia just in time to welcome the tanks of our liberators: ABASSO RE—VIVA STALIN!

Hearing some Czech and Slovak conversation I joined a small island of blond heads.

"Where are you off to?"

"To the Russian Embassy. Come along!"

But I was much too tired and even now still unable to bring myself to break the windows of embassies. More than ever before it was brought home to me that this was not a Czech custom. They were headed in the same direction. I told them what I thought of their idea, even though it was quite clear to me that they were motivated partly by the solidarity of the Italian youths and partly by their own feelings of frustration and despair.

"Seems to me," I told them, "that throwing stones is just the argument used by the world we have been fighting throughout our history."

A young man with intelligent eyes, who was embracing a Godiva with tear-stained cheeks, answered sharply:

"Yes, but we only won when we threw them back at our attackers."

With a sweep of his arm he pointed to the demonstrators, who were chanting angrily as if it were their own cause they were defending.

"Just look at them! If the tanks invaded this street, there would be gasoline bombs flying from every window!"

"And have you wondered why it is that no gasoline bombs are flying in Prague?"

"Because we're a lot of sissies, that's why! Because we don't deserve an independent existence!"

I had had just such an argument once before in my life. I had merely changed my standpoint. A question of age? No, my present views were then expounded by a boy no older than this one. The explanation lay somewhere else.

"We have just touched upon a problem which is called the Czech question. To fight or to compromise? Should we risk losing everything, or instead gain time and latitude with the aid of which we shall be able to return to our destined path, though by a detour?"

"If you're a Communist," he said, "and I guess you are because you talk just like my father, then I can tell you that I'm no longer interested in detours which lead through prisons and past the gallows. I don't ever again want to learn in school that it was Popov who invented the telephone and that President Masaryk shot workers. And I haven't the slightest desire to make the acquaintance of Siberian bears!"

I was put in mind of the man who had met *his* bears in Canada. The difference was that he had done so of his own free will. The young man and his girl friend lost all interest in me.

"Can't you see?" said another fellow in Slovak, "They're already arresting people in Prague. It's going to be exactly the same as in the fifties."

"Nonsense! This time they'd have to arrest a million people!"

"Well, why shouldn't they? Haven't they done it in the past? The Yanks or the Russians, they're all the same."

"What's your solution then?"

"Switzerland. They say that the Swiss accept all Czechs and Slovaks who ask for asylum. We'll remain in Europe, but at least it isn't part of the Byzantine Empire!"

I parted company with them in the Piazza Popolo.

"Where are *you* going to go?" the Slovak asked me.

"Home," I replied unhesitatingly.

"Give our love to the collaborators!" cried the young man. The Slovak waved in some embarrassment.

I walked on down the quiet street that sloped down to my hotel and I made up my mind. I no longer wished to drink Campari, glued to the radio, gab about the past, and be bored in striptease joints. It was now thirty hours since Perugia. I could still make up for lost time. I decided to wait until she returned and then put a last question to her.

As I reached the hotel a Skoda with a Brno license plate was just pulling away from the curb. The driver braked sharply. Out came the Moravian family, their gondola enthroned among the luggage behind the rear seat.

"The Italian Auto Club returned the car to us. They found it near Venice with this inside."

On the lid of a cardboard box containing shoes the car thief had scrawled:

EVIVA PRAGA ROSSA, PRAGA LIBERA!

"Now we're on our way home," the man said happily. "If worst comes to the worst, we'll try swimming the river. And what about you?"

"I'm going too," I replied.

"How about coming with us?"

"No, I have to wait a little longer. Till midnight."

Now I knew that midnight was the time limit I had set for her.

"Oh, well, in that case you'll catch up with us before we get to Milan. I drive slow on account of these women of mine."

"The way I look at it," put in his wife, "we've been occupied and had the car stolen, so we might as well remain in one piece."

They kept waving to me all the way to the corner of the street. Then I went in and asked for my bill. With my key the receptionist handed me a letter. It bore the letterhead of the American Embassy.

"Dear Sir," wrote the Cultural Attaché, "we have just received a cable for you from Iowa. Thanks to the kindness of your Embassy we are able to deliver it to you at once, and we await your reply."

DEAR SIR COMMA UNIVERSITY OF IOWA STATE IOWA CORDIALLY IN-VITES YOU TO PARTICIPATE IN ONE YEAR LITERATURE COURSE FOR YOUNG WRITERS FROM ALL OVER WORLD STOP THIS IS AN OLD PROJECT OF OURS WHICH WE DECIDED TO MOVE AHEAD OWING TO YOUR TRAGIC CIRCUMSTANCES STOP TRAVELING EXPENSES AS WELL AS STAY FOR YOU AND YOUR WIFE WILL BE MET BY UNIVERSITY OF IOWA ALSO GRANT $4000 STOP AWAITING YOUR REPLY YOURS SINCERELY UNI-VERSITY OF IOWA STATE IOWA END

---

28 X 55 / Pribyslav

"This is no coincidence," I laughed. "I saw your leaflets and so I had myself sent to your unit. I thought it would be fun for us to be on maneuvers together."

"Yes, but you see I don't ride in a tank. I'm on foot with the infantry."

"All right, take me with you."

"You'd have to get rid of that gold braid first."

He was in battledress. I had to admit that my spotless uniform was not suited to the occasion. I went to see the regimental CO, who only laughed at me.

"You should have got the theater to lend you a field uniform, Comrade Second Lieutenant."

He could not refuse to let me join them, though. I had the red-white-and-blue armband of the Maneuvers HQ and a written order issued by Colonel Prchlik. As I left the commander's caravan I heard him say to his aide:

"Have him attached to a crew that doesn't shoot its mouth off too much. Otherwise they'll let something drop, he'll write about it, and we'll be on everybody's shit list."

I spent the night in Peter's company, walking round and distributing bits of paper and colored pencils to the "agitators" so that they could produce their leaflets even during the attack. The work of political officers such as Peter was assessed by special umpires. All over the forest tanks were revving their engines as they prepared to take up their positions. About midnight it started to rain. The infantrymen did not even try to sleep, but sat silent under the low branches of fir trees, wrapped in tent canvas. Peter asked the nearest:

"Well, comrades, and how do you feel?"

"Plain bloody awful, Comrade Second Lieutenant."

The others laughed. His rudeness annoyed me, and I said:

"How about getting up when you speak to us?"

"I don't think much of the idea," he replied. "But how about you two saluting me?"

Before I had time to make a fool of myself once more, Peter snapped to attention and saluted.

"Sorry, Comrade Captain, I didn't recognize you!"

It was the infantry commander. He nodded to us, inviting us to sit down.

"My boys haven't had a bite to eat since early this morning, you know," he said. "So don't ride them any more."

They belonged to another regiment and their field kitchen had failed to show up. To test the efficiency of the supply units, they had not been issued any K-rations.

"Yes, but surely if there's any need for political work in the army at all," I protested, "then it's just in situations such as this. If soldiers have to go hungry, at least they ought to know why."

"But they do," he said. "Because of the bastards responsible for the food fiasco."

"No, you know what I mean: it's necessary to convince them that they must do their duty even on an empty stomach."

"That they know too. Trouble is, this man's army is all a lot of talk and no real action. The more wise guys there are telling everybody else what to do, the worse it gets."

I shared my last bit of salami with Peter. Then we smoked one

157

cigarette after the other, holding them in our cupped hands and sitting with our backs against the tree trunks like men about to be shot by the firing squad. I was glad to discover that there was still somebody with whom I could take up a conversation exactly where we had left off two years ago.

"We have grown complacent, that's what it is," he said. "This chap is a worker and a Party member. What can he expect of others?"

"Yes, you're right, but it is a scandal about that food. We keep blaming everything on the class enemy and yet we are responsible for most of the mess ourselves. After the trials of Slansky and the rest we thought we had put our house in order. What's wrong, then?"

"Lots of people have jumped onto our bandwagon using the Party to cover their own ineptitude."

"Yes, but whose fault is it?"

"Ours, of course."

"What do you think we should do about it?"

"Go on fighting as before. We must be uncompromising and demanding with others as well as with ourselves. We must set an example in everything, in the Party apparatus, in the arts—and now in uniform!"

The artillery barrage started at 6 A.M. I refused the cotton offered by the tank commander to plug up my ears. And when I found I could have used it, I felt ashamed to ask. The sappers' mines threw up mountains of earth. I was half deaf. At six-fifteen a mushroom cloud appeared on the horizon. The pyrotechnicians were simulating an explosion of a tactical atomic bomb. The first wave went in, dressed in antichemical clothing. Not an attractive sight, but I took comfort in the fact that they were on our side. We drove among the enemy bunkers, our infantrymen jumping off to clean them out. I caught a glimpse of Peter, running across a ploughed field and carrying someone's mortar.

SET AN EXAMPLE!

The day passed quickly. Once out of Olomouc we drove along the country roads. Hunger and rain no longer mattered so much because in every village there were flocks of girls standing at the roadside, waving to us. We reached the highlands just as night fell. The tank corps was part of a swift-moving Army group. It was penetrating the enemy defenses like the northern arm of a pincer movement aimed at reaching Pribyslav by six in the morning. From the earphones in my helmet came a torrent of orders demanding a swifter advance.

I was sitting in the turret of a T-34. This was forbidden; only two days ago a tank had keeled over with some reserves who had lost the basic reflex of ducking inside the tank. They were literally cut in half. But I could not help myself, being an extra with the gunner sitting right below me. I was drenched to the skin and terribly cold, and I envied the infantrymen who had strapped themselves to the turret with their belts, lying close to the ventilation outlets where the engine gave off heat. The men turned from side to side at regular intervals.

SET AN EXAMPLE IN EVERYTHING!

Now the tank corps kitchens had also become hopelessly lost along the route. While it was still daylight we had plucked sour apples off the trees as we went. I had smoked at least a hundred cigarettes since yesterday. And I had not a scrap of information: the regimental CO's orders had been conscientiously fulfilled— the crew of my tank spoke nothing but Hungarian.

It was raining violently. We again entered the forests, the paths now turned to quagmires. The tanks left deep ruts behind them, while the jeeps would often become stuck by their axles like beetles on pins. The men were seized by a silent rage, no one having the energy any more to curse aloud. The crews of the bogged-down vehicles simply jumped out and pushed them forward silently, inch by inch, until the wheels got traction again.

Umpires with white armbands stood at their posts, beetling their brows ferociously and writing cruel reports. The commanders of the units taking part in the maneuvers looked upon them as on their own death. And then we got stuck completely. Our engines stopped. I waded through the mud to see what lay ahead. There was a fine bridge that could take very heavy loads. It had one drawback: stretched across the road was a piece of string with a notice reading THIS BRIDGE HAS BEEN BLOWN UP. A hundred meters away some engineers were busily constructing a pontoon bridge in the dark. I pictured the long lines of tanks and armored cars stretched out behind us. Many kilometers away from here thousands of men were waiting, cold, wet, and hungry.

It was quite clear to me that the attack was collapsing. As I reached the bridge I heard a hoarse and angry voice.

"What orders did I give you?"

"I was to carry out a political briefing, Comrade Major."

"You were to carry out a briefing, you were to call together all the Communists and members of the Youth Union, you were to ask them for their pledges. You had time; this is the third time we are at a standstill."

"Comrade Major, most of the men were asleep—"

A small fat Lieutenant Colonel who was acting as an umpire asked:

"Did you issue any flash or leaflet?"

"No, I didn't Comrade Lieutenant Colonel."

"What *did* you do, then?"

"I was trying to find the field kitchens."

The major now started to shout, obviously in an effort to create an alibi for himself in front of the umpire.

"Did I give you any such order? We are not a charity institution. We have our tasks, and we are assessed according to the way we fulfil them. Thanks to you the entire division will get a lower mark! We're all hungry, but just because the supply units have failed to do their duty it doesn't mean that the political department should do the same, that least of all! Carry out my orders at once!"

"May I have your permission to speak, Comrade Major?"

"Permission refused! Dismissed!"

He stalked off into the darkness, with me at his heels.

"That fucking quartermaster!" It was the first time I had ever heard him swear. "I'm going to report this to the Central Committee and through them to the Political Administration. As a civilian he has only one salesgirl to boss about, and now he's bossing about a whole division."

"Where are you going, Peter?" I asked him.

"I'm going to wake all the Communists and members of the Youth Union to tell them that we are stuck, tired, and hungry but that at 6 A.M. we have to conquer Pribyslav. I'm sure they will be surprised and delighted by this news."

"Can I help you in any way?"

"Yes, you can," he replied, changing his tone suddenly. "You can help me a lot." He did not look angry any more, his face assuming its normal eager expression.

He and I started at opposite ends, working our way down the endless line of T-34s; the men we had awakened stumbled behind us. The heavy sleepers I left. When we met in the middle we had about forty men with us. Not much for a whole regiment. Peter and I climbed up on the nearest tank. Fortunately it had stopped raining.

"No smoking," Peter said. "They have planes up there looking for us. Comrades, I guess that you would later chew me out if I didn't reveal that we have a well-known poet in our midst. Here he is. Luckily he has a good memory and doesn't need a light."

Some of the soldiers had never heard of me, but most of them were interested. A poet under the present circumstances came as more of a surprise than if they had met Snow White in the woods. And so, seven years after February 1948 I gave a repetition of our front-line poetry readings. But the repertoire was different. Though I had originally meant to recite some political verses, of which I had written a good many recently, when I saw those boys there below me, stiff with the cold, sleepy and covered with mud, I changed my mind and gave them more lyrical stuff as well as some comic verses. Some of them laughed and there was a faint burst of applause. Another one. More soldiers now came up, their automatics rattling as they walked in the dark.

"Anyone got any grub here?" called out a hungry baritone.

The others shushed him. I don't know if he stayed, but many others now rolled up, climbing the neighboring tanks as if they were grandstands. The applause grew stronger.

"How about that letter to the bitch who ditches her boy friend?" someone suggested. The poem had a different title, but on the whole it was an accurate description. Spontaneous applause followed. My audience now included some of the tank corps gentry, and I saw several officers among the crowd. Poetry was feeding the hungry. This was the proper time for the verses I had written about the Army.

> You soldiers on our western border standing
> My homeland's peace and happiness defending . . .

The applause did not decrease, and I decided to make use of this.

"Comrades, I think I ought to tell you that my friend the Second Lieutenant from the Political Department is also a poet. I'll ask him to take over from me."

I jumped down from the tank and left him to it. I was sure he would rise to the challenge. I wanted him to take up poetry again, which he had so unaccountably abandoned. Perhaps he was waiting for it. He held a copybook in his hand.

"Yes," he said, "I do have one poem here, Comrades, but I want all of you to recite it with me. It is called "A Pledge" and here is the text: *We shall fulfil our task!*"

One after the other they picked up the pencil and solemnly signed their names. The whole thing was marred only by a dialogue between two infantrymen.

"Seems to me we'll have to go on ahead on foot if we are to do it."

"Oh, come off it! I didn't say *when* I'd do it, did I?"

Peter counted the signatures in his copybook.

"A hundred and seventy-one. Thanks."

"Why did you dodge?"

"Oh, that. I've finished with poetry once and for all. A man has to make his choice."

They found a ford near the bridge. The tanks moved forward. I had my work cut out finding mine. All the vents had been closed, the water reached right up to the turret. I put my hand in it and found it was like ice. For a moment I thought of the sappers and the tank drivers, and of all those behind us.

And of those who had driven tanks like these from Stalingrad to Prague. I thought of all the people who again had to resort to arms to defend the poetry of life against brutal force. Would my son one day also have to ride in one of these steel coffins? The roar of the engines and the rattle of the tracks died down. I entered my room. D_____ was sitting on the settee, holding one of our children on each arm. Her face bore the smile of the Sistine Madonna. My head bumped against the turret. I realized I had been dozing. We had stopped. From the tank in front, two infantrymen were carrying a third who was writhing in agony. Looked like a gall-bladder attack. The column moved on, leaving the sick man at the side of the road waiting for a doctor. The night of truth was not over yet. I turned around so that I would not be facing in the direction we were going, because my face smarted from the wind. An infantryman was standing behind the turret, holding onto a metal rung. He was dressed in the German Afrika Korps uniform that our soldiers wore immediately after the war. His coat collar hid his face from view, his forage cap was rammed low over his forehead. I had the impression he was smiling at me.

"Where are you from?" I asked him.

"Prague."

"Haven't I seen you before somewhere?"

"Sure."

I swallowed in sudden excitement. But surely I must be dreaming, I thought. Yet as the automatic slung over his shoulder bumped against the tank turret, it produced a clear metallic sound.

"What's your name?"

He turned aside his collar and I saw an earnest boyish face.

"Robek!"

Just then I heard an explosion very close at hand. He threw up his arms and fell into a blaze of brightness.

At the second explosion I opened my eyes. Our tank was standing still, encircled by fog. A third burst from a self-propelled cannon somewhere not far away. Then came the weaker roar of antitank guns and a staccato of machine guns. And all the time a rhythmic noise of hammering. I clambered down clumsily. My shoulder against the ice-cold turret was quite numb. The whole crew was busy repairing a broken track. They motioned to me, indicating that I was to find myself another tank. I started running through the sparse forest. The others seemed to be very far ahead by this time. The ground rose sharply, and I struggled on, sweating profusely. I had been so intent on hurrying in the direction of the gunfire that I failed to notice the steep hill in my way. Now it was too late to do anything but crawl upward. I thought my heart would burst with the effort. It was like climbing Everest. Then suddenly I was on top, panting and trying to recover my breath. The fog was lifting. A stout civilian with a huge head of hair was standing by a tree a few paces away. He looked just like

Jan Drda, the Chairman of the Writers Union. When he had finished and turned round I thought I must still be dreaming.

"Johnnie!"

He looked at me uncomprehendingly. Realizing that I was unrecognizable in my uniform and with my face caked with mud, I told him who I was.

"For heaven's sake, what're you doing here?"

"Looking for mushrooms," I replied. "And what about you?"

He took me by the shoulder and led me a little distance away. A newly built asphalt road appeared in view on top of that barren hill. The apparitions of the night continued: the silhouettes of large tents and a lookout tower built of sweet-smelling timber sprang up out of the mist. The place was full of officers, colonel being the lowest rank. A small general was shouting at a tall one, whom he outranked by one star.

"That's your fault, Comrade General!"

"It's the fault of the meteorologists, Comrade General!"

"Any postman could have told you that there are frequent fogs hereabouts, Comrade General. You should have planned contact an hour later!"

"Perhaps they'll arrive late—" said the lower-ranking general with his dying breath.

"I hope not for your sake! Comrade Minister Cepicka is leaving at seven. If he doesn't see anything, he'll make you pay every penny of the cost of this little exercise!"

Now I saw that all this—the tents, the lookout tower, the new road—had been built to provide an hour's entertainment for the Minister of National Defense, member of the Politburo and Klement Gottwald's son-in-law.

SET AN EXAMPLE...

I went inside one of the tents. The first thing I saw were the long tables covered with white tablecloths and laden with every imaginable delicacy, beginning with caviar and ending with cognac.

SET AN EXAMPLE IN EVERYTHING...

I felt an inhuman hunger. As if in a trance I greeted a group of writers who had been invited to take part in the show, and heard a clear, melodious voice ask:

"When are the soldiers going to eat?"

The Minister had a youthful, slightly bloated face, the intelligent eyes of a lawyer and the carriage of a Crown Prince. A tall officer in charge of supplies stood stiffly to attention.

"At ten o'clock on the line Tiger. The field kitchens have been just behind the first wave all the time."

The small general turned up, reporting as if he were on parade.

"Comrade Minister, permission requested to report!"

"Go ahead."

"The first units of the Army group have reached their destination."

The tent quickly emptied. I made straight for the table. The general responsible for the fog came in and poured himself a glass of brandy. He looked like a man who had just walked through a herd of enraged elephants. Catching sight of me he said:

"To hell with this! Why didn't I stay on the streetcars?"

I went out. General staff orderlies were just distributing the last pairs of binoculars. When they saw my low rank they passed me by as if I were so much air. I had my hands full of sandwiches, anyway.

It was a clear autumn morning. Far below us the sappers were doing their best to make it look as if Pribyslav were on fire. With my mouth full I watched the iron beetles crawl forward across the fields, accompanied by running ants.

My watch showed me it was 6 A.M.

At that moment I irrevocably outgrew my poet's coat. I made up my mind that I would try and write a play about the night that had just ended.

---

30 June 1968 / Sazava
(From the diary of the writer PK)

Mr. Kulhanek, the farmer from Xaverov who helps out with my garden, has concluded his regular commentary on the conditions of the Agricultural Cooperative Xaverov and the United Nations, hung up his scythe, and set off for home. The sun stands above the monastery, the freshly cut grass gives off a pleasant scent, the cherries are ripening, and my dachshund Adam turns over on his back, drunk with bliss. It is time to put the record player under the birches and play the Eine kleine Nachtmusik to the whole garden. Perhaps that would drown the noise of all the allied tanks on maneuvers here, a sound we weren't used to in these parts.

At this time last year I listened to music here after my return from the Writers Congress. Sitting on the grass in the black suit I had put on that morning for my own funeral, I could not help thinking all the time about Ludovik Vaculik. Although our good Comrade Novotny had claimed that we were both in the pay of the same Western espionage agency, that was the first time I had seen him. If you did not know him, you might easily think that he was suffering from the Herostratus complex, wishing to set fire to the temple once a year in order to boost his vanity. But even then, a year ago, he was terribly afraid. I am also afraid on occasion, but I try to hide it. Vaculik does not even try to. He is as rare as the Przewalsky horse, a man who speaks out, not what he knows he is supposed to think but what he really does think.

Exactly a year and a day later he now again entered the political arena in his typical fashion. He put together a document numbering exactly two thousand words resulting in a hurricane of admiration and anger, right from its second sentence.

"First the war endangered the existence of our nation. Then, more bad times with events imperiling its spiritual well-being and character. The majority of our people accepted the socialist program with hope. Its direction, however, fell into the hands of the wrong men. That they did not possess sufficient statesmanlike qualities and experience, knowledge, or philosophical erudition would not have mattered so much if only they had had more wisdom and the ordinary decency to listen to the opinions of others and allowed themselves to be replaced by more capable people."

I was fascinated. It was a political treatise coming from a future era in which I would dearly like to live. In contrast to the soul-destroying collections of unchanging phrases—including the buts, ifs, and althoughs and painstakingly avoiding all ideas not approved from above beforehand—he called a spade a spade, succinctly and in an admirably human fashion—with all the risk of making mistakes that this entails; and he was honest enough to

166

sign his name to the document. I recall his words when last April he was given back his Party card:

"The resolution in fact only states that some kind of procedural error has been committed ... it says nothing about the case in point, that is, about the views I expressed at the Writers Congress."

He was right—history was repeating itself. Nothing had really changed; they needed us to act as battering rams against the powers-that-be, whom they wished to supplant. Once they had achieved their aim, we would again become mere court jesters not to be taken seriously or rebels fit only to be punished. They had so far not shown us the instruments of torture they intended to use on us, but a year and a day after the Congress the tone adopted by the Party presidium was very similar to last year's:

"Regardless of the intentions of those who signed the two-thousand-word declaration, it is worded in such a way as to mar the reformatory endeavor of the present Communist Party leadership, making the Party as a whole responsible for the distortions and crimes of the fifties and en bloc condemning the results achieved through the work and self-sacrifice of millions of workers in the construction of socialism over the past twenty years."

Once more we had here millions of workers used as an argument, even though the text of the declaration did not speak of what the workers had achieved but rather what they were prevented from achieving by the stupidity of the ruling clique. And that is something for which we, the whole Party, are responsible, just as for the distortions and the crimes, because the Party card gave us, apart from certain rights, also the fundamental duty of making sure that the revolution should fulfil its ideals and not deny them. After all, it had been this very feeling of responsibility that had led these present-day critics of Ludovik Vaculik to launch their attempt to save the Party last January.

Had he voiced any doubts about their action? Had he crossed the Communist Party off the list of progressive forces, denied its leading rôle?

"We shall, first and foremost, refute any opinions, should they be expressed, that it is possible to carry out democratic reforms without the Communists, or even against them. This would not only be unwise but also unjust. The Communists have well-built organizations—it is necessary to support their progressive elements.

They have experienced functionaries, and after all they still hold in their hands the decisive levers and pushbuttons. The public has been presented with their Action Program, which is the first attempt to put right the biggest wrongs, and there is no one else with a similar concrete program."

Those who for twenty years had been cooking up their speeches from emotions and slogans could understandably be irked by someone speaking of such sacred matters without resort to the prescribed liturgy. Instead of "we must go with the Party in the name and in the interests of" Vaculik said "we must go with the Communists simply because they are there." But all this would not be sufficient reason for the press of our fraternal allies, inspired by certain voices in our own country, to speak of a signal having been given for a counterrevolution! Using a million words they extracted the following sixty-two to prove their point:

"If at this time," i.e., before the Party Congress and elections, "it is impossible to expect the central political organs to do more, we must achieve more in the districts and individual communities. Let us demand the departure from public office of those who have abused their power, damaged public property, acted dishonorably or cruelly. We must find ways and means to make them give up their posts. For instance by means of public criticism, resolutions, demonstrations, demonstrative working brigades, collections for their retirement presents, strikes, boycotts."

When the men of January created their pressure group in the Central Committee to serve the public interest by deposing the First Secretary of the Party and President of the Republic, I doubt that they felt guilty of treason or conspiring for a putsch. Yet socialist citizens who do not want to have at the head of their community a pocket edition of Antonin Novotny could "seriously imperil the constructive development of the socialist process of regeneration." This was stated in the presidium's resolution despite the fact that the incriminating text went on as follows:

"We must, however, refrain from using illegal, indecent or violent methods.... Our aversion to the writing of abusive letters must be universal.... Let us make sure that public order is preserved during our meetings.... If we hear strange reports, let us verify them.... Let us support the police when they are trying to apprehend real criminals. It is not our intention to create anarchy and insecurity. . . . Let us avoid quarrels and let us not indulge in barroom politics while under the influence of drink!"

Only a Czech could have written such a proclamation.

And yet over the reactions it provoked hovered the apparition of Hungary 1956. This forces me to ask myself a question that cannot be ignored:

IS A COUNTERREVOLUTION POSSIBLE IN THIS COUNTRY?

If my unhesitating reply is no, then it is not because it is a quiet evening and I am listening to the soothing tones of Mozart under my garden's birches. The reply is dictated by facts, nothing but facts, past and present:

Czechoslovakia is a country with one of the oldest traditions of popular social movements in Europe. (That was why the reactionary feudal lords of Germany and Hungary had attacked the Hussites of Tabor.)

Czechoslovakia lies on the crossroads of Europe, and its mighty neighbors, in particular Germany, Hungary, and Poland, have for centuries declared that it belonged to them. It had therefore become the nation's historical mission to belong to nobody but itself, to maintain its sovereignty and to establish an order in which the weaker should not be oppressed by the stronger. Even the aristocracy had been forced in the past to respect this principle. Since the Middle Ages the national consciousness has fostered a feeling for truth and justice, not only with regard to the outside world but also within its own society.

Czechoslovakia had accordingly become a country with a legacy of democracy and humanism, which had been present also in the twenty years between the wars, when Czechoslovakia was a bourgeois parliamentary democracy. We were taught in our schools that truth prevails while in German, Polish, Hungarian, and Bulgarian schools they taught that the mightier prevails, or at least that the nation stands above truth and justice.

Already in those interwar years Czechoslovakia had a strong and well-organized working class which sent dozens of its representatives to sit in the Parliament, so that in comparison with backward Poland, Hungary, and Bulgaria it was a bastion of the proletariat.

Already in those years Czechoslovakia had a Communist Party with a million votes behind it and several dozen members of Parliament, while the Communists of Germany, Poland, Hungary, and Bulgaria were being executed or sent to concentration camps.

Czechoslovakia became a pocket of resistance behind the Fascist front. Slovakia had cleansed itself of the treason committed by its clerical leaders by the popular rising against the Nazi invaders, while the soldiers of Germany, Bulgaria, and Hungary were supposed to help wipe the first socialist state in the world off the face of the earth.

Czechoslovakia was the first to conclude an alliance with the Soviet Union, as early as 1935!

Czechoslovakia and Yugoslavia were the only countries in Europe which after the war voluntarily chose socialism without the presence of foreign armies, and this at a time when the German Democratic Republic did not even exist, when Hungary was just getting rid of its kingdom, Bulgaria of its tsardom, and Poland was emerging from a civil war.

The difference in our traditions was thus obvious even to primary-school pupils. Czechoslovakia was linked with the German Democratic Republic, Poland, Hungary, and Bulgaria by their common experience of starting to build socialism and then by the long period of Stalinist distortions, which had begun with the fatal excommunication of Yugoslavia. But even in those years there had been differences which any impartial observer could not help noting.

As opposed to Poland and Hungary, Czechoslovakia had collectivized practically all its agriculture.

As opposed to the German Democratic Republic, Czechoslovakia had completely abolished the private sector in industry, trade, and services.

As opposed to Poland and Hungary, Czechoslovakia had deprived the Church of all political influence.

As opposed to Poland, Czechoslovakia had never accepted any Western loan.

As opposed to Bulgaria, Czechoslovakia had not opened its doors wide to Western tourists.

As opposed to the German Democratic Republic, Czechoslovakia had not oriented a major part of its foreign trade to West Germany.

But that was not all. What were the conditions out of which the Hungarian counterrevolution grew in that tragic autumn of 1956?

A reactionary peasant organization, a strong Vatican influence, powerful underground groups of former Fascist officers, old anti-Russian and anti-Communist sentiments which had been responsible for chauvinistic tendencies among the young people—and all this eight years after the Communist takeover and in the same year as the upheaval brought about by the Twentieth Congress of the Soviet Communist Party.

What conditions existed in Czechoslovakia for a counterrevolution today?

Twenty years since February 1948 and twelve since the Twentieth Congress, here was a country with a totally changed social structure. Two generations had grown up in admiration of the Soviet Union, following a whole century of pan-Slavism nurtured by both Czech and Slovak literature. The generals and other high-ranking officers had been with General Svoboda on the eastern front, the younger officers had joined the Army direct from the factories after February 1948. The police and State Security were staffed exclusively by trustworthy Communists. Most of the judges, lawyers, engineers, and functionaries were recruited from among working-class university graduates. All the young people under twenty had been born under socialism. Even the Club of Committed Non-Party Members had expressed its unanimous support for socialism. No one had demanded the return of nationalized property. Not one agricultural cooperative had disintegrated. Instead of thousands of shots being fired, only a few faces had been slapped in public houses. The last representative and unfalsified public opinion poll had produced a remarkable result: Would you like to see a return to capitalism? Yes—5 per cent; Don't know— 9 per cent. Do you think we should go on building socialism? Yes—86 per cent.

Who then was trying to make us believe that counterrevolution was lurking just round the corner? Where was the force capable of carrying it out? And if that were so, why were these assertions being made once more?

We agreed in the fifties with the tough measures against the class enemy while the cold war was in progress and because our leaders had told us that it was this class enemy who was behind all our economic and political failures. Since then we had been forced to look for a different explanation. Thinking people of all social strata had found a new cause in the distortions that had made it possible for bureaucrats and even criminals to rule the country in the name of the working class. Now that we are at last trying to transform our knowledge into action, why was someone intent on reviving the version of the fifties, with who knows whose name in place of Stalin's and Gottwald's?

Let us have the truth. Either they believed that we had succeeded in building the foundations of socialism—and in that case we had nothing to fear from the 5 per cent who were against and 9 per cent who did not know. Or they did not believe this —in which case they were themselves nihilists, marring the twenty-year-old endeavor of millions!

Last January Dubcek and the others had, on the contrary, tried to give new life to that endeavor. The changes taking place in the advanced countries of the world may result in such a solution of social problems that a bureaucratized socialism will become the tombstone of revolutionary ideas. The January reforms represented an attempt to make socialist society consistent with the demands of the scientific-technical revolution, an attempt to make socialism capable of developing all its potentialities and throwing an eagerly expected lifeline to the emergent nations of the Third World. This attempt was essential and progressive in every respect. It was the forces trying to conserve society in a primeval socialist age that, regardless of their past merits and their slogans, were truly counter-revolutionary.

True, it is a daring experiment for a Party with no intention of giving up its leading role in a disturbed society to change its methods, its organization, statutes, and leadership. But why should it not undertake such an experiment if the process of reform was so sympathetically received throughout the land? What was there to fear when even priests gave their blessing to the new leaders, not because these had betrayed socialism but because they were giving it a human face?

What cause did these leaders have to be angry when a Communist writer who alongside them—and perhaps earlier than many of them—had helped break the vicious circle of ignorance and malice by writing two thousand words that should have given them food for thought:

"We consider federalization primarily a means for the solution of the problem of nationalities, otherwise it is only one of the important measures aimed at bringing about the democratization of our life. By itself it will not necessarily provide better conditions for the Slovaks because it does not solve the problem of the regime —separately in the Czech lands and in Slovakia. The regime of Party and State bureaucracy may survive in Slovakia all the easier for having, so to speak, 'helped to achieve freedom for the Slovaks.'"

If the politicians do not rid themselves of their conditioned reflexes, if they do not learn to answer a question with an argument instead of an insult, they will once more begin to erect a Tower of Babel in which there can be no communication. Here are two arguments from impeccable sources:

"The chief cause of their collapse lay in the fact that they became attached to one particular form of growth of the working-class movement and socialism, that they forgot how one-sided it was and did not see the sharp clash which became inevitable as a result of objective conditions, so that they went on repeating elementary and at first glance indubitable truths: three is more than two. Unfortunately, politics is more like algebra than arithmetic, or perhaps higher mathematics would be an even better comparison. In actual fact all the old forms of the socialist movement had gained a new content, so that a minus sign had appeared in front of all the numerals, but these wise men of ours still go on stubbornly trying to make themselves as well as others believe that minus three is more than minus two!"

Who said this and when? Vladimir Ilyich Lenin, Collected Writings, vol. 31, p. 97 (Czech edition).

"The question of power has been solved in Czechoslovakia's internal politics: our reaction will not on its own be able to overthrow the regime of people's democracy, so that without outside intervention it does not represent any danger."

Who said this and when? Klement Gottwald, at a meeting of the Party's Central Committee on 9 April 1948!!

How paradoxical in this context is the sound of the tanks which have lost their way and cannot make it back to their frontier. I am

173

very much afraid that the evocation of ghosts will not increase their traveling speed.

It is a beautiful summer in a beautiful country, the grass smells sweet, Mozart is being played, but I keep reading and rereading two thousand words which contain my hope as well as my anxiety:

"This spring, just as after the war, we have been given a great opportunity. We can once more put our hands to our common cause which is called socialism and shape it to correspond as much as possible to what used to be our good reputation and the relatively good opinion we had of ourselves. This spring has just ended and will never come back. Next winter we shall know everything."

---

28 X 56 / Prague

As during the war, we again listened to news bulletins in English, French, and German. Now there was a TV set as well as a radio. Through the closed door we heard laughter and crying. D_____ was bathing the children. On the TV we again saw men hung on lamp posts and set on fire after they had been sprinkled with gasoline.

I cast my mind back to the ninth of May. These two evenings had something in common. In May fireworks had lit up Prague and lilacs were in bloom for the dead Robek and our living liberators. D_____ and the children went to watch the display without me. I remained at home feeling miserable.

A copy of that day's paper lay on Father's writing desk. In it were the photographs of the latest Laureates—my friends.

"It's all so unjust," I complained. "What do they have against me? It wasn't the Writers Congress which came out with the criticism, but its Party organization. I was annoyed to hear Hendrych announce that they had fired Cepicka as if by doing that they had finished off the personality cult in our country. I don't have to be told that Cepicka made the Army a state within the state—who should know that better than I?—but after all there were other people in the Politburo besides him! People who spent the whole war in Moscow! Did they have to wait for the Twentieth Congress? Didn't they know *anything*, anything at all before then?"

"You were also in Moscow," said my father. He was already in his pajamas, drinking his nightcap of milk as he sat behind his desk.

"And so was I," he added.

"Yes, only I was twenty at the time! Why didn't the rest of you tell me anything?"

He put on another pair of glasses.

"Look, I'm sorry," I told him. "I'm not trying to put the blame on anybody. But one such self-criticism is more than enough where I am concerned, enough to last me a lifetime. I just asked them to leave Stalin alone and tell us instead in what way it manifested itself in this country. After all, damn it, Cepicka wasn't the Party boss!"

"But Zapotocky was."

"Zapotocky repeated a number of times that he wasn't arguing with me as President but as a writer like myself. He even sat with me in the plenum. When he had finished calling me names, he said that they would never again punish anybody for views expressed at Party gatherings. So why did they have to cross me off the list of those who received the State Prize, having made me pose for a photograph for this purpose only the day before? And a State Prize I was supposed to get for writing a play which treated this very subject before the Twentieth Congress ever took place!"

"Surely you must have reckoned with something like that when you decided to get up and speak."

"I don't see why I should have."

"Well, now you do, don't you?" said my father.

"So what am I to think, then? That a State Prize is awarded to Communists for keeping their traps shut?"

"Maybe not exclusively for this, but I suspect it may be one of the reasons."

"But I don't intend to keep my trap shut! If they make such a fuss about discovering the distortions and are then incapable of taking the next logical step—how can I be sure that the political trials, for instance, weren't rigged?"

"The worst of it is," said my father, "that I have been thinking about this too. When they arrested Evzen Lobl I couldn't believe him guilty, but when I heard the broadcast from the courtroom it seemed absurd *not* to believe. Now it seems absurd that it could ever have seemed absurd."

"Well, that makes two of us in this flat alone! What about the millions of non-Communists who have been whispering this long before we tumbled to it? What if *they* take the next step instead of us?"

Now it was October and those who were burning on the lamp posts of Budapest were Communists. My father and I were drinking vodka, but it did not help to dull the senses. How could it have happened? Was it really possible that an innocent Rajk had been executed in a country in which Communists were in power? I kept hearing the voice of Jaroslav Seifert when he addressed the Second Writers Congress on 28 April:

"Several speakers have stressed that the writers act as their nation's conscience . . . I wish we really were that at this moment. For, believe me, I fear that we have not been our nation's conscience for very many years now. We have not been the conscience of millions, no, not even our own!"

What was he trying to say? That I, my father and mother, my relatives and friends, had given eleven years of our lives to a game in which people stole and murdered? But surely, I had read my Marx and my Lenin, where was there a single page that I could not sign with an easy conscience? Where and in what had I lied? Or had we truly been so frightfully ignorant? When, at a confidential Party meeting, they had read to us Khrushchev's speech, I ran straight to Peter. I had never seen him so agitated before.

"How could they do this?" he asked.

"Do what? How could they do all those terrible things or how could they reveal them?"

"Both. Can you imagine how the French or the Italians must feel at this moment?"

"But can you imagine how *I* feel at this moment?" I retorted.

"The same as me. The thing is I can't help asking whether the Communist movement can afford to wash its dirty linen in public like this, with the whole world looking on. Why didn't they do something? Why did they have to toss it at our heads like a ton of bricks?"

"I agree. But they *have* and now we have a bump on our head and in our soul. What do we do with it?"

"Above all, let's not give way to hysteria," he said. "We threw our arms round their necks like little helpless babies. That's because those who spent the war years in Moscow have always had the main say in our leadership. Zapotocky and particularly the younger ones like Novotny and Hendrych must lean more on our own revolutionary traditions. Not to copy others but to try and find our own model."

"Like the Yugoslavs?"

"Why the Yugoslavs? Why again go shopping in someone else's store as if we didn't have our own? There were always enough ideas in stock. Let's return to it, then. After all, Gottwald was our store manager, not Stalin!"

"Are you quite sure he didn't give too much of the stock away?"

"I hope not!"

When I got around to asking him about the political trials his wife showed up and he changed the subject to my TV commentaries, criticizing me for speaking with a cigarette in my hand. Why did he never wish to discuss politics in front of her? Was she perhaps even more critical than I? Was he afraid that she would get him into trouble? I always sensed some secret between them. And I invariably thought how much we had both been changed by our marriages.

I met him again last June, after the extraordinary Party conference, at which an unexpectedly tough speech was made by Vaclav Kopecky, member of the Politburo and Minister of Information:

"Certain writers have come to hold a completely erroneous idea of their own mission regarding criticism in our Party. They gave vent to this idea at their last Congress, seeing and hearing nothing, so that their speeches created nothing but a great sensation for *Literární noviny* and, alas, also for Radio Free Europe. The latter of course now expects that we shall take some severe measures as reprisals against the writers who spoke against the regime. Well, Radio Free Europe will wait in vain. It will be up to the writers themselves to adopt a standpoint on those speeches!"

"I don't agree with Seifert," I told Peter, "and still less with Kopecky. Why does he hide behind the regime when it was he who criticized more than anyone else? Why do they threaten those Party organizations which demanded an extraordinary congress? Why do they even have to refute ever having done so? Why are we climbing stepladders to take Stalin's portraits down from the walls when he is quite evidently rising from the dead?"

I was furious, and it seemed to me that this year, instead of a hammer and sickle, we ought to have a big question-mark on our flags.

"Brother," he said, using this appellation for the first time in many years, "the time has again come when to be a Communist means to fall into line. They loosened the reins in Poland and the regime all but collapsed."

"But this isn't Poland!"

"It can happen anywhere. Just because we have a few idiots at the top I don't intend to assist at a funeral of socialism. And least of all at my own."

It was October and on our TV screens we saw Hungarian blood being shed. The children came running into the room to say good night. I looked at that clever and still handsome man, watching him change in a fraction of a second into a grandfather. When we were alone again I asked him:

"Tell me, Father, when does a man become a father?"

"That depends."

"Somehow I feel I'll never be one."

"What makes you think that?"

"Oh, I don't know. I like kids, but to be absolutely honest, they get on my nerves."

"Maybe it's because you're more suited to your typewriter than to married life."

"If that's so, why didn't you talk me out of it?"

"Don't you think you're asking a bit too much of me? And in any case, I am not complaining—I quite enjoy being a grandfather."

"I've noticed."

"If it's any consolation," he said, "I can tell you that in time I even got used to you."

"Yes, but when did you actually begin to feel like a father?"

"I can tell you that to the day: it was when I found that on your own initiative you had learned *Cyrano* by heart. Since that time one can occasionally have a sensible conversation with you."

Mother came in, returning from a Party meeting tired and depressed.

"It was awful," she told us. "Just imagine, no one turned up except us on the committee. And our personnel manager today received a letter asking him to pick the lamp post he wants to hang on."

"Oh, take it easy," said my father. "If I know him, he wrote that letter himself. People don't do that sort of thing in this country."

"Oh, come, Father," I corrected him. "Don't forget you and I actually saw things like that back in forty-five."

"Yes, that's right, we did," he said. "But we shan't see them again."

"How do you know?"

"Because the Soviets will not permit it."

"In Hungary they even have their Army. And yet they're pulling out of Budapest."

"They'll be back, you'll see. There won't be anything else for them to do."

"I hope to God you're right," said my mother. Turning to me, she went on: "While we're on the subject, would you tell D____ kindly not to hang her washing so low over the bathtub. How is one to bathe?"

"First of all, Mother, you do have the strangest associations of ideas. And secondly, why don't you tell her yourself?"

She left without a word and went into her room. The phone rang. They were calling me from the theater.

"Sit down and don't get excited!"

"Why should I?"

"We have stopped rehearsing your play."

"Why?"

"Special precautions because of Hungary."

I downed a large vodka. It did not help in the least.

"Father, for the first time in my adult life I feel I'd rather be dead."

"Oh, nonsense, son," he replied. "From my own experience I can tell you the first seventy years are the worst."

"But you're only sixty-four!"

"That's just what I mean."

The room I had entered did not remind me of any room I had
ever lived in with her. I was conscious of a fleeting feeling of relief, being as carefree as I had been before I met her. The occasional pang of loneliness could be overcome, but it was fantastic
and soothing to realize that after so many years of sharing my
privacy with others it was suddenly I and I alone who decided
the condition of my home. The fat and extremely nice elderly
lady from the Old Town who did my shopping, cleaning and
washing had learned to move about my tiny flat like an arche-
ologist: she dug objects out from beneath layers of dust without
disturbing them the slightest bit. And there was also my wonderful old uncle who looked after my archive and who watched
over my housekeeper's ministrations with all the vigilance of a
former bank manager. All that was a thing of the past. Ever since
that first morning when *she* had wakened there for the first time,
the objects in the room had started their frenzied locomotion,
which then accompanied us wherever we went like a swarm of
angry bees. Today for the first time it had been different. She
had only time to open a suitcase containing her summer dresses;
the other pieces of luggage were still in neat array in a corner of
the room, where I had put them yesterday from the car.

I opened the window to let in some cooler air and switched
on the wireless. It was almost eleven and the free, legal Radio
Czechoslovakia came on the air with its signature tune, Smetana's
"Blanik," as in the days of peace when this late hour had been
reserved for the lovers of classical music. I shut my eyes. For the
first time in many months I again saw my mother, bent over her
knitting needles.

YOU HAVE A LONGER WAY TO LOOK!

Yes, I was again myself. It was as if the decision I had made in
front of the hotel had completely altered me. The certainty I
had felt in Perugia had returned. I knew that in exactly one hour
I would get up and set off for home. The idea that it would be
without her no longer grieved me. The shot fired by that tank on

the front page of a newspaper had drowned out more than one trauma.

Now I was again capable of rational thought and it seemed incredible that fifty hours ago I could have decided to change my whole life for her sake, to abandon what was most important in it: my work, which had always meant far more to me than just the invention of fictitious characters and plots. In an unknown inn at the foot of San Marino I had thrown aside the relay baton which was my heritage and my only legacy: the five-hundred-and-fifty-three-year-old legacy of the Czech spirit.

On 6 July 1415 Power committed one of its bloody errors when in Constance it had a Czech preacher burned at the stake in order to save the peaceful Slav minds of his flock from his heresies. He had had a toothache, and I often think of writing a play on the subject of what would have happened if they had taken him to see a doctor and then sent him home with a few fatherly words of admonition, as the Emperor's safe-conduct had assured? Who knows if this would not have bowled him over, as had happened to so many other intellectuals before and after him when instead of a kick in the pants he had been given some award or other by a wise ruler. Who knows what our history would have turned out to be if he had returned to Bohemia thus enlightened, to teach with greater vigor than ever before obedience and humility. But as usual they found the stake more attractive, naïvely scattered his ashes in the Rhine, and thus provoked the anger of the whole nation down to the last swineherd— similarly the Prague hippies were tonight scrawling DUBCEK on the steel plates of Russian tanks. They had called into being a movement in the heart of medieval Europe which became so democratized that even after the Hussites were defeated it brought to the Bohemian throne the capable Czech politician Jiri of Podebrady, who was chosen in an almost modern way in preference to the anointed heads of Europe.

On 6 November 1620, in another battle for the throne the Catholic Habsburgs defeated the armies of the Bohemian Protestant Estates on the White Mountain, two miles distant from the Ruzyne Airport, where the invading Soviet armies were now landing for the third night running. Once again Power has had a fine opportunity to gain the sympathies of a weary and corrupted land by its magnanimity, which would have defeated the losers a second time, this time in the minds of the people. Perhaps the nation would have accepted the religion and culture of the victors, if these were thrust at them less. But they again preferred to stage a show trial and then on a June morning in 1621 hanged, beheaded, and broke on the wheel the elite of the Bohemian nobility. Its remnants and the Protestant intelligentsia connected with it, led by Jan Amos Komensky, had to flee the country, vainly seeking allies abroad until they found peace in their grave. Then Power closed down Czech schools and burned Czech books, forcing thus the poorest peasant to sit up at night copying the Kralice Bible, just as after last year's writers congress the speech of Ludovik Vaculik has been copied. As a result the new Czech intelligentsia was born two centuries later under the thatched roofs of cottages and in the working-class suburbs of Germanized cities, and it became overnight the most democratic intelligentsia of Europe. Teachers, poor priests, and itinerant actors, themselves educated in German schools, gave the forgotten language of their ancestors back its sound, figured out grammatical laws and supplemented its depleted vocabulary, not only that it should reflect modern thought but also to become the nation's weapon in its struggle for national liberation and social justice.

That was why Comenius was present in my primer, not just through his pedagogical principle *schola ludus* but first and foremost by his humane democracy. That was why the poems, novels, and plays that accompanied my schooldays had captivated me not only by their modern literary methods but equally by their markedly socialist character. That was why, when I wrote my first unskilled verses, I quite naturally became "committed."

Such a tradition and such a content—and yet it had allowed itself voluntarily to be manipulated into what threatened to become almost another Dark Age. All it had needed was the gap in universal education caused by the war and the postwar change in thinking, when an organized allocation of emotions began to take the place of objective information. The Czech and Slovak Communist intelligentsia functioned like an electronic brain that had been wrongly programmed. No sooner had the error been spotted, however, than the voice of the Czech writers sounded as the first of all voices, when they in 1956 admitted their mistakes and drew the necessary conclusions from them. How important were Seifert's and Hrubin's speeches, which I at that time was still unready to accept because of my idiotic innocence! It was above all thanks to them that literature was able so quickly to become part of the new avant-garde, which was beginning to form inside as well as outside the Party to liberate it from the feudal bonds of the First Secretary and his apparatus. Even though its program was drafted by economists and political scientists, even though its chief bases were in the factories and scientific institutes, it was the voice of literature which gave it unity, repairing the artificially severed communications.

What were my friends of the Prague Spring doing, where were they at this moment? I will find them the day after tomorrow!

"Blanik" had just finished when I heard two people coming up the stairs. I literally jumped into my trousers. I had not expected him to accompany her all the way to our room. But at least, it occurred to me, with him present, our talk would take place without any hysterics. I now began to be curious what *his* reaction would be. Would he advise her to go home with me or would he offer her his selfless aid? I could not, of course, altogether rule out the possibility that they had already agreed what to do beforehand. This hurt, and the fact that it hurt worried me. Come what may, I had to suppress all sentimental feelings and all vanity. I must at last get off the train that was carrying me in the wrong direction and return along my own road to find myself.

By the time the footsteps halted outside my door I was quite sure I could do it.

---

25 XI 60 / Prague

The chef of the Olympia was busy behind his glass wall as always, and the cocktails were still being mixed by the same fixturelike barmaid. E____ had literally dragged me here in spite of my protests.

"I can't! When I look at that dance floor I'll keep seeing him as he danced the rock-'n-roll on his sixty-fifth birthday."

"Look, Maestro," she said affectionately, "it's time you gave up this morbid habit of yours—erecting little tombstones at every step."

"Well, in that case why do you wear mourning for a whole year for a man you've never seen in the flesh?" I asked, pointing at her black dress.

"Gerard Philippe is a dream," she replied. "A yardstick of purity in life and art that I carry about with me as a seamstress carries her tape. It doesn't stand in my way, whereas you keep stumbling over those little graves of yours all the time. I know that your father, whom I only saw once, would have loved to drink to his own funeral in the very place you and he used to clink glasses!"

Whenever she spoke in this vein my edgy resignation began to vanish. The headwaiter, small in stature but great in that special gift which changes water into wine and a mere professionalism into art, greeted me like a prodigal son, warmly welcomed E_____ as if he had always seen her with me, and led the way to my favorite table. I was telling E_____ how eight years ago I had asked him for two crowns change and how ever since he gave me two crowns with every bill. Just then I caught sight of A_____.

She was dancing with a youngster who might easily have been her son, except that she went out of her way to make it obvious that he was a lover. She again had close-cropped hair, perhaps to emphasize her girlish face. But her yellow dress with a metallic thread accentuated her womanly figure.

For a very long time she did not betray that she had noticed my presence, but no sooner had E_____ left the table to go to the powder room than she deserted her companion in the middle of a dance and sat down in her place.

"You're looking well. And you have a pretty girl. Is she a drama student, by any chance?"

"How did you guess?"

"I'm glad that you've come back to the fold. Are you single again?"

"Yes."

I was beginning to find her tone rather unpleasant.

"And what about you?" I asked her.

"No, I'm not single."

With a single gesture she consigned her boy friend to oblivion.

When she married that prosecutor I no longer had the slightest reason to feel jealous, yet I felt personally affronted. He had insulted her in front of me in a way that for the first time impaired my certainty that a Communist invariably acted humanely. Her decision to marry him therefore seemed utterly incomprehensible to me.

"Is this a serious romance?" she asked.

"I see that he has taught you the art of interrogation."

"He hasn't taught me a fucking thing.... Sorry. But bad language is just about the only thing I have learned from him. You live in Charles Square now?"

"How did you know that?"

"Alone?"

"Yes."

She waited until E____ had almost reached our table. Only then did she get up and say with a beaming smile:

"I'll call you some time. Bye—"

She picked up her juvenile and led him back to the dance floor. E____ was mistress of the situation, as usual.

"Well, sir, when you give your last supper, don't forget to invite me. I think it should be a merry gathering."

The past almost always hits me like a salvo. Next morning I was awakened by the ringing of the phone. An unknown voice that used the familiar form of address wanted to know whether he could come and call on me. I said that I didn't catch the name.

"This is meant to be a surprise," the man said, laughing. It was a pleasant laugh.

I very rarely refuse. Perhaps this is due to exaggerated politeness or to professional curiosity. The most sterile of conversations sometimes provides germs of ideas out of which months later a play is born.

I had scarcely time to wash when the bell rang. I went to open the door in my pajamas. My visual memory, the only gift that had been lavishly and purposelessly put in my cradle, did not tell me a thing this time.

"I guess you don't remember me," he said. "I remember you, though."

He showed me a small card which said he was a member of the State Security Corps. I sat down on the bed.

"I can't say that this fills me with gladness and joy."

"Sorry, I didn't mean it like that. You and I worked together building the Collective House at Litvinov. I studied in Moscow when you were at the Embassy there. In both places I was in your recitation group. You saw so many faces at once but we saw only you."

"Sorry," I said in my turn.

"That's all right. It's part of my profession to be on good terms with the crowd. You have to stand up in the limelight."

"Does the State Security Corps wish to start a recitation group? In that case I'm not sure that I'd be the ideal man to lead it. If I'm not mistaken, you must have a pretty large dossier on me by now."

"Oh, don't overestimate yourself," he grinned. "We treat you writers as a natural catastrophe."

"So what is this all about, then?"

"I wanted to tell you that we let a pal of yours go the day before yesterday."

"Slavek?"

"Yes. Let out on probation under the amnesty. I thought you'd like to know. You see, the first few days are the worst. Perhaps you wouldn't mind taking a look at him. He behaved himself inside, but he might do something silly out of pure exhilaration."

"But what on earth is he going to do? What kind of a job can he get if he's out on probation?"

"We've found him something."

"Yes, but he was studying to be an actor—"

He showed his teeth in a triumphant smile.

"Look, don't get us wrong. We're cops, not thugs. We put in a good word for him in a decent provincial theater."

I took the address. I reached the town of K⸺ shortly after ten in the morning. They had already started rehearsing. The stage doorman fortunately recognized me and promised to call Slavek.

"Don't tell him who I am," I said. "I want this to be a surprise."

It was—for me as much as for him. The man who came out into the street was thin and pale and gray-haired. In one hand he was holding a cigarette, in the other his text. When he saw me the book fell from his hand. I bent down and gave it back to him. His cigarette dropped from his hands, I bent down and gave it back to him. Again, the book fell from his hand, I bent down, but it fell from my hand too.

"You know what," I told him, "let's leave it right there."

We embraced, and under the loosely hanging pullover I felt the sharpness of his bones. I had a good look at him.

"I see they let you out just in time. What you need is a good tailor."

And he replied just as he would have done years ago, with Cyrano:

> *I carry my adornments on my soul.*
> *I do not dress up like a popinjay....*

We found a bench in a nearby park. He had an hour to spare. It was a cold, damp day and he had come out without his jacket. I therefore suggested that we should go to a coffee house.

"No, no," he said quickly. "Let's stay here. In the park over there . . . there is a lot of room . . . that is, if you don't feel cold."

"I don't, but you must be."

"Cold? Good God, no. I even have a shirt . . ."

He quickly changed the subject and told me how well they had received him at the theater.

"You don't want to talk about it?" I asked him straight out.

"About what? Prison? No, I'd rather not."

And then he added, as if by way of apology:

"I signed an agreement, you know."

Now I understood. But there was one thing I did want to know, something I had wondered about all those years.

"Look, I still can't understand why she left you the way she did? How could she run away and leave you behind?"

He answered without hesitation.

"She was expecting a baby. I only learned later. She had an abortion in the States."

"How could she do it, though?"

"To help me. She knew that if she told me I'd stay with her and she realized it wouldn't work. She never wanted me to leave the country . . . you see, I belong here like bacon with eggs."

I was not sure that this was not merely a fantasy he had invented to help him come to terms with life. But as I drove back to Prague and thought about him I grew quite certain that he had managed to find himself and was now unlikely to lose himself again.

A_____ came to see me last night. I had quite forgotten about her in the month since our unexpected encounter in the night club.

"I'm downstairs. Won't you let me in?"

Had she phoned to arrange a meeting I would have found some excuse to put her off. Like this I felt I could not very well send her away. In the lift she brushed my cheek with her lips.

"I hope you're not annoyed with me because of last time. It wasn't my day, that's all. And if you have a date, just kick me out."

Her tone was so friendly that I could not feel angry with her. I brought a bottle of whisky and found her standing in the middle of my tiny attic flat, looking round in astonishment.

"How many square meters is it? Four?"

"Ten."

"Did you hate her so much that you left that beautiful place for this?"

"Why should I hate her? We just didn't get on too well."

"Tell me about her."

I refused. I made a point of not gossiping about the people who had played any part in my life, least of all about D_____. Passionate love affairs petered out and were forgotten. D_____ remained in my subconscious like a neuralgic pain. I could still hear her voice as she said to the divorce judge:

"Your Honor, don't ask us to break plates over each other's heads. Surely a husband and wife can separate because they respect each other. If it's really the children you are concerned about, then give us the divorce we ask for. That way they'll at least always know us as decent people."

A_____ asked for Cinzano. I offered her the only chair, but she sat beside me on the couch, and drank with long swallows, as if it were lemonade.

"I'm glad you like it, but you'll soon be under the table at this rate."

"Don't worry. I've got more thirst than you've got money."

"What about your liver?"

"You ask just as my husband does. Shall I give you the same reply I give him?"

I did not insist. Instead I asked her if she still acted.

"The theater? Sure I do, in B———. That moronic youth you saw me with is our glittering star. Need I say more?"

The theater in B——— was a hole.

"You like it there?" I asked cautiously.

"No, I don't. But *he* absolutely loathes it."

I did not understand the logic of this statement. She poured herself another glass.

"Do you ever see Peter nowadays?" she asked.

"I wouldn't put it like that. Now and then we meet on an official footing. After the Twentieth Congress he was quite approachable for a while. Now he reproaches me for being a Titoist revisionist."

She took off her shoes. Then she asked me a question that took my breath away.

"You two hate me, don't you?"

"Why? Why should we?"

"For marrying him."

At last I understood. It was she who hated. She was so full of it that she was unable to talk of anything else. I told her as much. She smiled at me as you smile at a child who has just solved a simple riddle. She put her straight, strong legs across the armrests of my armchair. Just as on the night before the trial, I felt she was telling me someone else's story.

She had met the young prosecutor again a year after the trial. The Minister of Information, that tragic clown, had been in the habit of inviting young artists and actors to his banquets. As one of those who had rid the Party of "that coil of adders" at the Slansky trial, the prosecutor enjoyed great popularity.

"Look after her, won't you, Eddie," the Minister asked him, and he almost fainted. He looked after her for the rest of the evening. "Don't you understand?" he kept telling her. "That was the only way I could get you off Scot-free!" After the banquet he took her to the Olympia. They drank champagne and he claimed that she had taught him to dance. In the car on the way home he put his arms round her. She extricated herself, asking him whether he was trying to prove to her that he had been right in telling the court she was a whore. He apologized profusely. Next day he came to the theater, having first sent a huge bunch of roses. He sent her flowers every day; she kept refusing to meet him. He was frantic, and finally proposed to her.

"He was married and it all but ruined his career. Luckily for him his wife committed suicide in time."

I had no idea, I told her.

"No, they hushed it up. You see, she had been ill for some time. The authorities could not allow a scandal connected with his person. That was the time when people started saying that the trials were rigged. He himself sent several people to jail for 'slandering the regime.' And it was then that we were married."

"But did you love him?"

She left the stage on his account. He wanted a wife who would make a home for him.

"But it wasn't a home, rather a night club frequented by what must have been the greatest idiots of the entire peace camp. Generals. Ministers. Secretaries. Daddy Novotny himself showed up one evening. And when he left that ass I married said to me: 'In former times the President used to visit writers, now he visits a prosecutor. Just goes to show that it's we who are writing the drama of today.'"

I could not help asking:

"Do you know anything about the trials?"

"No. I made him promise that he wouldn't mention his work in my presence. I have enough on my own conscience, thank you."

One day she received an anonymous letter and found him in his secretary's flat. He admitted that he had been having an affair with her all the time they had been married. On his knees he begged A⎯⎯ not to destroy him.

"I first wanted to apply for a divorce, but then I thought, why should I? He would only get out of it again and I'd be left high and dry at thirty. So I put the fear of God into him and then dictated my conditions. Sometimes I feel sick of it all, but I make sure that he feels even sicker."

I was speechless. She stroked the back of my hand.

"Sorry to unburden myself like this, but I had to tell someone at last."

Then, I don't know how, we started talking about the summer of 1944 when we two had first met.

"Strange, isn't it," she said. "There was war and death all around us and yet I know that was the only time I felt at peace with myself . . . I wonder if you ever guessed that I was desperately in love with Robek?"

How was it possible that this had never occurred to me?

"He alone knew what he didn't want. That's why he had to die."

At midnight we were out on the terrace, listening to the bells of Prague.

"Can I stay with you?" she asked.

How many years I would have been willing to leave any of my loves for her single caress, a single word. . . .

"Sorry, I have to get up early," I said. "You wouldn't get any sleep."

She did not betray any emotion, but kept the conversation going for a little longer. She talked gaily about nothing in particular. When I opened the street door for her I suddenly remembered.

"I've forgotten the most important news of all. Slavek is out!"

"Yes, I know," she said. "I have just spent a week with him in the mountains."

Again I was speechless.

"My husband was the first to prove I was a whore. I'm doing my best not to disappoint him."

Thursday, 22 August 1968 / Rome
(Continued)

Instead of a knock on the door I heard a key turning in the lock. How did she get it? A bald gentleman was staring at me, astonished to see me as I was to see him. I discovered that when an Italian stammers he sounds just like a Czech. His companion, on the other hand, was quite undisturbed. In her miniskirt, which revealed her thin legs, flat-chested, handbag under her arm, she might have stepped right out of *Nights of Cabiria*. The bald gentleman glanced at the room number on his key and opened his door. I saw now why his hand shook so much—the girl was no more than fifteen. Apart from sheltering guests from Czechoslovakia the hotel evidently fulfilled yet another important social purpose.

I closed my door, still trying to button my shirt. Behind the thin wall drunken laughter, while my friend's voice again spoke from my radio. He was reading a sentence written less than a month ago, yet it now sounded like the echo of a faded parchment.

"*We'll not abandon this road alive!* Do you remember this sentence, dear friends and listeners? A million signatures attested our determination to stand firmly behind it. It was contained in the Declaration of Czechoslovak Citizens to the Presidium of the Central Committee of the Communist Party of Czechoslovakia just before its departure for Cierna, where it was to hold its talks with the Politburo of the Soviet Central Committee. Maybe at the time we did not really understand its full meaning. Now the time has come when our determination will be put to the test. Now is the time to give that sentence its true meaning. We cannot abandon this road! Having once said as much, it is our duty to keep our word!"

That sentence from a declaration signed in the city squares and village marketplaces recalled all the other declarations drafted by Czech and Slovak writers from the days of Munich to the present. The world of literature might justifiably reproach us for having written more manifestos—some of them dubious—over the past quarter-century than books of real artistic merit. It could scarcely deny that whenever our national existence was threatened we had our readers and our opinions were taken seriously as perhaps nowhere else in the world.

For the third night running half a million nervous invaders, armed to the teeth, were standing face to face with fourteen million of my outraged and angry fellow citizens. They too had weapons—a whole modern army that had been confined to barracks—and the knowledge that they were in the right. How much was required for a desperate action to flare up which would at last take the place of the nonexistent counterrevolution and give the much-needed pretext for reprisals?

For the third night running, too, one heard a handful of voices from the legal broadcasting stations that were being kept going by sheer will-power rather than by technical skill. For the third night running hundreds of journalists and writers were working away to prevent the decimated Party leadership from losing contact with the people, so that every morning there would again dawn the hope that now had two names: Conscience and Commonsense. BEHAVE AS IF THEY WERE NOT THERE!

These were the rules of the game; they helped to paralyze superiority of arms and to save human lives. The Battle of Britain, Tobruk, Sokolovo, Dunkirk, Nazi concentration camps and places of execution—all these had Czech and Slovak victims during the last war, and they had not died a shameful death.

However, in this catastrophic and absurd situation there was little sense in committing grandiose suicide; this would bury more than just two small nations in the heart of Europe. The protracted disease of socialism would give rise to a malignant tumor.

Gigantic China, when it was still a choice, defenseless morsel for well-trained warriors, could defend itself by swallowing them up slowly and quietly but also surely and without trace. Small, beleaguered Czechoslovakia today, as always, had only one possibility: to fight injustice by its hereditary intellect and experience. It was saving not only itself but also, in the final analysis, its misguided allies. By its superhuman discipline, it had so far not allowed them to lose the last vestige of reason and commit something still worse through which they might isolate themselves for whole generations from the world's revolutionary forces.

Small, occupied and once again abandoned Czechoslovakia was during these dramatic hours rescuing the prestige of socialism, as well as the human dignity of the inhabitants of the five countries of the Warsaw Pact. Its actions decided whether their own children would one day call this invasion a mistake—or a crime.

For the first time since the evening of last Tuesday when in San Marino I wrote them a dozen postcards, cheerfully announcing that I was leaving the turmoil of the world for the silent shores of art and love, I again thought of my friends in Moscow and Leningrad. How often had we pooled our *rubles* to go out at midnight and buy stockpiles of bottles and then continued our endless arguments. How short were those exciting nights in small rooms! People, tables groaning under the weight of books and caviar, sausages and lithographs, notebooks, cheeses and vodka. I could only admire the determination with which they tried to overcome the handicap of the Soviet intelligentsia— their artificial isolation from the rest of the world. They thought of me as the courier of the ideas of European Marxists, which the local postmen had refused to deliver. Gramsci, Garaudy, and Fischer shocked them much as they had shocked me a few years earlier; yet only a year later they were ready to admit their error. I liked them for the spontaneity with which they struck up new friendships as well as for the devotion which made them capable of extreme self-sacrifice. They thus made up by their touchingly archaic attentions for the damage done to the relationship between a superpower and her tiny fellow traveler by their heavy-handed leaders.

Our history, our culture, our thoughts as well as our endeavors provoked them to indulge in a constant confrontation, which was all the more meaningful as Czechoslovakia was a fraternal socialist country. In contrast to the Russian stranger I met in the Monastery winecellar, whose hatred was in direct proportion to his ignorance, my friends in Moscow and Leningrad entertained no doubts about the nature of the Prague Spring.

Guta cavat lapidem non vi sed saepe cadendo ...

It was one of these friends who said that perhaps Czechoslovakia would turn out to be the drop which would help them erode the rough surface of the Russian rock. Not by force but by constant action.

Now the Russian rock had landed on top of us.

What were they doing, what were they thinking at this moment—the actors Vladlen and Oleg, translator Volodia, or Lala the playwright? I had no doubt that they had immediately grasped the enormity of the wrong that had been done to us. In that case there was nothing left for them to do but what enlightened Russians have always done since the beginning of time when their Tsar went mad: to drown in alcohol their *Gore ot uma.*

The one who did not need to do this was most probably writing in his wooden cottage near Kazan. Although he had never set foot outside his native Russia, his works were filled with the same universal experience as those of geniuses who with their dog Charly or with their hunting rifle had been all around the globe. He was Alexander Solzhenytsin, a man I had never met, a Russian, and yet the only person I wanted for a companion this night.

Thinking of him like this, with admiration and respect, I once again realized that our frontiers lay somewhere else than where dictators and chiefs of staff had drawn them. When the five countries of the Warsaw Pact came to realize how nonsensical their action had been and to remove its direct consequences, we would be faced with an even harder task than standing up to tanks armed with nothing but arguments.

I shall never forget that moment one morning in May 1945 when the rumble of tanks heralded the resurrection. Out of a million similar moments had grown an international feeling that together with a long-existent sympathy for Russia had permeated the thinking and the action of the liberated country. This feeling was so strong that it had survived even the ordeal of Stalinism. The criticism voiced during the Prague Spring had not destroyed, but only cleansed it. The newly acquired freedom and equality had acted as an impulse for brotherhood, for the equation has always been and will remain:

$$\text{LIBERTÉ} + \text{EGALITÉ} = \text{FRATERNITÉ}$$
$$\text{FRATERNITÉ} - \text{LIBERTÉ} - \text{EGALITÉ} = 0$$

What could our people have felt during those moments around midnight on 20 August 1968? What were the feelings of the commanding officer in charge of the frontier post at C_____ when he saw around the bend the winding snake of armored vehicles so similar to those in which he himself had fought at Kiev and the Dukla Pass—did he feel sorrow or hatred? What did the elderly Communist lady working in Prague Radio weep most for—the burned-out houses or her burned-out love? How did the miners, drunks, and lovers react when they came from their night shifts, pubs, and beds to find themselves confronted by guns in the hands of those they had been used to calling brothers? What kind of feelings would grow out of these millions of moments and how would it influence the thinking and action of so humiliated a country in the course of the next twenty years?

Another test would be in store for us, without which our moral victory would not be complete: when the time of reckoning came, it would be up to us to forget the affront we had suffered and show the same magnanimity the Yugoslavs had shown to us when we offended them twenty years ago.

Revenge is no policy. It merely provokes a new revenge; it merely replaces one wrong by another; it harms those who have been led astray while those responsible for leading them astray settle themselves more firmly on their thrones.

The relay of hope passed on by a dozen legal radio stations had again reached Prague. My friend's voice read the latest news. Even after two days, military intervention had not succeeded in creating a political solution. The occupation forces were to spend their third night without food under the stars. Their dream of a new Czech government that would throw open the doors of barracks and stores had come to grief on an indomitable people and an indomitable President. The white-haired man at the Castle put up a brave defense—as he had once defended Sokolovo. The Fourteenth Extraordinary Congress endorsed the post-January policy and condemned the infringement of a socialist country's sovereignty. A new Central Committee was elected, without the fools and the traitors. The names of the interned leaders had been put at the top of the list of candidates. I shut my eyes and saw in front of me the faces of the First Secretary of the Party Alexander Dubcek, of the Chairman of the National Assembly Joseph Smrkovsky, of the Premier Oldrich Cernik.

What film ran through their heads when foreign parachutists broke into their offices and aimed their automatics at them? Did they put up a struggle or were they resigned to their fate? Had they expected death? Were they afraid? Did they cherish any hope? Did they believe in anything? Did they think of anyone? Of their wives, Lenin, or perhaps God?

For the first time since the death of the Stalinist leaders, whose myths as well as bodies were turned to ashes by the Twentieth Congress of the Communist Party of the Soviet Union, I felt moved by the fate of politicians.

"The second day of the occupation is coming to an end," said the voice of home. "Let us remain faithful to the objects of our sworn allegiance."

In the pause that followed I could hear the bedsprings creaking from the next door. The bald gentleman was not wasting any of the time he had paid for. I thought of that thin, childish body. Across three frontiers I suddenly felt the anxiety of my daughter, who I hoped would never know what it was to be humiliated. The castle I had been trying to build for her vanished in the sand.

Our national anthem sounded on the radio. I turned the volume up to wash away my sorrow and disgust. It was midnight. I started to pack.

◻

12 July 1968 / Sazava
(From the diary of the writer PK)

It was five o'clock in the afternoon and I was still lying under my birches.

"You really aren't going?" she asked me.

For the past twenty-four hours I had been cursing myself for having allowed myself to be talked into becoming a candidate for the Czech National Council. In Parliament I had quite logically not been elected, just as last March at the regional conference, the writer Jiri Hanzelka was another political corpse, while Professor Sik scraped through with a majority of a single vote. True, our nonelection made us very popular with the nation and gave me renewed hope of a seaside holiday, but I was nevertheless annoyed by this triumph of the hard-liners, able once more to score an easy goal.

"I'm fed up to the teeth with politics!" I said. Ever since that morning I had been brooding over a screenplay, but it again hatched as a letter. This time to His Excellency the Soviet Ambassador in Prague.

I wrote for three hours, and when I had finished I felt calmer and was able to tear up what I had written. But the desire to write was irrevocably gone. I was lying on my back, looking up at the birches, fed up with everything and everybody, and, most of all, myself.

"You promised to drop politics when you're forty," she remarked, to my surprise. "Can't you stick it out these few more days?"

"I think that if I start a little prematurely it will be all to the good," I said. "I'm glad I've lived to see a time when I can correct the mistakes of my youth and I don't intend to start making new ones. I will gladly leave that to your enlightened generation, which is convinced that it has inherited this land from fifty generations of utter idiots—the first of whom no doubt was our Forefather Cech himself, who instead of sailing to the shores of Manhattan settled his tribe in this dull country with neither a sea nor Coca-Cola. I have decided to take your advice and spend the rest of my life devoting myself to my fictitious heroes, who are hardly likely to do any serious damage. Perhaps I have played a modest part in bringing about the astounding upsurge of democracy in our country, the helm of which has at last been grasped by men who possess integrity, education, and the nation's confidence. Let them henceforth, under the vigilant eye of your mature and critical contemporaries, see to the building of highways, the further growth of striptease, and the early departure of the allied armies which seem to be enjoying their maneuvers so much that they cannot bring themselves to end them. I want out!"

"In that case why did you write that letter today?"

"Just force of habit, my love. In senility, which according to you I entered the moment I joined the Communist Party, people find it most difficult to rid themselves of their old habits. That's all the more reason why you should congratulate me on my decision and go and make strawberry dumplings to celebrate my return to the womb of innocence."

"Have you ever been invited by the Premier before?" she asked cunningly.

"You know as well as I do that I have not, my sweet. All the former Communist governments considered Communist artists to be mere clowns, the one point on which you and they are in agreement."

"Oh, shut up!" said Z____ sternly. "Why this self-pity? We hadn't the slightest reason to love you while you allowed psychopaths to rule us in the guise of Party discipline. Surely you must understand that we could not very well distinguish between you. Now that you have done it yourselves, we're beginning to trust you."

"We thank you!" I cried, grinning with gratitude, for she spoke as if her generation and mine were jostling there on the lawn, between the birches and the fence. But, not to be deflected, she concluded with dignity:

"If the Premier has chosen to invite those who only last autumn were expelled from the Party to dinner, then not to go would be not only impolite but downright insulting. Have you forgotten how happy you were when Ludovik Vaculik accepted his Party card back without a fuss? I don't see why you should have to crown your victory over your own stupidity by behaving like a spoiled brat."

An hour later I was in Prague, where I changed from my jeans and washed my neck so as to be fit to represent Czech hacks in the presence of the highest in the land.

At the stroke of eight we were convulsed with laughter when we saw one another making for the Hrzan Palace. Goldstucker, Prochazka, Vaculik, Liehm, Klima, Hanzelka, Havel, Skvorecky, and so on. Twenty people whose literary as well as nonliterary activities had in the past few years kept several hundred Party watchdogs and State Security men busy.

Premier Cernik personally led us out on the terrace, offered us drinks, and introduced us to a part of his team. It was good to see personally the best government this country had had in the fifty years of its existence. The number of academic titles exceeded the number of its members, the Minister of the Building Trade alone having four.

"Good evening to you all," we were greeted by Josef Smrkovsky's familiar deep voice.

"But weren't you dining with the Press tonight, Josef?" asked the astonished Premier.

"I was supposed to be, yes," replied the Chairman of the National Assembly, "but my spies told me you chaps were here, so I postponed it."

A white open-neck shirt gleamed under his gray crew-cut hair. He towered over us, taller by a head. When he pressed my hand to express his condolences on the election at which he had presided yesterday, I could not resist asking him why he did not bring a surgeon with him when he shook hands with people.

"I'm glad you took it like good sports," he told Hanzelka and me. "Democracy applies to everyone alike, ourselves included.

But they've played a dirty game, no doubt about that. They keep paying lip service to Party discipline, and yet when it comes to a secret ballot they quite cheerfully ignore our resolutions."

Someone pointed out that Jiri Hendrych had been one of the organizers of the move to prevent the election of Hanzelka and myself.

I had met Hendrych quite recently in the building of the Central Committee. We came suddenly face to face in an empty passage. He returned my greeting with the good-natured smile of a philatelist who had just risen from his beloved collection.

"Glad to see you," I said sincerely. In this most human system of ours men who had been deprived of power used to be put into isolation and suffer various slights; I wanted to show him that we did not intend to tread Asian paths ever again.

"What're you doing these days?"

With evident pleasure he started telling me how he was collecting material on the thirties for the Historical Institute of the Communist Party of Czechoslovakia. So immersed in his subject was he that he did not even repeat himself or make those long pauses so typical of his big public appearances. And as I watched him depart down the long corridor, stooping with the weight of a packed brief case, I erased from my mind the nasty memory of last year's writers congress.

Obviously I will remain hopelessly naïve to the end of my days. All theory is gray, but the tree of life eternally green.

The sun was just setting and the smoke above the roofs of the Little Quarter created a huge postcard. We turned our backs to it. Power and literature mingled on the terrace, launching into a long and necessary dialogue which was terminated only by the arrival of Alexander Dubcek without announcement or fanfare. As always, at public meetings as well as on TV, he was preceded by his perpetual hesitant smile which seemed to be asking forgiveness for his very existence.

Hanzelka and I stuck to Josef Smrkovsky. This was the fourth time in my life I had talked to him, yet I felt I knew him intimately. Perhaps it was because I had been with him at those two stormy gatherings in March, at which politics ceased to be a subject to be feared. And perhaps there was a sentimental connection with the days of the Prague rising in May 1945, when Smrkovsky, then a thin, long-haired young man, had acted as vice-chairman of the Czech National Council.

Where are the snows of yesteryear. . . .

I was still unable to decide whether Smrkovsky looked older than he was or was older than he looked. His rich, emotional voice and boyish eyes did not seem to suit his tired gait and slack carriage. The contrasts one often finds in people who have spent many years behind bars. As if they were concentrating the remaining energy of their whole body into several points where they are most needed and can best be put to use.

On this small terrace there were three men who had been sentenced to life imprisonment in the fifties. Josef Smrkovsky, Dr. Husak, and Professor Goldstucker were now serving the balance of their terms as Chairman of the National Assembly, Deputy Premier, and Chairman of the Writers Union respectively. I couldn't imagine them standing at attention, their caps pressed to their side, reporting to a conceited nonentity who watched over the food, sleep, and hard work of these accursed traitors of the revolution.

"Tell me," I asked Smrkovsky, "are you really convinced that you now effectively control the Security Service?"

"I understand." His typical phrase with which he answered most questions. "Probably no government in the world is capable of doing that today, because the police aren't so much a state within a state as a world within a world."

"I quite agree," said Jiri Hanzelka, "but isn't that all the more reason to keep a check on them as a priority? I'd be quite willing to wait a while longer for the opportunity to travel, for instance, as long as I can rest assured on this score."

"That's why we made Pavel Minister of the Interior," Smrkovsky replied. "Surely that speaks volumes!"

It did. I had rarely met so many enthusiastic people as I did the morning after Pavel's first radio interview. A man who had fought in the Spanish Civil War and led the People's Militia in February 1948, he brought to his new post an intimate knowledge of all our jails and an inability to sign the confession that was demanded of him. Having assured his listeners that he would remain Minister only for as long as he would be able to ensure absolute legality, he spent half an hour giving expert advice on a subject learned during his years in the political wilderness after his release from prison: how to grow strawberries in adverse conditions at higher altitudes.

"Yes," I said, "Pavel is a man who will go down in history as the first Minister of the Interior to receive messages from well-wishers, asking him at the same time for seedlings. But how can his Deputy for State Security be a man like Salgovic?"

"I understand," said Smrkovsky again, throwing his hands wide apart. But he did not seem inclined to give any real explanation. "I, too, can't say I'm overjoyed when I meet the secret policeman who put the handcuffs on me. On the other hand he was the only one who allowed me to say goodbye to my wife, and that was quite a lot in those days."

I saw Dr. Husak slipping away. It seemed to me all the time that he did not feel at ease in this company, although it had been these very people who had for many years fought stubbornly for his rehabilitation.

Ludovik Vaculik, leaning against the low wall of the terrace, was pointing out a nearby window to Dubcek:

"One machine gun over there and there would be no more trouble in this country for some years to come."

His remark was received with a burst of hearty laughter. Next to me Josef Smrkovsky was excavating one more cigarette from the packet in his hand and shaking his head.

"Let's hope it all stays nice and jolly . . ."

"Why, is anything up?"

"Don't ask me. Certain things have to follow protocol. We'll tell you everything when the time comes."

Now I put to him the question that had been burning my tongue all evening.

"You refused to attend the Council, didn't you?"

"What Council?"

"I mean the conference of the five in Warsaw."

His reaction was unexpected. He had been about to light his cigarette, but his hand with the match stopped halfway. He was obviously surprised and quite angry.

"How did you know?"

"Look out, you'll burn your fingers."

"Who told you this?"

I made a vague gesture.

"Oh, friends. I came tonight from the country. In Prague everybody knew it."

At last he burned himself and rubbed his fingers furiously.

"Well, I'll be damned!"

"Why're you so surprised? Your speech in December was being quoted the very same evening. That Svoboda was to be President— my barber knew before Svoboda did. And as for your refusal, people even know that Brezhnev asked whether Comrade Kolder agreed with your decision. So there's no need to be angry. Of course you can fire all the drivers, typists, secretaries, and the whole Presidium. But perhaps it would be simpler to conduct politics openly, to inform people about things faster than their barbers. Do you know what I think is the key to success for a Czech politician?"

"Well?"

"To realize that he is a politician in Bohemia."

"I understand!"

He gave one of his boyish laughs, a mere flash in the pan. The Warsaw business could not be dismissed so lightly. He stooped even more than usual and, dragging Dubcek out of a nearby group of people, went off somewhere to whisper with him.

It had grown cooler outside and our Hyde Park moved to the dining room. The Premier walked past me, engaged in lively debate with the author of the two-thousand-word declaration he had so resolutely condemned in Parliament. They were still arguing about it, but now Cernik was calling him just "Ludovik."

I remained on the terrace. Above the illuminated city, almost close enough to touch, I saw the dark silhouette of the large Petrin park. Whole generations of Prague lovers had successfully broken its lamps to go on searching for hidden treasure. I thought of my approaching fortieth birthday, my children, political meetings, future theatrical plans, my dachshund, and Z____. I was conscious of a gnawing anxiety that perhaps I had already thrown all my dice, and with this nostalgic feeling turned to watch our leaders through the glass of the window.

If I had wanted to write a play for three male actors with the most diverse characters, I could hardly have found a better trio as models.

Alexander Dubcek. When the news leaked out nine months ago that there had been a sharp clash between him and Antonin Novotny at the October meeting of the Central Committee, people in the Czech lands asked: Who is he? He turned out to be the fellow Novotny had appointed First Secretary of the Slovak Party several years ago, a good boy with a perfect class background; Dubcek did not talk out of turn, but worked quietly and persistently, implementing a sensible policy in his native Slovakia. As the spokesman of the most compact group, radical where Slovak national problems were concerned and moderate in general political matters, he was practically the only possible candidate for the new Party chief in January. He was supported by the progressives and had at least the passive approval of the hard-liners to whom he was certainly more acceptable than someone like Josef Smrkovsky. At that time no one could have imagined that what was at first sight an insignificant change in the leadership would result in producing a new socialist alternative which was to thrill as well as appall the revolutionary movements of East and West.

Alexander Dubcek had become a world political star but nobody had told him. He reminded me of that nonactor of genius who appears in Forman's films, reaping laurels at every festival from Cannes to Plata del Mar but not attending any of them because he has to be in Kolin every day to conduct his brass band. Under normal circumstances, Dubcek would doubtless have remained a mere sounding-board for the inventions of the Big Boss. As it was, his case served as a powerful indictment of Novotny's totalitarian regime, which had turned latent individualities into uniformly packed sardines. Dubcek was the perfect example of the way a seemingly mediocre man can grow into a real personality if society creates the necessary conditions for growth.

It was the first time a Slovak had become First Secretary of a party in which there was an overwhelming majority of Czechs. Yet he did not have to exert himself to overcome the obstacles of national feelings, he overcame them by his mere physical existence. Following in the wake of many Slovak politicians who had outdone themselves trying to speak faultless Czech without ever gaining any sympathy, Dubcek wore his Slovak nationality as visibly as his white shirt—and the Czech organism accepted him without the slightest difficulty. People in streetcars, in bars, or chatting with friends jocularly spoke Slovak, and though it may have sounded terrible to the natives of that country there was not a trace of ridicule in it. Prague always loved in an original fashion. And it showed its love only very rarely.

Dubcek was the first politician since February 1948 who again respected the wishes of the majority, as he demonstrated when he changed his views on the question of convoking the extraordinary Party congress ahead of time. But his real magic, with which he enchanted old ladies in retirement as much as university professors, lay in his weaknesses. After the divine leaders of the Stalin era, who had insisted that their photographers retouch every pimple and radio technicians remove all sibilants from their broadcasts, it was pure joy to watch a man who seemed to be dying of stagefright. His heavy-lidded eyes made him look as if he had just been dragged out of bed to appear in public. And the way he stammered! One suffered to hear him read a speech. Yet, strangely enough, as soon as he stopped reading from his paper and looked straight into the camera. . . .

"How is it," I asked him tonight, "that you speak so incomparably better off the cuff?"

"When I look at the paper in my hands I have a feeling that people are laughing at me."

He had of course scored his greatest triumph by bringing back into politics a simple, comprehensible language. He could hardly have won higher praise than from the famous comedian Jan Werich:

"He's a chap you can talk to."

And it was again Jan Werich who fished out of one of Dubcek's speeches a brief sentence consisting of two nouns, one adjective, one preposition, and an indefinite article, making use of it to describe a program the like of which had not been known in the world for a long time:

SOCIALISM WITH A HUMAN FACE.

Alexander Dubcek did not give interviews. He grew wooden in front of photographers. He had left behind his family with three adolescent boys in Bratislava and spent the past six months living in a hotel. Perhaps so as to have a home he could return to if things went wrong. In any case, he had studied hard to gain the title of doctor of social sciences, so if the worst came to the worst he could always open a practice.

He seemed to me almost exceptionally sensitive. I even suspected him of being able to blush. Looking close at him for a long time, I wondered how he would be able to withstand the brute force. But I immediately repudiated the thought as being unworthy of Europe, this century, ourselves, and our allies.

Oldrich Cernik. Standing next to the proletarian tribune Josef Smrkovsky and the poetic functionary Alexander Dubcek, he looked like one of a thousand men who after working hours forgather in the famous beer cellars of Prague. The only thing that might perhaps have set him apart was his staccato pronunciation, which indicated that he hailed from Ostrava. There is a game in which a number of people are shown a photograph and asked: Who do you think this would be if it weren't So-and-So? In Josef Smrkovsky's case seven out of ten replied "a farmer." In Dubcek's, five out of ten "a teacher." And in Oldrich Cernik's case the replies went like this: an office worker (2), waiter, dentist, shop manager, masseur, football coach, functionary (any kind), film director, actor.

In actual fact he, like the other two, had originally been a factory worker, one of the many for whom February 1948 had made it possible to develop their natural talents. As some people are born actors, he was a born manager. He too had for many years been an insignificant cog in the wheel of Antonin Novotny, who had made mediocrity a virtue. Then Oldrich Cernik gained rapid promotion, becoming the head of the Planning Office. He must have been one of the few people in the country who knew the full extent of the catastrophic economic situation. He was thus one of those who had been criticized by Professor Sik. Strictly speaking, he had played his part in helping to build up the sham image which Daddy Novotny intended to present to our children as a Communist oasis despite the fact that it lagged so badly behind the rest of the world as to be near the elegiac times when man invented the plow. But viewed in practical terms, it is just about the only way a man living in a monolithic system—moreover part of a power bloc—can pave the way for and then carry out reforms without profuse and futile bloodshed.

As time went on it became clear that Marx's laws were so accurate that they functioned even against his own Church. Our Iron

Conception, a product of the Cold War, Stalin's theses, and home-made dilettantism, had damaged our economy so badly that not even cries of There will be meat, comrade housewives! could avert disaster any longer. A group of economists represented by Professor Sik had proposed the introduction of a new model, whose counter-revolutionary nature lay in the fact that it intended to turn the thinking of a socialist society from voluntarist idealism back to Marxism. The ship was by this time listing very badly, and after some hesitation the captain agreed that it might be a good idea to construct pumps. But he categorically rejected that part of the project—unfortunately the decisive part—which demanded political as well as economic reforms. The new model was to be experimentally introduced in several selected factories, while the power to make all important decisions was to remain vested in the Big Boss.

The ensuing farce is best described by an anecdote which tells how the Prague Transport Corporation wished to improve the catastrophic state of the taxi service in the capital. When Daddy Novotny was informed that the best taxi service in the world was to be found in London, he sent his experts there to find out why this was so. Having pruned their report of all undesirable political connotations, he announced that he intended to launch an experiment: half of Prague's fleet of taxis would henceforth drive on the left.

Oldrich Cernik had at that time shown much enthusiasm for Sik's innovations. Now he had become the Premier of a government that was to put them into practice. A paradox? No, just reality: in the eyes of the hard-liners it was Ota Sik and not Alexander Dubcek who was the real cause of their defeat, for he had infected with his arguments even some of the people in the Party apparatus "with the effrontery of which only a university professor is capable," as Comrade Jodas would no doubt put it. Sik was dangerous because he wished to make knowledge and proper qualifications mandatory not only for factory directors but also for political functionaries.

Although I definitely belonged to that wing of our society which according to Hasbek might be called "Party of Moderate Progress within the Limits of the Law," I began to understand that to call someone a centrist need not necessarily be an insult. I guess that in a democracy—even a socialist democracy—there must always be someone capable of equalizing antagonistic pressures and establishing the necessary balance without which no democracy can exist, much less a socialist democracy which is as yet weak as a newborn chick. Professor Sik thus became Deputy Prime Minister and I had no doubt that Oldrich Cernik would provide him with the necessary latitude. It is not usual for a captain to torpedo his own ship. Especially if at long last it is sailing on a course that does him credit.

Oldrich Cernik, I found out today, spoke in exactly the same way on a public platform and in private—drily, without any show of emotion, almost monotonously. But this terse matter-of-factness seemed to suit him. And I, who could not bear the loud-mouthed garrulousness of the old guard, even found it engaging. I had heard it said about him that he liked to stand on his dignity and had no sense of humor. This was not my impression, although he really did sit for hours as if he had swallowed a ruler. However, I noticed that whenever anyone made a joke he smiled as if to himself, and when he followed this with witticisms I felt sure he would be appreciated as a humorist in England. I concluded that his reputation for humorlessness came from people who did not consider anything funny unless someone slipped on a banana peel or two men set about kicking each other. And as for his dignity, it was good to know that some time ago he had not felt it beneath him to sit for his examination at the Technical Mining College although he was the Minister of the Mining Industry.

He obviously possessed exceptional tenacity as well as stubbornness, this last manifesting itself whenever he argued. There was yet another layer, and this the most interesting of all because it was so patently hidden under the bulletproof vest of his self-possession. Somewhere in his make-up there was some kind of imbalance—perhaps of an emotional nature, I do not really know—but I could have sworn that he was in the habit of secretly writing verse in which he was quite different from the surface man. Such a second layer in the soul of a leading politician can be conducive to inner harmony or it can result in the break-up of his personality. Caesar, Napoleon, Stalin. As a citizen I should feel impoverished if Oldrich Cernik were not a member of the governing body. Should he ever become a dictator, I would feel endangered. I had exactly the same feeling about Dr. Gustav Husak.

I recalled the words of the economist Selucky, who opened his address at the public meeting at the Slavonic House last March by saying:

"I had a terrible dream. I dreamed that all of us sitting on this platform tonight were arrested on Cernik's orders!"

Everyone went out onto the terrace again. The full moon stood right above our heads, looking with its red ring like an enormous No Entry sign. It signaled either rain or very bad times indeed. They were talking about a man whom Dubcek, Smrkovsky, and Cernik all called Ludvicek, using the diminutive form of his name and meaning the gray-haired President himself.

"We owe you an apology," I told the First Secretary. "Once we came to you with a petition asking that someone worthy of the name should become the new President and occupy this disgraced seat. We emphasized that apart from his other qualities he should be young in spirit and physically fit. You understood from all this that we had managed to discover who your candidate was. Yes, why make any bones about it—the doctors were almost positive that he could not work at full pressure for more than two or three hours a day. We tried to talk you out of it, but in vain. You had your way in the Central Committee. And then we crossed ourselves when watching the election on our TV sets, seeing him laboriously climb the steps to the mike, seeing his hand shake when signing the Presidential oath, hearing his voice falter when he read it. Well, after that came the payoff. The old gentleman, who had long been sailing the seas of retirement from which there is no return, suddenly made land again and at once came to life like an old warhorse at the sound of the bugle. Within a quarter of a year he drove and flew all over the country. He visited places that had not seen the head of state for a full fifty years. He gave many forgotten things back their true meaning. I've had a tough training and I don't move easily. But whenever I now see the President's flag from my window as it rises above the roof of the Castle, fluttering like a dove's wing, I blow my nose loudly and pour myself a glass of brandy. The doctors claim it is a Biblical miracle. If so, you doubly deserve our admiration, for it was you who said to him 'Take up thy bed and walk!' "

Alexander Dubcek looked as if he might faint there and then. He backed toward his two partners like a young actor who is just starting his stage career and suddenly finds himself taking a curtain call together with Olivier and Gielgud.

"Oh, but we all thought he should be President."

Then the natural vanity of the professional politician won through after all.

"But I see that you writers have realized that even you can be wrong on occasion?"

"You are the first politician to whom I—reluctantly—admit this."

"And you are the first artist from whose lips I am glad to hear it."

However, we had not come here merely to exchange polite compliments.

"In one respect, though, it's quite definitely you who's wrong," Jan Prochazka told him. "It's a mistake to trust people like Salgovic and Bilak.

Dubcek threw apart his hands just as Smrkovsky had done earlier. But while the latter had thus passed the question on to someone in higher authority, there was nothing for Dubcek to do but answer it, which he did, evidently for the hundredth time and to little avail.

"True, Salgovic has made mistakes, but he's an honest man, as is Bilak. If we acted as you suggest, it would be most unjust to people who have devoted their whole lives to the Party. In this way we may be able to win them over to our point of view."

Undoubtedly some part in this magnanimity was played by an awareness of their common class and professional background, by the sentimental relationship existing between Communists who formed part of the apparatus created at a time when all the other Communists were thought to be the agents of imperialist espionage agencies. A famous speech came to my mind, which holds an important message for all revolutionaries:

> For Brutus is an honorable man,
> So are they all, all honorable men

"My poor Alexander—Brutus!" I thought. "Don't permit the Antonys to help you bury Caesar, since they will one day denounce you for a criminal and destroy you together with all of us!"

When we came out into the square it was the next day. And the next day meant new anxieties. We parted not unlike fellow graduates after twenty years, who know that next time their number will not be complete. The Chairman of the National Assembly again crippled my hand. I survived his handclasp and asked him: "Do you think you'll come through all this and not break up?" He shook his head with conviction, adding by way of farewell: "Ludvicek will help see us through."

I had less than two hundred meters to go to my Prague bed, but I preferred to make for my sofa at Sazava fifty kilometers distant. As always when I felt less than cheerful, I wanted to wake up among the cucumbers and the woodpeckers. I drove rapidly through the sleeping villages, trying to avoid one hare after another; they too must have been going through some enlightened era, for they displayed a mass tendency toward suicide.

I wondered why the three had chosen last night to meet those whom all their predecessors had used as a lightning conductor whenever they were in trouble. Had they at last grasped that we were the most loyal allies of any government that had clean hands and good intentions? Or were things really so bad that the country was in a state of national emergency?

It was one o'clock when I put the car away in the garage. Its walls were still hung with empty canvases left there by Pravoslav Sovak, who some time ago deprived my car of its shelter, having failed to find a more suitable studio anywhere in Europe. What fascinated him most was the nearness of my kitchen garden, and between pictures he cooked the vegetables according to recipes from five continents.

The white rectangles of the unpainted pictures were as mysterious as the approaching day and the days that were to follow.

The gravel crunched as I walked across to the house. Though everything was in darkness, Adam woke and welcomed his beloved master with a sleepy bark. The night was warm, the sky clear. And come to think of it, I felt much worse this time last year.

25–29 June 1967 / Sazava
(From the diary of the writer PK)

THE FOURTH WRITERS CONGRESS or HENDRYCH IN ACTION

A Tragicomedy in Five Acts, Prologue and Epilogue. (A brief summary of the play, supplemented by the slightly abbreviated text of Act Four.)

Dramatis Personae:

Secretary of the Central Committee of the Communist Party of Czechoslovakia and Chairman of its Ideological Commission .. Jiri Hendrych

Secretary of the Central Committee of the Communist Party of Slovakia and Chairman of its Ideological Commission .. Vasil Bilak

Head of the Ideological Department of the Central Committee of the Communist Party of Czechoslovakia ... Frantisek Havlicek

My cousin and his wife..........................JK and LK

Farmer from an Agricultural Cooperative.. Mr. Kulhanek/as a guest

Z____ .... Z____

P____ .... P____

The Duetted Voices from the audience ....

Writers, translators, critics and literary historians......Members and candidates of the Czechoslovak Writers Union

Villagers

PROLOGUE

Sazava and Sazavou, late afternoon on Sunday, 25 June 1967. The villagers are enthusiastically building family houses while in the fields belonging to the State Farm the hay rots. A westerly wind is blowing, so that only a few can smell the gunpowder from the Middle East. The writer PK has finished writing the speech he intends to make at the Congress and is climbing down from the roof to read it. He reads it under the birches, dressed in a swimsuit. His audience consists of his doctor cousin, the cousin's wife, with both of whom he is linked not only by family ties but also by membership in the Party, which they joined the same time as he did, Mr. Kulhanek, a farmer from the local cooperative, and Z_____, who is serving coffee. When he is finished, his listeners speak almost in unison.

LISTENERS: Wow!

For a moment the writer PK imagines that instead of the birches he is facing an assembly of the country's leading literary lights, and instead of his relatives and friends a delegation of the Central Committee of the Communist Party. He is conscious of a slight feeling of vertigo, remembering the hundreds of hours wasted over the past ten years by the writing of other similar speeches resulting only in a series of repressions and depressions. He looks around. Everywhere the newborn summer is making miracles. The grass, water, sun, and air are playing a magnificent quartet. Up on the roof a half-written play awaits him like a woman who has only just stopped saying no. He thinks that his amateur appearances on the political stage are not of the slightest use; his life's road has for years now been strewn with the corpses of thematic subjects he has not had time to write. It seems to him that this is the time to decide whether he wishes to leave behind him a number of theatrical works or a collection of ephemeral speeches. He makes up his mind not to attend the Congress, whereupon his cousin disagrees, Mr. Kulhanek nods understandingly, and Z_____ exclaims with pleasure. His relatives and the farmer depart. As he sees them off, PK finds a letter in his letterbox by the gate, which must have been lying there for some length of time. A friend from the Soviet Union who failed to find him in Prague has sent him a copy of the letter Alexander Solzhenytsin wrote to the recent Congress of the Soviet Writers Union. The letter is a passionate protest against censorship which is again threatening to disrupt communication, which has led in the past to the birth of an inhuman system that cost Soviet society and the whole world a countless number of

213

talents. PK reads the letter in the rapidly darkening garden, illuminated only by fireflies. This message from the man in whose
work he has again heard the voice of great Russian literature shocks
him to the core. He becomes aware of the existence of an invisible
link, which across thousands of miles gives people the strength to
hit their heads against the wall repeatedly for the sake of thousand-
years-young ideals. Z_____ brings him his favorite dish—lentils with
rice—and in a long monologue describes the advantages of a life
in the country. The Prologue ends with her promise that tomorrow the water would be still warmer than today and that they
would be having strawberry dumplings for lunch.

ACT I—EXPOSITION

The main hall of the Transport Workers House of Culture in
Prague-Vinohrady, Monday 26 June 1967, 2:12 P.M. The pre-
Congress meeting of the Writers Union's Party Committee begins.
After repeated requests for its convocation it has deliberately been
called without much notice so that there should be as little time
for it as possible. The writer PK greets friends he has not seen for
many weeks. The faces of those present betray their skepticism.
Enter the Head of the Ideological Department HAVLICEK, who
welcomes Secretary HENDRYCH and Secretary BILAK on the platform. Secretary HENDRYCH reads the letter sent to the Writers
Union Party Committee by the Presidium of the Central Committee of the Party. From this it transpires that the Party is disturbed
by efforts being made to deprive of union influence those Communist writers who maintain a firm attitude on Party policy. It
therefore demands that no "confused" people, much less those
to whom the endeavors of our socialist society are alien, should be
elected to hold office in any of the Union's bodies. The letter goes
on to criticize Literární noviny for a number of its articles which
have recently had to be censored, in particular for the attempt
made by the writers Prochazka, Lustig, and Klima to print a discussion in which they defended Israel and denigrated the historical
rôle of the United Arab Republic. Immediately after this the poet
Sotola comes forward and, as a former Chief Editor of Literární
noviny, reads an interminably long list of confiscated material,

which shows that for practically every issue of the weekly two numbers had to be compiled so that censored articles could be replaced by others. A similar account is then given by the writer TREFULKA on behalf of the Brno literary weekly Host do domu. The writer PROCHAZKA, who is the Chairman of the Union's Party Committee, reports on the activity of Communist writers in the period between the Third and Fourth Congress. His monologue presents a sad picture of a series of critical situations caused by the clumsy interventions of the Party and State apparatus. Prochazka goes on to read a letter from the non-Communist playwright Vaclav Havel, who asks that the Union should act as a guarantor on behalf of the writer Jan Benes, who is to become a defendant in a political trial. The writer Vaculik comments on the words of Secretary HENDRYCH, saying he sees no reason why citizens should not be able to criticize the actions of their government, including its foreign policy. The writer LUSTIG reads a letter which he, together with the writer Prochazka and chess Grand Master Pachman, sent to the Party leadership, stating that a socialist country's policy on the Middle East, to be effective and based on principle, ought to support the progressive forces on both sides. The writers of the letter point out the Arab doctrine of the physical liquidation of Israel, about which nothing is publicly said in this country. The writer HANUS, on the other hand, criticizes the editors of Literární noviny for exerting a negative influence on the work of the entire Writers Union. Asked by THE DUETTED VOICES to say exactly what he means, he demands a quarter of an hour in which to prepare his speech. The Head of the Ideological Department HAVLICEK hints at attempts being made to cultivate a split of the Union into factions; but fortunately for us there are people who contact the Central Committee and keep us informed. The writer PK says that, although he is not one of the blue-eyed boys for Literární noviny, he cannot accept the unfounded criticism made by the writer Hanus. Several more people have their say and there is a short interval.

Scene Two opens with a speech by Head of the Ideological Department HAVLICEK. He refutes the complaints about a large number of censored articles by saying that this is the fault of several individuals who deliberately write in such a way as to get themselves censored. He then suggests that the discussion should be ended because it is time to draw up a list of candidates. Former Chief Editor JUNGMANN, however, wants the Party Committee to adopt a standpoint on the letter from Vaclav Havel and the accusations leveled against Literární noviny. He also demands that Head of the Ideological Department Havlicek reveal the identity of the persons who go to the Central Committee to lodge complaints and to say against whom these complaints are made. This HAVLICEK refuses to do because he has had some similar unfortunate experiences before. Secretary HENDRYCH expresses his astonishment that no one has so far seen fit to say anything on the subject of the Party Presidium's letter. As for the question raised by Chief Editor Jungmann, Secretary Hendrych does not know whether we walk around with our eyes closed or with our eyes open. As regards the list of candidates, there is no need to beat about the bush; we all know how matters stand. The writer SPITZER moves that the Union should consider acting as guarantor in the case of Jan Benes, in accordance with valid laws. This is greeted with applause. The writer SULER, however, asks Chief Editor Jungmann to forgive him but the list of candidates has evidently been compiled with a bias toward the group favored by Literární noviny. Consequently, the writer HANUS suggests that Jungmann, Klima, and Vaculik be dropped. He does not like Klima's underhand methods. The writer KLIMA wants him to describe his underhand methods in more detail. The writer HANUS says it is not his duty to describe anyone's methods; he will simply not vote for Klima. The writer Vaculik is a nice fellow, he has written a decent book, but he lacks experience. The writer KLIMA insists that his underhand methods be specified. The writer HANUS withdraws what he said earlier, so that Klima should not feel offended, and says that his only reason for not wishing to vote for him was that he does not like his methods. THE DUETTED VOICES sum up by saying that Klima uses methods but these are not underhand. On the table there are now forty-five names of candidates drawn up in advance, as well as twenty-six more that have been put forward during the meeting. The writer PTACNIK points out that it is going to be a very difficult election and that as an experienced official of the Union he thinks he ought to take charge. Head of the Ideological Department HAVLICEK proudly proclaims that he is the one who was entrusted by the Party with the task of conducting this meeting. Shortly after this he succeeds in creating utter chaos. The voting is carried out by a show of hands, separately in the case of each candidate. Monitors report the results to the table of the Electoral Committee. As time goes by it becomes clear that the candidates whom the Party would most like to see elected are getting the least votes. Secretary HENDRYCH leaves his chair on the platform, which he had previously decorated with his jacket, and in his white shirt and braces goes over to the Electoral Committee's table to make sure that there is no hanky-panky. In spite of this precaution the unfavorable trend continues. It culminates when the writer PK suggests that the lady writer Smetanova should be put forward as a candidate, since there is every danger that the Union will be run by a lot of boring males. Everyone in the room knows that the lady in question is first and foremost a brave girl of very progressive views. She is elected by acclamation. Head of the Ideological Department HAVLICEK announces that the election is over and proposes that the Party Committee pass a resolution that at the forthcoming Congress the writers who are Party members will contribute to a positive solution of the problems connected with the further development of Czechoslovak literature in the spirit of the resolution adopted by the Thirteenth Congress of the Communist Party of Czechoslovakia. In a hoarse voice he then thanks all those present for their participation and ends the meeting at nine minutes past midnight on Tuesday.

ACT II—CRISIS

Scene the same, next day, Tuesday 27 June 1967. Enter the above, as well as the non-Communist writers and a very few guests. Newspapermen are admitted in limited numbers, and only after being carefully screened to make sure they are of the native variety. The writers glumly sip their coffee, assuring one another that, based on the previous day's experience they are wasting three long days in a short life. Despite this the writer PK hands in his application to speak in the debate. Though he is sure he is needlessly and voluntarily heading for disaster, he wishes at least in this way to pay his private tribute to the recluse of Kazan. The clock shows it is 10:06 A.M. *Yesterday's presidium comes out on the platform. After the formal opening, the writer* MILAN KUNDERA *gets up to speak. It is common knowledge that this introductory speech was revised by the Party over a period of several months. The text Kundera finally agreed to read without having to be ashamed of himself had been pruned to a mere two pages. Now that he has taken his place on the rostrum, however, he asks to be allowed to add a few words of his own. Then, quite unexpectedly, he begins discussing what culture means to a small nation which has always had to fight for its very existence. And he goes on to give a brilliant analysis of vandalism, in which category he includes the banning of artistic works beyond the comprehension of those responsible for their prohibition.*

KUNDERA: *Of course every freedom has its limits, which stem from the extent of contemporary knowledge, education, prejudices, and so on. But no progressive era has ever prided itself on its limitations. In our country, however, it is still considered a greater virtue to guard borders than to cross them. A variety of momentary socio-political factors are invoked to justify the curtailment of spiritual freedoms. . . . This nation has been through more in this century than most other nations, so that if its genius was not napping it might also know a little more. This greater knowledge could lead to that liberating crossing of the borders of our present-day knowledge of man and his destiny, which would give Czech culture its meaning, maturity, and greatness.*

This introduction, which suddenly raises the standards for the following discussion to an unexpected height, is heard in rapt silence. It is broken by the voice of Secretary HENDRYCH. *Following the customary ritual consisting of a summing-up of the extraordinarily difficult international situation, he astounds the Congress by expressing the thought that the Communist Party is the force capable of integrating the diverse interests of various groups of the population into a single stream of socialist development, the vast majority of those present having agreed on this more than twenty years ago. He then recalls the progressive and humanitarian tradition of Czech and Slovak literature—which again is something his listeners seem to have been aware of before this. He only hints at the dangerous tendencies within the Writers Union, about which he spoke at length in the introduction to Act I. Without so*

218

much as mentioning the problems of censorship, he promises that new ways and means will be sought in the sphere of the economics of culture, thus suggesting that there might be a hope of higher authors' fees and lower taxes. He expresses his firm conviction that the Fourth Congress will show that the Writers Union is at one with the Party in matters of ideology, and he wishes it every success in producing fruitful results.

The writer PTACNIK, who is in the chair, asks the writer PK to address the Congress. PK comes up in a gray short-sleeved sports shirt, and there is nothing left for him but make his speech. He opens with a historical allusion, saying that the inhabitants of a country that experienced Munich wish to be truthfully informed without any distortions about the situation in the Middle East.

PK: A citizen, however loyal he may be in principle, can have his own private view of the matter, and in this twenty-second year of socialism must have the right to make that view public. . . .

Then he goes on to criticize the new Press laws, and in particular the fact that the right of protest belongs not to authors but only to editors. These, however, are bound by a secret Party directive according to which any disagreement with the censors is not to be settled in court but solely by arbitration, the arbiter the Party apparatus, which is most frequently the defendant in the case. The writer PK speaks of the vast number of articles banned in the Union's magazines alone and asks how many complaints were lodged against the censors.

CONGRESS CHAIRMAN PTACNIK: Not one.

PK: I think it is the duty of this Congress to demand reform of the Press laws in the sense that every author should himself have the right to defend his freedom of expression within the framework of the socialist constitution.

He speaks of the damage done by distorted information in the state of our society and the world in general to the young generation, which is more and more alienated by the Party's present role of prohibitor and dictator.

PK: A revolution may be started by force of arms, but its further existence or nonexistence is decided exclusively on the battlefield of the heart and brain, in particular of the generations which inherit that revolution. . . . Historical experience has placed emphasis on the dialectics of Marxism. Czechoslovakia has a unique and single opportunity: to make socialist freedom of the spirit our own specific code.

While PK is resuming his place, the non-Communist writer KLIMENT is mounting the rostrum. He tells the Congress that a society can either replace literature with worthless trash or allow its intellectual minority a freely committed stand conducive to a fruitful dialogue. He, too, recommends the abolition of censorship, remarking that it is nothing short of a scandal if our writers have to learn of the existence of Alexander Solzhenitsyn's letter from the Parisian Le Monde, on sale in Prague hotels, and not from their own sources. Kliment demands that the Congress be acquainted with the contents of that letter. The writer PK automatically rises to his feet and calls out.

PK: I have here a Czech translation of Solzhenitsyn's letter. Does the Congress wish to be acquainted with it? [Applause.]

CONGRESS CHAIRMAN PTACNIK: Comrades, even though your applause indicated what your wishes are, you must forgive me but I have to ask you to take a vote on it.

They vote. One is against, two abstain. The writer PK goes back to the rostrum and begins to read. About a minute later he is interrupted by a slight commotion. He goes on reading and sees a white shirt rise behind the presidium's table, sees a jacket flash by as it is hurriedly snatched from the back of a chair, sees Secretary HENDRYCH hurrying away to the exit. He reads and hears a muted, angry voice: "You've buggered everything up!" Then the door swings behind Hendrych; he is gone and the crisis is upon us, a crisis of unprecedented dimensions, an unprecedented exit, and PK can only go on reading the remaining five pages of the letter in as loud and clear a voice as possible. Its author is then given a long ovation expressing solidarity, and the writer PK leaves the hall. Outside in the passage he has to hold onto the stair rail, suddenly feeling extraordinarily light and insubstantial, he looks down and is conscious of vertigo, which he feels whenever he is more than three feet above the ground, but he manages to get to the bar and order a vodka.

The rest of the day goes by as if in a fog. The reader is asked to refer to the text of this play, entitled "The Protocol of the Fourth Congress of the Czechoslovak Writers Union," which was published in Czechoslovakia as well as abroad, though of course without the Prologue, Epilogue, and Acts I and IV.

ACT III—COLLISION

The writer PK has such bad dreams that night that Z____ refuses to interpret them. Feeling that the genre of the play he is performing in has changed radically, he ignores the continuing heat wave and puts on a white shirt with long sleeves. From the beginning the dividing line is drawn not between the official Party delegation and the writers but right across the Congress itself.

The Slovak writer LAJCIAK states that the Congress is being cunningly manipulated by a small group, and that this makes censorship inevitable. The speaker in fact demands that his own work be censored too—surely a unique case in the history of literature. The writer PK now hears from the mouth of a man of his own generation the kind of phrases he himself was using fifteen years ago, and he thinks angrily of the Master Manipulators who are responsible for so many human tragedies. But now the philosopher KOSIK is getting ready to speak, and he reads a letter sent from prison by a Czech intellectual on 18 June 1415.

JAN HUS [quoted by KOSIK]: A certain theologian tells me that all will be well with me and I shall be permitted to do as I please if I only submit to the Council, and he says: If the Council declares that thou hast one eye, though thou may have two, then it is your duty to agree with the Council that this is indeed so. I replied to him: Even if the whole world told me this, I, possessing reason, could not admit it without outraging my conscience.

In his fairly brief but incisive monologue, the Marxist philosopher KOSIK concludes.

KOSIK: This fifteenth-century Czech intellectual defended the unity of reason and conscience, refusing the Council's offer as a false alternative, for a man who agrees with the Council that he has one eye knowing that he has two gains nothing but loses all, since to lose one's reason and conscience is to lose the very substance of humanity. A man who has supplanted his reason with private calculation and suppressed his conscience into a bad conscience becomes a man devoid of reason and conscience. Such

221

a man has lost everything and gained nothing. He has become a worthless person, a nonentity. And if we realize that Nothing is Nihil, then a man without reason and conscience is a true nihilist. That is why this Czech intellectual of the fifteenth century chose between conscience and reason on the one hand and nihilism on the other. And since the conflict between the truth and nothingness is a radical one, it seems that his choice could also be only radical.

The audience, moved, applauds.

The writer KLIMA presents a historical picture of the struggle of the Czech nation against Habsburg censorship, a struggle that was brought to a successful conclusion by the December Constitution of 1867.

KLIMA: It cannot therefore be denied that those who have just introduced Press laws which re-establish censorship, choosing the centenary of its abolition to do so, are not lacking in a certain absurd sense of humor.

The intensity of the conflict is growing. And although it is beyond all possible doubt on whose side the majority's sympathies lie, the balance is tipped in favor of the other party by a weight of extraordinary caliber: the empty chair behind the table of the presidium. Secretary HENDRYCH has not returned since his dramatic departure on the previous day. There are rumors that the Party Presidium is in session, with the Big Boss himself in the chair. Well-informed sources claim that sanctions are under discussion, and they advise moderation. Addressing the Congress is the non-Communist playwright HAVEL.

HAVEL: I am trying to convince myself of the wisdom of keeping the reading of Solzhenitsyn's letter an internal affair of this Congress. But since it has already been read, I can find no possible reason why it should not—again internally—receive comment. . . . I have a strong feeling that in it the author has said no more than he can guarantee with his whole life up to now. As if he did not use a single word more than is required to state the whole truth, nor a single word more than the author can at any time vouch for. . . .

The young writer then goes on to speak of the structure of the Writers Union, which was created in the early fifties as one of the notorious "levers" by means of which the powers-that-be exercised their authority, and he puts forward a number of proposals for its democratization. The writer PK meanwhile helps to draft the final Congress documents, for he was elected a member of the Proposals Committee and it is now late afternoon. THE DUETTED VOICES come running into the small conference chamber and run out again, shouting.

THE DUETTED VOICES: Come along, all of you, now the fat's in the fire and no mistake!

A man of about forty is standing at the microphone. He has a large crop of hair and a pair of horn-rimmed spectacles which go well with his trustworthy Moravian face. PK was very much taken by his novel The Axe, published last year and dealing with the life, faith, and death of an old Communist, but this is the first time he has seen him in the flesh. The writer LUDOVIK VACULIK is not an experienced orator, but neither is he a stammerer suffering from stage-fright. He looks more like a naturally shy man who is at this moment feeling the weight of a terrible tension which is communicating itself to all those present. The most striking thing about his speech is its style: frank, idiomatic, and absolutely original.

VACULIK: Citizen—that used to be a glorious, revolutionary word. It signified a man whom no one was able to govern in an uncontrolled fashion, someone who could only be cleverly ruled with the impression that he was ruling himself. To achieve such an impression in those who were governed used to be the aim of a highly skilled profession known as politics. The social revolution in our country was successful yet the problem remains. Although we caught the bull by the horns and are holding him, someone keeps kicking us in the backside and will not desist.

The buffet and the tables in the passage outside are deserted; everyone is crowding into the hall. The writers of the country are listening in suspense to ideas they have a hundred times wanted to express themselves. It is a long speech, the most courageous and honest speech to be made here, and yet it is not until it is almost over that the first burst of applause interrupts it. The majority of those present are experiencing a mixture of admiration and anxiety. Admiration at the way the Communist on the rostrum has at one blow struck down all the existing taboos and given a practical demonstration that reason and conscience can work in concord five hundred and fifty years after Hus, anxiety at the fact that the unwritten rules of the game have for the first time been flagrantly broken, rules according to which the retention of the taboos was the condition for the continued existence of the Writers Union, its publishing house, and its weekly.

VACULIK: In conclusion I should like to make it quite clear, though this should perhaps be implicit in my whole speech, that my criticism of the powers-that-be in this country is not aimed at socialism, since I am not convinced that it had to develop the way it did and since I do not identify those powers-that-be with socialism, as they do themselves. . . . And if the people who represent that power were to come here and ask us all one question—whether this dream is capable of realization, they would have to consider it an expression of our good will and our profound civic loyalty if the answer was 'I don't know.' "

Suddenly it is all over. There is some listless applause. Hardly anybody is discussing the speech behind the scenes, as is usual here. The writer PK goes out into the corridor and wanders about as if in a daze. He catches sight of VACULIK, shaking hands with two or three friends. Apart from these, he is surrounded by an almost tangible silence. Everyone is wrapped in his own thoughts. The writer PK plucks up his courage and walks up to that man he has never met before.

PK: How do you feel?

VACULIK: Awful. I haven't eaten a thing these past two days, and now it's even worse.

PK: Do you need anything?

VACULIK: I guess so. Something that would make me sleep tonight and then something that would make me get up tomorrow morning.

The writer PK calls Z_____, asking her to get hold of one Valium and one Librium at once. The discussion continues, but few people are aware of what is being talked about. One single item penetrates our consciousness. The Head of Department HAVLICEK announces that an extraordinary meeting of Communist delegates to the Congress is to be held at nine o'clock tomorrow morning. The others are asked to come an hour later. The strictly limited time set aside for this Party meeting is the first omen of impending catastrophe. The intermission follows.

ACT IV—PERIPETEIA

Same place, Wednesday 28 June 1967, 9:07 A.M. The characters who appeared in Act I are carefully checked before being allowed inside. The non-Communist writers are left outside behind closed doors, drinking coffee and murmuring disgruntledly. In view of the situation the writer PK has instinctively put on a black suit and a tie. Secretary HENDRYCH again takes the chair he had abandoned on the previous day.

SECRETARY BILAK [in Slovak]: Dear Comrades, at the request of many delegates and upon the recommendation of the Presidium of the Central Committee of the Communist Party of Czechoslovakia we have called this branch Party meeting of your Union to consider the very grave situation that has arisen at the Congress. I do not wish to preach to you, only to remind you of certain principles which every Communist must respect. Our Party practices broad inner democracy but also democratic centralism. Anyone who does not respect these principles, whether on purpose or not, is attempting to change our Party from a revolutionary organization into a shapeless association. We have not come here as the representatives of our own persons but rather of the Central Committee of the Communist Party.... I call on Comrade Hendrych, as leader of our delegation, to speak.

SECRETARY HENDRYCH: Comrades ... I think that what occurred at this Congress, and in particular in some of its stages, cannot leave any genuine Communist unconcerned. He must be seriously disturbed by the lengths to which some individuals have gone. It is obvious that this is a group of people acting together, mostly Party members who have come forward with views that are fundamentally opposed to the policy of our Republic, the policy of the Communist Party, the Party line adopted at the Thirteenth Congress.... We cannot ignore the fact that Comrade PK, in spite of what was said at the meeting of the Congress Party organization, considered it necessary to air his incorrect opinions on the problems of the Middle East also at the Congress itself. We can understand if something is not quite clear to anyone, but we can neither tolerate nor forgive that a Communist should publicly criticize the government's policies, attack the government and his own Communist Party at a time when the tension in the world has dangerously mounted and when there is shooting. Equally we must criticize Comrade PK for making public a document that was not addressed to the Congress, nor published as a document of the fraternal Writers Union. This action can only be described as an irresponsible step which seriously damages our fraternal ties.... We must necessarily ask what Vaculik and others like him really want, what Havel and others like him want? What is it you want, Vaculik?... We can't leave matches in the hands of irresponsible people! Patience has its limits, and so has indulgence. We'll not allow anyone to subvert this Republic! Those who come here—like Vaculik—to make various anarchistic attacks are separating themselves from the Party. These are attacks such as this Republic has not had to cope with on the part of certain people since February 48, and thus in this respect we make short work of them. I do not wish to argue with Vaculik in concrete terms about the speech he made here yesterday. He showed himself to be completely unqualified; the attacks he used clearly reveal his intentions. If we should publish what Vaculik said, God help us! What a picture! And then we'll add that there was long-lasting applause!... I think that what happened at the Congress must be reflected also in the list of candidates for the Union's Central Committee.... I'd like to remind you of the passage in the letter sent by the Central Committee of the Party. It says that the list of candidates should not include people who are no guarantee of ideological strengthening of the Union. Apart from the preparation of the Congress, the Congress itself was also a criterion of this maturity. For that reason we recommend that the list of candidates be supplemented predominantly with those writers who on Monday received fewer votes than the thirtieth candidate. I also recommend that after any possible minor amendments the list should be approved as a whole ... in other words, make it incumbent upon all the Comrades present to vote for it. The Central Committee of the Communist Party of Czechoslovakia demands that if the Congress resolution and the composition of the new body are not in keeping with what we have been talking about, all Communists should leave the Congress. That, of course, would mean the end of the Writers Union! [Excited murmur in the hall.]

SECRETARY BILAK: You have heard the standpoint of the Central

Committee delegation. The situation does not permit us to discuss any individual points. . . . Now, does anyone have anything to say? [*The first to recover is the Slovak writer Hela Volanska.*]

VOLANSKA [*mounts the rostrum, speaks in Slovak*]: Comrades, I did not think I would have occasion to speak at the Congress and so have not prepared a speech. I must ask you to excuse me, for I am very excited. I only wish to ask the comrades from the Central Committee to consider that these are young people who lack experience. . . . I am under the impression that a mistake was also made on the other side of the table. . . . I beg the Party to consider whether this would not be a false step to take!

SECRETARY BILAK: I'd like to recall that at the Party meeting here on Monday which lasted until late at night a letter to us Communists from the Central Committee was read and Communists were asked to adhere to the principles contained in it. . . . What they are trying to push through here is no joke. It is an attack against the very foundations of the Republic. . . . We have no time to discuss details. . . . If anyone else has any comment, all right, but otherwise we must continue. [*Murmur in the hall. Vaculik goes up to the rostrum.*]

VACULIK: Comrades, I have come forward because I was directly challenged to do so. My activity has been called openly anti-State, my personal standpoint said to be part of some preconceived plot by a certain group. I made my speech because I wanted once and for all to put my own mind in order. I thought that by saying what I wanted I'd eradicate one curse that lies upon us: that no one any longer speaks his mind openly but censors his own words, resorting to metaphors, vague expressions, and so on. . . . No one who has any political aspirations speaks as I spoke. I did not appeal to people to subvert the State but rather to think and be frank; I made it clear that I understood the special position of people who have to wield power. I did not throw all those things at socialism, since that is linked in my mind with scientific methods of ruling society. . . . I mentioned that a process of regeneration was taking place in the ruling circles. Without any ulterior motives I sided with those among them who find themselves in a tricky situation. I refute terms such as "anti-socialist" and ask Comrade Hendrych to reply to what I have just said. Does he still mean to stick to it? I put forward suggestions for improving legality and examining the Constitution, and the like. If the Party wishes to respond to what the nation is thinking, it must support me. If it does not, it will solve the question I have posed for myself.... Even in my writings I have separated myself from all endeavors to link the critical movement with the hopes of those who expect help from the West. I could not care less about the West; I have never been there and do not long for a visit. The only thing I am concerned with is what and how our working people had to build. I appealed for calm reflection on how, decently, to reconcile the two poles that exist in this country, that is, the pole of power which is necessary, and the pole for everyone who works in science and—I do not like to say this—the arts. To stand and talk here like this is not arrogance; for that one needs modesty. I have been afraid and am afraid.... But apart from voting in the hall, there is also the voting inside men.... Try and understand this. I do not accept your accusations. Tell me what you think!

SECRETARY BILAK: Comrades, I must repeat once more that the delegation has already stated its point of view. If Communists do not see to it that the Congress ends with dignity, the delegation will have to leave and other measures will have to be taken. I do not think it would serve any useful purpose for Comrade Hendrych to reply to individual points, which would only give rise to argument.

VACULIK: I am asking Comrade Hendrych to reply! To try and feel all this as deeply as I do!

SECRETARY HENDRYCH: Comrades! What has been said is over and done with. We can pass Vaculik's speech on to the Party and we shall see what standpoint it adopts. What the ordinary people will have to say about it. Because it is a speech that is full of insults, it insults the workers, the representatives whom the workers have elected. What do you call these people? The entire State apparatus, including teachers, members of Parliament, local authorities, and so on? You call them people thirsting after power, obedient by nature, with a bad conscience, congenitally stupid, without moral scruples, with an abundance of fear and of children. Thank you very much! [Part of the audience murmurs in disagreement.]

SECRETARY BILAK: Quiet, Comrades!

SECRETARY HENDRYCH: Your speech, Comrade Vaculik, quite obviously, beyond all reasonable doubt, is the speech of an anarchist, with a considerable dosage of aristocratic bias. [The murmur in the hall grows stronger.] It is arrogance to our people and to this regime, regardless of who wields power.... You are demanding the abolition of working-class rule. That is the real gist of your demands!

VACULIK: Certainly not!

SECRETARY BILAK: Comrade Vaculik, let's not have any shouting here.

SECRETARY HENDRYCH: What is the aim behind this criticism of power? On a nonscientific, demagogic basis you are building the ideological foundations for anarchy in our society. That is something the consequences of which we have already seen on other occasions.... As for intentions, the way to hell is paved with good intentions! That's how it is! [A minority applauds. Dressed in black, the writer PK goes up to the rostrum.]

PK: Dear Helenka Volanska, I wish to thank you for your defense plea, but it was really like a defense attorney who cannot plead any mitigating circumstances for a mass murderer but his youth and the fact that he comes from a broken home. Being thirty-nine years of age I consider myself old enough to take the responsibility for all my actions. If anyone says that the reading of Alexander Solzhenitzyn's letter was deliberately staged, then that is an untruth! It now appears that there were several other comrades who intended to read Solzhenitzyn's letter at the Congress. I'm not saying this in order to create some sort of alibi for myself. I think about what I did on Tuesday on the spur of the moment, and I believe I would do exactly the same today. The fact that our writers cannot learn about so important a document any other way is not, I suspect, so much my fault as rather yours, Comrade Hendrych, since you are head of the Ideological Department. If, Comrades, you think that what I said imperiled the Congress—since I am among the first thirty candidates on the list —you must do as you see fit. Aviators must also occasionally throw the ballast out of their balloon if they wish to save the crew. But whether you manage to cross the nearest peaks or make a forced landing, remember that this time the ballast did not consist of bags of sand. [He walks away to applause that is interrupted by the chairman.]

SECRETARY BILAK: It is quite natural that the comrades are trying

229

to justify themselves, but I must ask you not to continue the debate on this subject. No one can consider it right for the Central Committee of the Communist Party of Czechoslovakia to publish a letter addressed to a fraternal congress and no one from the Soviet Union has asked us to propagate it. Communists must have a certain amount of feeling, of responsibility, one Party must behave tactfully toward another. This item is finished, Comrades. It was my task to acquaint you with the standpoint of our delegation. I ask Comrade Havlicek to read a certain proposal regarding the list of candidates. [Tension mounts.]

HEAD OF DEPARTMENT HAVLICEK: Comrades, please consider this suggestion. [Havlicek reads out the names of the candidates. Eleven are missing! They are replaced mostly by those who did not get sufficient votes on Monday.]

SECRETARY BILAK: Thank you, Comrade Havlicek. You have heard the proposed list of candidates. Any comments? No. We recommend that the Party organization accept a resolution ... binding all Communists to vote for this list of candidates. Yes? [The first to recover from the shock is the writer LUSTIG. He almost runs up to the rostrum.]

LUSTIG: Comrades, this just isn't possible! Some people have been left out with no explanation at all. If we accept this without discussion, we ourselves would be infringing Party democracy! [Applause.]

CERVENKA: Comrades. I have compared the new list of candidates with the old and I would like to ask a few questions. For me the Central Committee of the Writers Union is first and foremost a representative body of writers whom I respect. I judge them by their work and not by fortuitous emotional public appearances. For me Ludovik Vaculik is first and foremost the author of an exceptionally poetic and interesting book called The Axe.

On the other hand I see that Jiri Hajek is again one of the candidates, though I consider him a critic of extremely changeable and unstable methodological foundations who discredits socialist criticism!

PROFESSOR GOLDSTUCKER [rises]: I do not wish to be a candidate, Comrades! [Astonishment in the hall and on the platform. The writer Jindriska SMETANOVA approaches the rostrum.]

SMETANOVA: I'll be brief; even a shred of self-criticism tells me that with so many names important to Czech literature absent from the list of candidates, it would not be right for me to be there. [*Applause. As she passes him, PK kisses her hand.*]

SKACEL [*shouts in a hoarse voice*]: *I too withdraw!*

THE DUETTED VOICES: *We also!*

HANUS [*goes to the microphone*]: Comrades, time is short and so I'll only say a few words. I find myself in a very unfortunate position. You all know that my standpoint is to a large extent the same as that of the Central Committee of the Party and the Presidium, but I cannot agree with the practical steps that are being proposed. I am not one of the candidates, and therefore cannot withdraw, but I wish to say openly that I relinquish my vote because I am unable to vote on a list of candidates that has been drawn up in this way. [*The applause grows in strength, and the Party delegation shows increasing signs of nervousness.*]

SECRETARY HENDRYCH [*pulls the chairman's microphone across to himself*]: Comrades, we're not pleased that it should have come to this conflict, but you must understand that we as a Party organ, as the Central Committee, can never countenance the appearance on the Union's list of candidates, which is approved by the Party organization, of people we cannot be sure will act in a responsible manner, as they have demonstrated at this Congress! [*The writer PAVLICEK raises his hand at the table.*]

PAVLICEK: I wish to be crossed off the list of candidates because I now see that I do not belong there.

SECRETARY BILAK [*quickly*]: Let us vote on whether to lay before the plenum a revised list of candidates against the original list adopted by the Party organization on Monday evening. [*But the critic BRABEC puts up his hand to speak.*]

BRABEC: Comrades, we have heard that people who cannot be trusted have been dropped from the list of candidates. This touches me personally, since I was on the original list. I should very much like to know why the following people cannot be trusted: Sotola, Civrny, Vrba, Vaculik, Trefulka, Kosik, Klima, Havel, Brabec, Jungmann, and PK. I think we ought to discuss this, certainly as regards the Communists among them. [*Applause. The other side is sending its third man to the microphone.*]

HEAD OF DEPARTMENT HAVLICEK: Comrades, as far as the omission from the list of candidates of the writer Vaculik or Comrade PK is concerned, I think that is absolutely obvious. When Comrade PK declared that he would act in exactly the same way it is impossible for him to become a member of the Union's Central Committee. People who put the Party, the government, and the like into impossible situations in international socialist relations cannot be members of the Central Committee . . . after all, the Central Committee of the Writers Union has to deal with the Union of Soviet Writers and many others. If things go on like this, what's going to happen to our international cultural relations? I recently had talks in the German Democratic Republic. Even though we are not in agreement with the German comrades on various tactical matters, we can't have them reproaching us with the irresponsible behavior of some of our comrades.

SECRETARY BILAK [having in the meantime conferred with Secretary HENDRYCH]: Comrades, I propose that we adopt the following resolution: The Party organization of the Fourth Congress instructs the Communists in the Election Committee not to include in the list of candidates for the new Central Committee of the Writers Union any of those who at the Congress spoke against the Party line. I put this to the vote. Who supports this motion? [The attempt fails once more, the writer SPITZER asks to be heard.]

SPITZER [in Slovak]: Comrades, I appeal to all of you, on the platform as well as in the hall, not to allow prestige, stubbornness, or emotions to make us do something rash, something that we shall later very much regret. Let us rather consider a little longer how to find a way to prevent this election from causing a crisis.

SECRETARY HENDRYCH [having realized at last that the original proposal would not get through]: Comrades, I think it would be right to take a vote on the motion put forward by Comrade Bilak, that is that the list of candidates should not include those who opposed the Party line at this Congress, i.e., Vaculik, Klima, Havel, and PK. [There is an angry murmur from the audience when it realizes how the resolutions of the Party's Central Committee can be altered according to need.] I'm sorry, but we can under no circumstances agree to these Comrades being on the list of candidates. This has nothing to do with prestige. It does not mean that we shan't continue to talk to these Comrades, to seek to clarify the position, but they have shown so little responsibility that they cannot be candidates. The Election Committee must be instructed to replace them.

SECRETARY BILAK: *This means that not all those whose names were read here will be omitted from the list. The Election Committee will handle it.* [*Head of Department* HAVLICEK *is taken completely by surprise.*] [*The critic* JIRI HAJEK *asks to speak.*]

JIRI HAJEK: Comrades, I have learned here today that I have again been put on the list of candidates in an acutely critical situation, for which those who wanted and prepared it are fully responsible. I took the proposed list of candidates, as it was originally put forward here, to be an attempt to save the Writers Union. That was how matters stood. In this power struggle provoked by certain of our comrades, it was the last chance, the offer of a certain platform of cooperation. Under these circumstances my name has again appeared on the list, together with people with whom I no longer wish to sit at the same table. . . . I wish that in all future discussions on this matter my participation in any of the Union's bodies should not be considered.

SECRETARY HENDRYCH [*he has been busily writing and crossing out and now he goes to the rostrum without bothering to ask*]: Comrades, just to speed things up I wish to make a suggestion from the Chair. I recommend that the original list is retained, without Comrades Vaculik, Klima, Havel, and PK, these to be replaced by Comrades Skala, Hanzlik, Fryd, and Suler.

SECRETARY BULIK [*quickly*]: *I put this suggestion to the vote. Will those in favor of this amended list of candidates put up their hands?* [*The first hands go up.*]

VOLANSKA: A question. Do those comrades who withdrew their candidature remain on the list?

SECRETARY BILAK [*without consulting anybody*]: Yes. This should be further debated in the committee. *How many in favor?* (137) *How many against?* (12) *How many abstentions?* (34) *There is thus a clear majority in favor of the amended list of candidates. Kindly remember that Party discipline demands that we Communists abide by the majority decision. Since most of the Communists were in favor of this change, you must all vote accordingly at the Congress. I declare the meeting adjourned.*

The clock shows 10:39.

ACT V—CATASTROPHE

The non-Communist writers are now allowed in. They do not ask too many questions. The atmosphere is heavy with catastrophe. Each of the four deleted candidates is surrounded by a group of friends. Some explain that they only voted for the compromise solution in order to save the Union, its publishing house, its weekly, and the Literary Fund. Others condemn this as moral suicide. Not even the late Minister Kopecky, after the Second Congress in 1956, had dared to go quite that far in brutally manipulating the Congress proceedings. No one can really say which of these two opinions is right. At 10:57 the last session begins. Secretary HENDRYCH *makes his final speech. In contrast to the one he made in the second act, this time it is brief and harsh. The Congress, he says, had been manipulated and misused. The Party expects that at this final session appropriate steps will be taken, as a way out for our literature. When the amended list of candidates is put up for discussion, the non-Communists again demand that Havel, Klima, Vaculik, and PK be included. The Communists, bound by their resolution, vote against. A secret ballot then confirms the list of candidates as amended by Hendrych. The writer PK goes out into the corridor, where he again meets his old friend, as he had done three days ago. P_____ is visibly shaken, having played an important part in the preparation of the Congress. It had been a matter of honor with him to try and convince us of the Party's requirements, but also to seek a compromise that would avoid a conflict at all costs. Now he looks like a man whose wife has just run away with his best friend.*

PK: I would be grateful to you if you would pass on a query from me. Does the Party again intend to take more than purely inter-Party disciplinary measures against us? If so, I won't tonight sign the proposed contract with the Hamburg Schauspielhaus for the staging of my adaptation of Schweik next September. I'd like to save myself a lot of trouble and this country unnecessary disgrace.

P_____: I wonder that you can think of such things at a time like this. And I admire you for being able to concern yourself with them just now.

Nevertheless he goes off and returns with an assurance that the staging of plays naturally has nothing to do with the Congress. Secretary HENDRYCH, he tells me, is satisfied with the way things turned out in the end. Only tomorrow would he discover that in the general chaos no one had thought of doing anything about the Congress documents. The resolution passed by the Congress, as well as the letter sent by the writers to the Central Committee of the Party, defend the views expressed in the discussion and repeat the main arguments. The new Central Committee of the Writers Union is urged to seek a new Press law which would give the right of protest to the author. The writer PROCHAZKA, closely observed by the Secretaries, concludes the proceedings.

PROCHAZKA: Dear friends, to pass any kind of judgment at the end of our deliberations is at this moment more than anyone can attempt to do, for already our Congress is part of history and therefore subject to far more profound and lasting criteria.... The writer will never want to be at the mercy of various doctrines and dogmas; he will stubbornly wish to make them subservient to him. As long as he does not betray his mission he will refuse to accept the ideal of man lost in a crowd and in uniform as being unworthy of mankind. For the writer himself has found many times that to be alone with oneself is as nothing compared to being alone in a multitude.... The Congress is over, the search goes on; it is the good fortune of literature that nothing lasts for ever.

[Exeunt victors and vanquished together, left.]

EPILOGUE

Back at Sazava, it is again evening. The writer PK, still in his black suit, feeling thoroughly miserable, puts his record player under the birches, so that the whole garden resounds with the Eine kleine Nachtmusik. And even though he did not take the well-meant advice, he is rewarded with the promised strawberry dumplings. Not that he feels particularly hungry. The curtain of night comes down.

THE END

Everything was just as we left it last Christmas. Only the price of our room had gone up once again. We decided to take it nevertheless, for the fat little angel among the tall flowers—a piece of sustained *kitsch* by some unknown master, who, instead of settling his bill, had presented Mr. Pupp, the hotel proprietor, with a garishly colored picture of his youngest offspring—was to us the insignia of our brief holiday from daily life.

The *fin-de-siècle* Christmas crib that is Karlovy Vary lay nostalgically silent in the drizzling rain. The first spa guests were making their way to the springs. Apart from the usual Soviet visitors there were now the first strange swallows from America, which had not been seen here for years. The two flocks had something in common—the loud colors of their clothes and the endearing naïveté of the ordinary people from vast continents amazed by what they see on their travels among unknown barbarians.

Everything was very much the same, only we two were different. E_____ was at her wits' end after her first season on the professional stage (for which, she said, she did not have the necessary gift of healthy cynicism), and I at mine after my tenth season as a professional writer, which had begun by the banning of yet another of my plays. She was, moreover, beginning to resent what she incorrectly believed to be competition offered her by my children. I was once more almost penniless, my mother had been ailing for some time, and Antonin Novotny had had himself re-elected as President for another term. Prospects were pretty grim in every way.

Having reached the end of my term of office and at the same time of my youth, I decided to make a speech in the Central Committee of the Youth Union about the crisis in which this organization found itself. I was annoyed at the Chairman's opening speech for glossing over the May Day demonstration in Petrin Park by students and apprentices. I said that blows with police truncheons, even though dispensed for the first time by Communists, could not make up for the work of an organization that had become part of the Establishment. It had been transformed into a State institution and no longer represented the vital interests of the young. In the discussion that followed the Union's officials took me completely apart, the *coup de grâce* being administered by the Chairman himself, Comrade V_____. I could not resist copying out one sentence from the shorthand record because it reflects the level on which that body conducted its business.

"I think that the Comrade, Comrades, has given way to various petit-bourgeois, various erroneous tendencies which can be seen in certain sections of our intelligentsia, and he, I'm sorry to say, though I believe that he is sincere and means well, is sometimes becoming a bearer, and he thus harms not only himself, Comrades, but all of us, I think the Comrade understands that today we weren't concerned with berating him here in the Central Committee but want to make him understand that we all feel responsible for what goes on in our country, that we as Communists also feel responsible for the further development of our Youth Union, that we must all really rally round the Party, Comrades, and help her solve her problems which she is trying to overcome, and that the members of our Central Committee had just this in mind when they criticized him, their critical words meant to show him what this is all about."

Which they certainly did. For several weeks I retired to my tiny maisonette, writing during the day only to throw what I had written into the waste-paper basket in the evening. Finally I stopped writing altogether. I borrowed my old books from my children and every day started reading as soon as I woke, reliving all the familiar adventures of Garibaldi, Mikhail Strogoff, and the Three Musketeers, putting the books away only when I was too sleepy to read any more. In spite of all my famous victories at the side of my heroes, my dreams were filled with dismal dark corridors at the end of which always waited the two men in black, holding the knife with which they killed Josef K_____. I only saw E_____ in the clubrooms of her provincial theater, where I went to present her with flowers on a first night, vainly seeking the right words to give her back her lost self-confidence.

Despite all this, we had now taken this holiday together, hoping that Karlovy Vary, which had been our asylum in the past, would throw us a rope with which we would draw closer together as well as to life. But no such luck. We were nice to each other, but about as close as two caryatids holding up the same balcony. We both had our hands full with our own burden.

She walked alongside me up the colonnade, sipping her mineral water through the narrow nozzle of her china beaker, while I crunched my beloved Karlsbad wafers, both of us equally taciturn. There had been times when the presence of a third person had been an intrusion—now it brought welcome relief.

Slavek was his usual slim, boyish self, though his hair had gone almost completely white. I stressed that this gave him an interesting appearance, turning to her for confirmation that woman must find him irresistible. She agreed courteously, only to excuse herself immediately afterward, saying that she was sure we had lots to talk about.

Slavek and I sat down at a table in the Pupp café, exchanging the customary information about old friends and old flames, whose light still burned in the universe even though all the stars had long gone out. We spoke of Robek and Peter, both of them equally distant and irretrievable. I ordered two vodkas, but Slavek said sorry, he wasn't allowed to drink.

"Go on," I said gaily. "Surely you're fit as a fiddle."

He merely shrugged his shoulders, and I fell silent, suddenly swamped by the darkness of the Jachymov uranium mines where he had served his sentence. He dispelled the gloom with a smile.

"Oh, I didn't tell you—I'm no longer working in the theater."

I was startled.

"What on earth went wrong?"

"Nothing. I've got a job on the radio. As an announcer."

"You're joking!"

My good humor returned, for the first time in many days. If they had taken him on at the Radio, then it could only mean that the leather jacket of our "cadres policy" was rapidly losing its toughness.

"If the secret police are showing so much confidence in their former guests, that surely is a good omen for the future," I said.

"More likely just a bad conscience on their part," he remarked, lost in thought.

"Why do you say that? Surely they treated you very magnanimously once before?"

He hesitated a little before making his decision.

"Oh, my dear chap—you, a writer with a vivid imagination, don't you still see the truth about my case?"

I had no idea what he was driving at.

"I only came back across the border once as a foreign agent. I was so fed up with the whole thing that I went straight to the police and gave myself up. All the other trips were on behalf of our own lot. I was repaying my debt. But then they unexpectedly charged me interest."

Friday, 23 August 1968 / Rome
(Continued)

The avalanche was set in motion two minutes after midnight. As soon as the last strains of our national anthem died away his voice came on the air again.

"Citizens! It is expected that arrests will be made in Prague tonight. Paint over or remove all street signs and house numbers, the names of tenants in your houses, as well as the remaining road signs throughout the country!"

The avalanche was fast approaching, and it would annihilate almost everyone who had helped write the story of my life. I stood numb over my suitcase. I took her things; my hands trembled. A porter I had never seen before came into the room, not even bothering to knock.

"Il telefono per Lei."

I raced downstairs, unable to fight off an uncontrollable panic. Until now I had imagined my return home as if it were taking place outside time, as I had experienced it a hundred times before: the long ascent comes to a sudden end and the long panorama of Prague lies before me; the distant St. Vitus Cathedral reminds me of the pigeon-haunted turrets rising up right above my roof. Ever since my decision to return home, I had only worried about the closed frontiers. I was convinced that once over the border I would immediately become part of the resisting nation. Now it occurred to me for the first time that although the man scrutinizing my passport might be a Czech, he

239

could be far more of a hate-filled enemy than any foreign soldier. An earlier incident I had had at the frontier, which hitherto I had thought of more as a farce, suddenly smelled of blood.

There was no phone booth in my hotel; the receiver was simply lying on the receptionist's desk, in front of which stood yet another unlikely pair. I didn't give a damn. About anything. As the receptionist handed over the key to the man and his girl friend, I picked up the phone.

"Hello. Hello! Is that you?"

"Yes," she said.

I heard her very indistinctly, but she was here, not far away, in this city. The barrier of arguments I had for so long and so painstakingly been building between the two of us against love and habit, fell apart like a house of cards.

"Come and join me here, I'm waiting for you," I told her.

She said something I could not understand.

"I can't hear you. Speak louder."

Like people who can't hear, I started shouting.

None of the Italians present took the slightest notice. This, after all, was their usual manner of conversation. The man and his girl friend vanished upstairs, embracing as they went. The receptionist immersed himself in the sports page of the *Corriere della serra*. South of the Alps there existed only one human being whom I could burden with my own anxiety.

"Where are you?" I shouted into the receiver.

"In Prague."

Now her voice came through more audibly. On the other hand my condition grew rapidly worse. My heart started racing madly, and I had to lean on the desk.

"Stop fooling, can't you, there isn't time! Where are you calling from?"

"From Prague!"

Only then, more by instinct than by any rational process, did I realize that this was the phone call I had asked for twenty-four hours ago. I was speaking to my ex-wife.

"I'm so glad you're still there," she said. "We were afraid you'd come back."

I pulled myself together.

"It's I who am afraid on your account. How are you all? What about the kids?"

"They're okay," she said. "We had to give them a spanking yesterday because they slipped out of the house in the morning and went around all day carrying a flag."

"Lock them up, for heaven's sake," I told her. "Don't let them out. Is it very bad in Prague?"

"Yes," she said, "it's bad all right. Our street is full of them. Don't come back."

"I'm just packing my things," I said. "We'll be in Prague tomorrow night."

"No, you mustn't!" she almost shouted. "Please stay where you are. We're so glad you're out."

"But why?"

"Dozens of people have called to say you mustn't return."

"Yes, but tell me why?"

"There was some shooting near your flat. Your windows have been smashed."

"Oh, nonsense!"

I knew she never lied.

"It's true. Nobody sleeps at home any more. Your friends have all disappeared."

"Disappeared? What do you mean?"

"We don't know. Nobody knows anything. It's just like during the war. Please promise me that you'll stay, or we'll go crazy worrying about you."

"Oh, for God's sake," I said, "don't make it harder for me than it already is."

"Don't you make it harder for us."

"Have you any idea what it would mean to me?"

"Yes, I have," she said. "But I let you go when you wanted to, so now you can do something for me for a change. If it comes to the worst, perhaps you'll at least be able to get the children out. . . ."

I heard the orchestras of the sinking *Titanic*. I was incapable of speech.

"Do you want to talk to them?" she asked.

"Don't wake them."

Yet I wanted to hear them so badly.

"I think I *will* wake them," she said. "They'd be sorry about it tomorrow if I didn't."

"Yes, that's right," I said. "Go and get them."

The television of my mind followed her out of the once-beautiful hall, marred by a brick partition, down the passage and into the room in which the light of the street lamp outside illuminates the gay colt painted by Chi pai-shi, who had presented the picture to me himself. I saw her bending over the settees and waking them one by one, taking great care not to startle them. I saw their bare feet fumbling for slippers, their sleep-dazed eyes avoiding the light. Then she walked back at the head of a sleep-walking procession, back to the phone from which a wire led all the way to me here, thin like my hope. I waited expectantly, only to hear a female voice:

"*Tre mille sette cento lire, signore.*"

I yelled so loudly that even the receptionist grasped the urgency. But they told me the only thing I could do was to order another call. I just didn't have the strength for any more. Dragging myself up the stairs to my room I pictured them standing around the silent phone, while underneath their windows the tanks menacingly pointed their guns.

Still the room was filled with his voice. The Fourteenth Extraordinary Party Congress had called a general strike for twelve noon today. The sirens drowned the *Titanic* orchestra. The sirens of the occupation, the sirens of February 1948, the sirens of State funerals, the sirens of the occupation. We had come full circle. And I was out of it.

"Citizens!" he said once again. "Stop cars with the license plates AE 40–01 and ABA 71–19. They have been sent to arrest our people. I repeat. . . "

The voice of the free radio was blotted out by static. Like a landscape suddenly revealed by a flash of lighting I saw in front of me the six hundred pages of Solzhenitsyn's novel *The First Circle*, which I had read last year during three nights in a Moscow hotel. Even in the almost illegible copy which my Soviet physicist friend had bought for a month's salary, the averted face of socialism, as created on the Seventh Day of the Revolution by the tragic genius of Stalin, was clearly to be discerned in every detail.

Lasciate ogni speranza voi ch'entrate!

The crackling and buzzing in my radio was driving me mad, and so I switched the set off. Again I heard the creaking of bed-springs from the room next door. I leaned against the wall and examined my room, whose squalor seemed now to achieve a new dimension. It was the dimension of infinite time, and suddenly I experienced the hopelessness of Remarque's heroes.

Then I took out my car keys, slammed the door shut behind me, ran downstairs and out of the hotel, unlocked the car, got in and drove away like a madman.

□

16 August 1967   /   Hamburg
(From the diary of the writer PK)

A TRIP TO HAMBURG or SHOW HIM THE INSTRUMENTS!

A screenplay. [The film is meant as an unusual combination of a crazy comedy and a political horror film, the treatment to be serious in the farcical scenes and frivolous in the serious sequences.]

CAPTION: Tuesday

SCENE 1   Exterior—day. A Bristol Britannia coming in to land.

SCENE 2   Interior—day. PK is returning from EXPO 67, his head full of memories and impressions. He is looking forward to sorting them all out and putting them on paper to the soft music of the Sazava weir.

SCENE 3   Interior—day. Z_____ is waiting in the airport lobby. She tells PK that his Schweik in Hamburg goes into rehearsal day after tomorrow. PK faints.

SCENE 4   Interior—day. Fast motion. PK is darting about his flat, looking for things, finding them, losing them again, phoning people, writing, passing on messages, giving instructions. His pri-

vate correspondence he throws into his suitcase. He opens the official-looking letters and his eyes rest on one with the letterhead of the Central Committee of the Communist Party of Czechoslovakia. The camera comes to a stop, then picks out the words: YOUR PRESENCE IS REQUIRED IN THE CENTRAL CONTROL AND REVISORY COMMITTEE WHICH IS TO CONSIDER YOUR BEHAVIOR AT THE FOURTH CONGRESS OF THE WRITERS UNION. U_____. Z_____ advises him to send Comrade U_____ a card from Hamburg with the following text: GO JUMP IN THE LAKE! YOUR SWEETIE. PK rejects this with some heat and picks up the phone.

SCENE 5 Interior—day. The Central Committee of the Communist Party of Czechoslovakia. Comrade U_____ listens as PK tells him he is only passing through Prague and will not have time to come before September. Then he suggests that PK come over at once.

SCENE 6 PK curses aloud and Z_____ expresses her conviction that he will not manage to get everything ready before he has to leave for Hamburg. PK tells her not to worry, that he'll be back in no time.

SCENE 7 Interior—day. A pile of documents on a table. Looks like a collected edition of all PK's speeches over the past ten years. One of the four men is reading out the four points of the indictment: attack on the Soviet Union (the reading of Alexander Solzhenitsyn's letter), attack on Czechoslovakia's foreign policy (criticism of the official Czechoslovak attitude toward the war in the Middle East), attack on the Party's internal policy (criticism of censorship), and bourgeois defeatism (his assertion that the young generation doesn't give a tinker's damn for such a Party).
    "Well, what have you to say about it?" asks Comrade U_____.
    "There's a lot of it, I must say," replies PK. But it would seem they had not read their Schweik for some time. Then he rejects the accusations. The comrade who is taking down what he is saying in a school copybook wants to know how to spell the Soviet writer in question, and says:
    "Here you are making him out to be almost one of the classics and nobody even knows how to spell him."

PK says he does not think his arguments will be recorded accurately enough and asks to be allowed to put them to the whole Central Control and Revisory Committee. This seems to offend them. They tell him that the Committee has too much on its plate as it is, and retaliate by dissecting his Congress speech as if it were Holy Writ. They keep looking for nonexistent hidden meanings. Then they come to the following passage:

"Most of my young friends are university students. It can therefore be argued that my view of this generation, thank the Lord, is somewhat distorted, for in the factories and fields—at least according to certain functionaries of the Youth Union—there are still pure and unspoiled young people whose life's aim is to become members of the Communist Party."

Comrade U_____ suddenly shouts:

"This sentence shows you have for years been making a fool of the Party!"

PK turns pale, folds his arms across his chest, leans back in his chair and refuses to say any more. This gives rise to a comical situation, for they pretend they have not noticed and strenuously keep the conversation going among themselves. They make frequent references to his worthier past until in the end they give the impression of discussing a dear departed friend. Half an hour later they realize that he is quite capable of staying offended all night, and Comrade U_____ asks with pretended surprise:

"Aren't you on speaking terms with us any more?"

PK replies that if what Comrade U_____ said is correct, then they are only wasting their time trying to talk to him.

"Oh, come now," cries Comrade U_____, "don't sulk just because of one slightly exaggerated turn of phrase!"

PK replies that they have for three hours been trying to concoct proofs of his anti-Communist attitude out of his turns of phrase, which may also sometimes be exaggerated. He recommends that they go out into the street and tell this to the first man they meet who had read his poems or seen his plays, and he would be sure to laugh in their face. The scene suddenly becomes a dialogue between four fathers and their only son. His case, they tell him, is naturally quite different from that of Ludovik Vaculik and Company. They will gladly forget the whole thing if only he will be a good boy and write his Party a letter in which he will retract his views. PK says that he does not intend to mock the Party in the future either and asks that, in keeping with the Party constitution, he be allowed to be present at a discussion of his case by the whole Committee when he returns from abroad. Now he really has to go. They ask him in severe tones whether he realizes that it is up to them whether he will remain a Communist or not.

"No, you're wrong there," he says. "You may at most be able to decide whether I am to remain in the Party or not."

Since he has already got to his feet they want at least to make sure that there will be a replay. They urge him in his own interests to turn up again the next day. He says that by this time tomorrow he will be on his way to Hamburg, as in his spare time he dabbles in theatrical authorship and production. The camera zooms to take in their astonished faces.

SCENE 8 Interior—night. PK in a state of considerable excitement is throwing books, typescripts of the play, tape recordings, and newspapers that had accumulated during his fortnight's absence in Montreal, into his suitcase.

"That Party of yours," comments Z_____, "is the most comic outfit under the sun."

CAPTION: Wednesday

SCENE 9 Exterior—day. A brilliant morning. Z_____ and PK are loading the car with a vast quantity of suitcases and bags, since they will be away for almost two months. The concierge waves goodbye from her window.

SCENE 10 Exterior—day. At high noon they inch forward in a queue of cars, packed with tinned foods and children, moving slowly toward the passport and customs check at the border. They are given the necessary rubber stamps and have therefore theoretically left the country, but then the official takes another look at their passports, stammers something about being back soon, and goes off. They wait a long time, while the other vehicles flow past them, as if they were a torpedoed vessel. Z_____ prophesies that PK will not see the other side of the frontier. PK advises her to calm down. He is well aware that they are capable of all kinds of foolishness, but he does not believe they would really make asses of themselves. They know that, as opposed to Z____, who shoots her mouth off in the bar and suchlike places, he says what he thinks at political meetings and public platforms. It would not surprise him if she were told that she would have to stay behind. At last a group of uniformed men comes out of the customs house, led by the Second Customs Officer, who says:

"Well, mister playwright, it seems to be your turn. Drive up onto the ramp."

SCENE 11 Exterior—day. The inspection is being carried out by the Second Customs Officer, who is assisted by a buxom female colleague. He is a tough guy who evidently has hopes of promotion. First of all he wants to see all PK's books, magazines, and texts. Piles of the stuff are carried off to the customs shed for closer scrutiny. Their interest in the printed word is so obvious that PK cannot help remarking: "If by any chance you are looking for a transcript of the Fourth Congress of the Writers Union, then you can save yourselves the trouble. I of course do not have anything like that with me."

He gets a surprising reaction. As if waiting for something of the sort, the Second Customs Officer drops all pretense at civility and says curtly that no one's interested in his opinions. From that moment on it is open war.

SCENE 12 The same, a little later. Articles of clothing, shirts, underwear, and socks are spread out on benches and draped over the fence. The camera swings round to show the car, its seats taken out and its trunk ransacked. PK and Z____ are ironically commenting on the actions of the Second Customs Officer, who retaliates by significantly examining every bra and every lipstick. The drivers of both Czech and foreign cars taxi past the strange group with incredulous eyes. The number of the customs officers dealing with the case grows every minute.

SCENE 13 Interior—day. Inside the customs shed. PK has gone to protest to the Chief Customs Officer himself, telling him that he has a thousand kilometers ahead of him and isn't it time to call it a day. He also informs that dignitary that he is going to lodge a complaint in the proper quarters because the behavior of some of the officers conducting the examination leaves much to be desired. The Chief Customs Officer advises him not to worry about when he will be leaving. That is up to others to decide.

SCENE 14   Marked differences of attitude begin to be displayed by the customs officers concerned. When he is sure no one else is listening, the First Customs Officer says quickly and sotto voce that PK is quite right and that he mustn't let them bully him.

SCENE 15   The same a little later. There is a great deal of nervousness in the air, for the people in uniform feel that they are making a hash of things. The climax approaches. The Chief Customs Officer in person reads out to PK and Z____ the text of the Act permitting a bodily search of people suspected of smuggling or other offenses. His anxiety makes him read this with a pathos that is more suited to the passing of a death sentence. Then he asks if they have anything to say. Z____ tells him she has only one last wish—she would like one of the younger men to carry out the search in her case, and she suggests the Second Customs Officer. Regardless of this, the Chief Customs Officer hands her over to one of his female subordinates, while he escorts PK upstairs.

SCENE 16   Interior—day. The Chief Customs Officer's office. A writing desk, a sofa, a safe. Fir trees provide a poetic backdrop outside the window. PK takes off his underpants, puts out his tongue and says Aaah. Two uniforms and a naked human body— the most typical genre picture of this century. The First Customs Officer evidently has a similar thought, for without waiting to be told he starts handing him his clothes. PK tells them that bearing in mind his shady past they ought not to rule out the possibility that he had made microfilms of the material they are looking for and that he had managed to swallow them in time. Were they equipped to deal with such an eventuality? He is led out of the office without a word.

SCENE 17   Interior—late afternoon. The hall of the customs shed. The Chief Customs Officer approaches with a triumphant smile and asks PK to accompany him inside.

SCENE 18   Interior—late afternoon. Inside the customs shed. A savings book containing the sum of 1900 German marks is lying on a table. PK explains that the money was officially allocated to him by the State Bank out of his foreign royalties. Since it was to cover four journeys, he was advised to put the remainder in a savings account to simplify matters. That was why he had the savings book with his other papers in his brief case. All this is duly taken down in a signed statement.

SCENE 19   The same—a little later. On the table are two hundred Czech crowns and six Danish crowns. PK explains that the two Czech banknotes had no doubt been left in Z____'s purse by his absent-minded companion by mistake; the six Danish coins she had been carrying around in her pocket for years. As the lot would be exchanged for a mere twenty-two German marks, no one could surely suspect that they had actually meant to exchange this money, seeing that he had been given so large a sum quite legitimately. PK therefore considered the whole thing to be no more than a very minor offense and was sure that Z____ would be quite ready to pay the small fine prescribed for such cases. However, the Chief Customs Officer states that all in all it constituted a criminal offense.

SCENE 20   The same—a little later. A new climax. On the table lies a pillow slip that has been found cunningly concealed among the travelers' clothing. Close-up of the pillow slip: a theater has been painted on it in red crayon. In front of the building is a crowd of people, a dachshund with nine puppies, and a bed full of girls. On the other side, this time in blue, is a picture of a large gateway with the inscription KSC (Communist Party of Czechoslovakia) over it. A huge foot is kicking out a small figure of a man. There is a tense silence as PK is challenged to explain the meaning of this provocation. He collapses with laughter and asks for the author of the painting to be brought in.

SCENE 21   The same—a little later. Z____ explains that she executed the pillow-slip painting a short time ago as a birthday gift for PK. She points to the two inscriptions—What I wish you in red and What I don't wish you in blue. The whole work of art is thus meant to say: Z_____ wishes PK to be successful with his audiences, with girls, and with dogs. She does not wish him to be expelled from the Party for his part in the writers congress because she suspects that this might be the death of him. Z_____ points out that she had made use of a commodity called humor when she painted those scenes on the pillow slip. The Chief Customs Officer refuses to recognize such humor. Z_____ indicates that the pillow slip had not originally been intended for his eyes. The Chief Customs Officer wants to know why the pillow slip was being taken abroad to a capitalist country. Z_____ declares she took it with her in order to please PK. The latter remarks that she had succeeded admirably. The Chief Customs Officer and the First Customs Officer leave them to consult higher authority.

SCENE 22   The same—a little later. The Second Customs Officer, on his own responsibility, takes Z_____ to the buffet so that she can at last get something to eat. The First Customs Officer suggests to PK that he too ought to call someone higher up. He therefore puts a call through and holds a brief chummy conversation with the operator on the local exchange. As a result PK gets a priority call to Prague free of charge.

SCENE 23   Interior—late afternoon. The Central Committee of the Communist Party. An official says that Comrade P_____ is not present but promises to give him PK's message as soon as possible.

SCENE 24   Interior—late afternoon. The customs shed. PK asks the Prague official to get P_____ to call him at the earliest opportunity. He reminds the man at the other end of the line that he had only signed the contract with the Hamburg theater after consulting Comrade Hendrych. A whole team from Prague was waiting for him in Hamburg and they were already putting up the scenery. Any delay could have serious repercussions, economic as well as political.

SCENE 25   Interior—night. The Chief Customs Officer's office. The confiscated printed matter has been spread out on the desk, chairs, and sofa. The Chief Customs Officer is holding fourteen copies of Rude pravo in his hand, his questions reflecting his conviction that he has succeeded in bringing off a great coup.

"Explain what purpose lay behind your exporting to a capitalist country a large number of Czechoslovak daily newspapers!"

PK dictates into the protocol:

"This question is as ridiculous as it is undignified."

The First Customs Officer types this with obvious distaste. PK declares that at a very early age he acquired the habit of reading the daily press, and especially the Czechoslovak variety, in particular the Party newspapers. He does not see why he should be deprived of all the remarkable information contained therein during his absence abroad. The Chief Customs Officer picks up a bunch of private letters.

"Explain what purpose lay behind your exporting to a capitalist country this letter from A.V., Prague-Vinohrady, Kourimska Street."

PK asks to be acquainted with the contents of the letter, which he has not yet had time to read. It seems that the unknown Mrs. A.V. from Kourimska Street, Prague-Vinohrady, had taken it into her head to thank him for the speech he made at the writers congress. The camera shows us the text in close-up: I don't know what exactly you said about Israel, but I wish to shake your hand for it!

PK dictates:

"This question is as ridiculous as it is undignified...."

The First Customs Officer bangs his fist on the table and announces that he has had enough. PK is wrong if he thinks he can make a monkey out of official representatives just because he happens to be a writer. PK says that one of the very few rights he still has left is the right to reply to questions as he sees fit. The First Customs Officer informs him that he is not going to take down such answers, whereupon PK says that it was not his idea to write this protocol and he does not insist on it. Bidden to continue, he dictates:

"This question is as ridiculous as it is undignified."

The sentence is again not taken down and the argument continues. The Chief Customs Officer claims that it is they who formulate the protocol. PK points out that he will never sign any such statement. The Second Customs Officer now comes in to put on his driving jacket because his stint of duty is over. Over the heads of his superiors he winks encouragingly at PK.

SCENE 26   The same—a little later. The First Customs Officer gnashes his teeth as he types that the question is as ridiculous as it is undignified: PK has always been in the habit of replying to letters, and has every intention of doing this in Hamburg.

SCENE 27   The same—a little later. After more heated argument, the First Customs Officer adds a postscript in which PK asserts that the principle of presumption of innocence had been infringed in his case, as he is being treated as a culprit even though nothing has yet been proved against him. That done, PK signs the statement with an easy conscience.

SCENE 28   The same—a little later. The Chief Customs Officer and his First Officer are compiling a List of Confiscated Articles. Under Item 9 they put 1 postcard from Yours as Ever, Aunt Mana, under Item 21 1 pillow slip hand painted with sketch for Birthday. In conclusion PK states that they have confiscated all the material he needs for the staging of Schweik, so that all he can hope to do in Hamburg now is to feed seagulls. He estimates the loss the theater will suffer at approximately 250,000 German marks and enquires who is going to pay for it, since the contract was negotiated on his behalf by the State Theatrical Agency. The tired Chief Customs Officer sends him downstairs so that he can once again consult higher authority.

SCENE 29   Interior—night. The customs shed. Prague is calling. An official of the Central Committee of the Communist Party gives PK a message from P____ who says that the case can only be handled by the customs authorities and the Party cannot intervene in matters that come under the jurisdiction of a State organ.

SCENE 30   Interior—night. The hall of the customs shed. Z____, asleep, curled up in an armchair. The Chief Customs Officer comes in and wakes her. He tells PK that his passport is to be confiscated. He is to return to Prague, where he will be visited by certain officials, briefed to deal with his case. Z____, on the other hand, is free to continue her journey to Hamburg. Z____ starts to laugh hysterically and is about to make a speech, but PK restrains her.

SCENE 31 Exterior—night. PK and Z____ are throwing damp clothing into their suitcases, with the Chief Customs Officer and First Customs Officer looking on silent and motionless. This takes place on the dark ramp of the customs shed. There follows a gay interlude when PK falls into a large hole under the car and bruises his knee. The Chief Customs Officer asks him what has happened and the writer replies with an unprintable word, which is mercifully muted by the night. Then he and Z____ get into their car and drive in the direction of Prague without a word of farewell.

CAPTION: Thursday

SCENE 32 Montage—exterior—interior—day. Rapid cutting. While Z____ waits at home for the officials briefed to deal with his case, PK sneaks out under the concierge's windows and pays successive visits to his legal adviser, the Writers Union, the Theater Union, the literary agency, the District Prosecutor's Office, the General Prosecutor's Office, and the Supreme Court. He leaves out only the Central Committee of the Party, for he does not intend to speak to P____ again in his life. In the end he is capable of telling the whole incident in eleven minutes flat. He is told, however, that no suit has been filed against him. They all advise him to go and bathe in the Sazava and stop worrying because he is not to be held responsible for the damage caused by his failure to show up in Hamburg. Finally he arrives at the Ministry of the Interior, but there he does not get beyond the information desk, where an unknown official likewise assures him that they know nothing about the whole business.

SCENE 33 Interior—late afternoon. At home a surprise awaits PK in the shape of two men, one of whom introduces himself as Blatny and says with a smile that he is the Interior Ministry's postman. They have come to return the confiscated material, which they do, checking every item carefully against a list and keeping up a constant flow of light chatter. They cannot tell him

253

anything about his passport, though. PK recounts his experiences at the borders in eleven minutes flat, estimating for their benefit how much this little improvisation is going to cost the country in hard cash. The phone rings. The caller is a friend of PK's, a chief editor who has just received, through Party channels, the information that PK had been apprehended as he was about to flee to the West in possession of a considerable sum of money and compromising political documents. As the chief editor appears to think that this might possibly be true, PK tells him where to go and hangs up. The man who gave his name as Blatny suggests that PK write a complaint to the Minister, which he does at once and the two men take it away with them.

CAPTION: Friday

SCENE 34   The same—next morning. PK cannot come to terms with the fact that because of some anonymous pig the Republic is to be shown in a bad light and pay for the privilege in foreign currency. He therefore gets dressed with the intention of making some more official calls. The telephone rings and the man who yesterday introduced himself as Blatny says that he had been up all night trying to sort this thing out and by way of a reward invites himself for a cup of coffee. PK and Z——— stare at each other in wonderment.

SCENE 35   The same—noon. The man who introduced himself as Blatny at last arrives for his coffee. Looking like someone who has just brought off a coup, he instructs PK and Z——— to pack their bags once more. PK is then to cross Hradcany Square and go to the Passport Office of the Interior Ministry, where he is expected in Room 200. There he will be given back his passport. The Chief Customs Officer will be informed that PK is in a great hurry.

"You'll go across that border like greased lightning," says the man who introduced himself as Blatny.

SCENE 36   Exterior—day. An official of the Ministry of the Interior helps PK and Z——— carry their luggage to their car. The concierge looks on behind her window, smiling uncertainly.

254

SCENE 37   Interior—day. Room 200. Behind the desk sits a man with the inscrutable face of a Chinese, who introduces himself as Benda. PK cheerfully takes a chair opposite him.

"I have been instructed to inform you," says the man who introduced himself as Benda, speaking in slow, measured tones, "that your passport is to be rescinded for good."

PK's face suddenly assumes the expression of a half-witted child. Haltingly he tells the man that he has been sent here by an official of this very Ministry who introduced himself as Blatny, and who even helped him carry his bags to the car. The man who introduced himself as Benda says, speaking in slow, measured tones:

"I'll check what you say and find out how things stand."

SCENE 38   The same—a little later. The man who introduced himself as Benda comes back. Not a muscle moves in his face when he says, in slow, measured tones:

"I have checked your story, Comrade. You did not lie. Only the situation has changed meanwhile. You will not be given your passport."

PK feels he is on the point of breaking into either hysterical laughter or tears. He controls himself and in eleven minutes flat recounts his woes to the Chinese, entreating him to inform the Minister. PK is willing to stand on the pedestal of the statue of St. Wenceslas and declare publicly that this country is being run by some demented policeman. Should he be arrested, he will repeat this in court, enlarging on the subject as part of his defense plea. The man who introduced himself as Benda emits an indeterminate sound which can be taken to mean anything.

SCENE 39   Interior—night. PK asks a friend to his flat and does his best to get drunk, in which attempt he does not succeed. Like his father before him, he knows how to hold his liquor. Producer Pistorius brings his analytical brain to bear on the problem and suggests that in the morning PK call the Deputy Minister of Foreign Affairs Klicka.

CAPTION: Saturday

SCENE 40   The same—next morning. PK calls Deputy Minister

255

Klicka, whom he has met twice in his life. Nevertheless, he is immediately summoned to the Czernin Palace.

SCENE 41 Interior—day. The Deputy Minister's office, coffee, brandy. In eleven minutes flat PK recounts his story. Deputy Minister Klicka calls the Deputy Minister of the Interior Klima.

"Comrade Deputy Minister," says the Deputy Minister, "I have with me a friend who is unhappy ... ah, I see, you're dealing with the case already?"

Deputy Minister Klima listens for some time, nodding his head. Then he says that all the same he would be very grateful if the Deputy Minister of the Interior would intervene on PK's behalf before the whole affair is referred back to the Deputy Minister of Foreign Affairs as a faux pas in our international relations. He hangs up and tells PK that his passport has been taken away from him because of his attempt to smuggle out of the country two hundred Czech crowns and six Danish crowns. The customs authorities can deal with a case like that in two ways: either by imposing a fine on the spot or by leaving Prague to deal with the offender. In PK's case they had chosen the latter alternative and the Ministry of the Interior was powerless in the matter. His case was to come up for consideration in September. PK has an overpowering urge to get up and smash something. Deputy Minister Klicka promises to exert himself further on his behalf. However, it is Saturday, and in two hours' time the whole city will be heading for the country. PK is also told that yesterday, just as he was crossing Hradcany Square going from the man who had introduced himself as Blatny to the man who introduced himself as Benda, the news had arrived that the writer Ladislav Mnacko had defected.

SCENE 42 Interior—day. PK comes home, throws himself on the sofa, and wishes he did not exist. Z____ does her best to mollify him, again extolling the delights of a life in the country. She promises him more dumplings, this time with plums. The phone rings. PK refuses to get up. It is P____, asking him to come to the Central Committee of the Party immediately. PK does not want to go. Z____ uses force to persuade him, saying that if they have to stay behind, she will insist that he marry her.

SCENE 43   Interior—day. The Central Committee of the Communist Party of Czechoslovakia. P_____ explains that after receiving the first report of PK's border incident he was unable to do a thing for him, because that report spoke unequivocally of a criminal offense. It had taken him a full two days to ascertain that the case was at the very least a doubtful one, since the customs authorities in Prague had themselves only learned of it yesterday. He had therefore come to an agreement with them that, although PK's offense concerning the two hundred Czech and six Danish crowns would not be dealt with until September, there would be no objection to his going to Hamburg in the meantime to produce the stage version of Schweik. There was no danger of his defaulting on the fine, which might amount to as much as fifty crowns, for he was leaving all his property and savings behind in Prague. P_____ asks PK to drive at once to the Ministry of the Interior and ask the porter, who would be informed. PK is advised to hurry because office hours will be over in twenty minutes. PK silently but warmly presses P_____'s hand and flees.

SCENE 44   Interior—day. PK arrives breathless at the porter's lodge of the Ministry of the Interior. Ministry officials are hurrying in the opposite direction, making for the woods and rivers. The porter states categorically that he knows nothing. PK stammers as he asks to be allowed to use the phone. The porter declines, saying it is forbidden. PK runs out into the street.

SCENE 45   Exterior—day. PK runs two hundred meters in record time and jumps inside a phone booth which, surprisingly enough, is not out of order. He calls the Central Committee and, near to suffocation, informs P_____ that he has become the victim of some fantastic plot. P_____ asks him to take things easy and to return to the Ministry of the Interior, promising to phone them at once. PK hangs up without so much as a goodbye, for he has no breath left for any more words.

SCENE 46   Exterior—day. PK makes it back to the Ministry, ready to barricade the exit with his own body if need be. As it turns out, it need not be, for standing in front of the yellow-tile building is the man who on the previous day at the Passport Office introduced himself as Benda. His Chinese face glows with a delighted smile. In his outstretched hands he holds a passport. PK thanks him feebly and staggers back to his car.

SCENE 47 Exterior—day. Once more in the yard, PK and Z_____ are for the third time loading the car with their baggage, with the concierge again looking on from the window, her face reflecting the considerable confusion of her mind.

SCENE 48 Exterior—day. PK and Z_____ are again inching forward in a queue of cars packed with food tins and children toward the passport and customs control on the frontier. They are both dressed exactly the same as on Tuesday. So is the Chief Customs Officer, who is just emerging from the building. For a moment he seems to think that he is having a nightmare, then he salutes woodenly and disappears from view. The Second Customs Officer also salutes, again winking an encouraging eye. The First Customs Officer gives a weak wave of the hand. The car crosses the border.

"Well, what do you make of that?" says PK exhaustedly. "Blow me if I can understand it."

"Brecht, Galileo, the scene of the Pope being dressed," replies Z_____.

"What?"

"They showed you the instruments."

SCENE 49 Back projection—night. Interior of the car. Hundreds of kilometers of the monotonous Autobahn pass under the wheels of the car. Z_____ is fast asleep, curled up on the seat like a dachshund. PK has plenty of time to think. He thinks of the border. Not the one that runs between states, but that other dividing line, absurd and terrifying, which on Wednesday night crossed the office of the Chief Customs Officer, dividing three men: two captains on active service and one reserve; three members of the Youth Union, all now reserves; three Communists, all of them still on active service. What had happened? Where did that dividing line, that frontier come from? Who put it there? In the name of what? Who was to benefit when two Communists considered a third one to be a scoundrel and he thought of them as fools? The revolution? The Party? The country? The people? Had he been there alone against them? Had they been alone against him? Or were all three of them their own best enemies? Was it all to begin again? And where would it end? PK drives on through the summer night. He winds down the window and lets the fresh air play on his forehead.

SCENE 50 Exterior—night. The car recedes from view.

CAPTION: The End

Friday, 23 August 1968 / Rome
(Continued)

There were two cars following close behind me, one in the left-and the other in the right-hand lane of the one-way street. When I indicated that I wished to move out of my lane, a horn was sounded peremptorily behind me and I had to carry on as I was. Perspiration broke out on my forehead: so they had found me even in Rome. The street was absolutely deserted. Both the cars increased their speed and drew abreast of me. They were full of men who looked straight ahead of them. I was sure they would shortly force me to pull in to the curb. This was a scene I had watched a thousand times in films and on television. Now I was myself playing the leading rôle. In front of us the traffic lights changed to red. The two drivers applied their brakes. I accelerated and my car went in against the lights. The last thing I saw was the looming bulk of a shiny limousine. There was a loud crash, my Renault was thrown into the air and burst into flames. . . .

No, my nerve failed at the last moment and I stepped on the brakes too, jerking to a halt between the two cars. Their drivers gave me a nonchalant glance and as soon as the lights changed drove off, one to the left, the other to the right. I watched their disappearing taillights with relief, but could not rid myself of the fear that gripped my throat as I imagined the streets of the city in which my nightmare was becoming reality. Among the patrolling tanks cruised cars with the Czech plates AE 40–01 and ABA 71–19. In front sat a blond man with sharp features and cold eyes.

He was not taking away Solzhenitsyn's Innokenti Volodin, though. He was taking away my friends.

I realized that I had now been standing for quite some time in front of the strip club. I left the motor running and went inside. They were gone. I asked the headwaiter how long ago they had left, but he could speak nothing but Italian and did not understand a word I was saying. Only when I had for the third time pointed to our table and then to my watch did he smile and lead me to the bar. He offered me a stool next to the stripper whom I had offended several hours ago and who looked at me with a mixture of disdain and expectation. I tossed some banknotes from my pocket to her and hurried out. As I drove away I caught sight of her as she followed me into the street.

I drove straight to his house, my feelings of fear replaced by anger. I had been right: his car was parked at the curb, yet all the windows were in darkness. I left my car round the corner and returned to ring his bell. He answered it without much delay. From the door phone a panting voice responded.

"Who is it?"

I did not answer but went on pressing the bell. Then the lift came down and the hall light went on. He unlocked the door and remained standing there uncertainly, dressed only in a pair of canvas trousers and his undershirt.

"Where is she?" I asked him.

"Who? I've been asleep."

I did not care whether he was really drunk or only pretending it, and shoved him aside. He staggered but managed to hold onto my shoulder.

"Have you gone mad?"

The whole gamut of sorrow, indignation, and emotion of forty years merged into a single impulse. The last inhibition gave way— I struck him so hard that he reeled back and hit the wall. But by that time I was racing upstairs.

10 August 1968   /   On the border
(From the diary of the writer PK)

On the last Wednesday in July we learned that the delegations of
the Czechoslovak and Soviet Communist parties were to meet
somewhere in Czechoslovakia within the next few days. The units
of the Warsaw Pact forces which had taken part in the June
maneuvers were still making the show of forced march of military
history to reach their borders. The tension increased. On Thursday
we went for lunch to The Cloisters. It was raining slightly. A
foreign young man joined us at our table without a word. He was
fair-haired, with an odd, long, sharp-featured face. We took in his
presence with silent disapproval and went on studying the menu.

"Pochemu taxi nieyediet?" he asked me.

I was surprised to hear him address me in Russian, and curtly.
He directed his bright eyes at me. His eyes gave the face that strange
look. The cool, challenging glance would have been more suitable
if he had been speaking to a woman, as long as she did not have
a jealous companion. He repeated his question and I realized
that he had been drinking. I replied politely that whenever it
rained the dispatcher's office tended to be kept busy and it was
therefore best to wait outside in the street in the hope of catching
a cab.

"Then come with me," he said in Russian. "I don't like waiting
alone."

Z____ stared at him as if he were a lunatic. I explained to him
that we were just about to have our lunch, but that even if that
were not the case I did not see why I should act as his escort. His
eyes suddenly narrowed.

"Why do you speak Russian so well?"

How strange that he should ask why I spoke such fluent Russian!
Z____ was looking at me now, her eyes wondering how much
longer I was going to stand for this. However, I had been quite
well brought up, I felt compassionate toward drunks, and he was
beginning to interest me.

"I simply have learned it," I said.

"But why? Who are you?"

"Sorry," I said, "but before I tell you who I am you'll have to introduce yourself."

He ignored this.

"Davay, speak! Are you Russian?"

"Why Russian? I'm Czech."

"Strange! And why have you learned Russian so well?"

I made up my mind to teach him a little manners. Turning to Z____, I continued our discussion about food. He watched us for a time, then decided to play along.

"Fine then. I'm a tourist, and you?"

Both in clothing and behavior he resembled a Soviet tourist about as much as a hawk resembles a sparrow. And anyway, all tourist trips from the Soviet Union had just been suspended.

"If you are a tourist, then I am simply a native," I told him.

"My Czech!" he said angrily. "And how you behave! What have you done to Novotny? Novotny—the only friend of the Soviet Union and the best Marxist in Czechoslovakia!"

"How old are you?" I asked him.

"And why must you know that?"

Seeing me again incline my head toward the menu he said quickly:

"I'm thirty. So what?"

"Well, you're thirty. I am forty, and yet I don't address you by the familiar form. You're ten years my junior and yet you don't hesitate to use it. I'm afraid that is typical of the present mutual relationship between our two countries and parties."

I was curious to see how he would react.

"Fine," he said to my surprise, apologizing. "Excuse me."

"Novotny, whom you consider such a friend of the Soviet Union and our best Marxist, was responsible for Marxism almost becoming extinct in this country. We're trying to revive it. But in any case that is our own and nobody else's business. We don't send you letters telling you how you should live and what you should think."

He smiled. If one could call it a smile. Too much irony and cool malice. And then, as if speaking to a criminal who had just given himself away, he said:

"You know what you are? I'm going to tell you! You are a counterrevolutionary! But you won't laugh for long!"

Z____ and I got up simultaneously. Outside in the passage the headwaiter caught up with us.

"He stood for half an hour by the bar and then made straight for your table!"

"He says he's waiting for a taxi."

"Well, he certainly didn't ask for one."

On the street Z____ said to me:

"I'm scared."

"Oh, come on, why? He's from the Russian Embassy or the trade mission and has had one too many, that's all."

"His malicious eyes!"

"Who cares? Even if he were from the secret police, he can go to hell as far as I'm concerned. No one is going to make me be afraid in my own country."

"Weren't you afraid during the war?"

"Well, there isn't any war, is there? Unless you count the war of nerves. And fortunately my nerves are perfectly in order."

"Let's hope Dubcek's and the others' are too."

It could not be denied that our lunchtime incident was in keeping with the strange atmosphere created after the five Warsaw Pact powers had sent their letter and received the reply from the Presidium of the Czechoslovak Central Committee. We spent a long time discussing the situation in the editorial office of Literární listy. I suggested that before the conference of the Party delegations Ludovik Vaculik ought to write an article explaining what was at stake. He said that after the fuss there had been over his Two Thousand Words, he was afraid he might start a third world war. In the end they left it to me to do the writing. It took me a long time to decide to whom I should address my article. Then I wrote:

FROM THE CITIZENS OF CZECHOSLOVAKIA TO THE PRESIDIUM OF THE CENTRAL COMMITTEE OF THE CZECHOSLOVAK COMMUNIST PARTY.

"The moment has arrived when our country has again, after many centuries, become the cradle of hope that is not only our hope. The moment has arrived when we have the opportunity of showing the world that socialism is the only real alternative for our entire civilization. We expected that socialist countries especially would welcome this with great sympathy and understanding. Instead, we are being accused of treason.

"Everything we are struggling to achieve can be summed up in four words: SOCIALISM—ALLIANCE—SOVEREIGNTY—FREEDOM. The first two are our guarantees to our fraternal countries and parties that we shall not permit such a development as would jeopardize the true interests of the nations with whom we have for the past twenty years been fighting for a common cause. The other two, on the other hand, are guarantees for ourselves that there will be no repetition of the grave errors which recently threatened to erupt into a crisis.

"Explain to your opposite numbers that the extreme voices which can occasionally be heard in our debates are a product of the bureaucratic police system which had for so long strangled creative thinking that in the end it drove a great many people into inner opposition. Convince them by means of innumerable examples that the authority of the Party and the existence of socialism in this country are today far stronger than at any time in the past.

"Comrades [14 names], it is possible that not all of you share the same point of view. Some of you, in spite of having helped to bring about what is known as the January policy, are severely criticized for your earlier mistakes. Such is the lot of the politician, but the seven months that have passed since January have shown that no one intends to turn that criticism into a bloodbath in order to take their revenge.

"Negotiate, explain, but whatever you do, unified and unconciliatory, defend the road on which we have set out and which we shall not abandon as long as we live.... We are thinking of you and ask you to think of us! We appeal to all our fellow citizens who agree with us to support our message."

We considered what to do with our text. Someone suggested a special number of Literární listy, but Chief Editor Jungmann said the printer was working to full capacity as it was and would tell us to go to hell. At that moment we received a phone call from the printing house asking us whether we did not want to do an extra edition of Literární listy; if not, they said, they would print something themselves.

I could not for the life of me see how we were to get the necessary signatures, since we were not organized for any such undertaking. Then I slipped on a winding staircase and sprained the middle finger of my right hand.

Late that evening someone rang the bell at my door. It was S——, who had come for copies of the text. When I offered him one of the two existing ones he grew indignant, saying he had a contact from the employees of the Municipal Sewer Department in the car; eleven other people were waiting at home. He therefore asked me to retype the text. I showed him my swollen finger, whereupon he sat down at my typewriter and started to hammer away like a woodpecker.

In the morning the editorial offices were full of students from the Charles University who had heard about our special number on the radio and came to offer their services. They would take the text round the factories and gather signatures. The telephones got busy, everywhere the Message was being read out, and well-known names were bandied about over the air. I saw that Z—— had signed herself immediately after the National Artists.

I paced the office, wildly excited. Suggestions and supplements kept pouring in and I at once read them and worked them in. S—— arrived with eleven hundred signatures and as a reward I took him to lunch. We talked about a female fellow pupil of ours whom we had teased every day by hiding one of her shoes. Z—— declared that this helped to explain many of the later distortions.

When I returned, the Chief Editor had already left for the printing house. We discovered that they had forgotten to give him the most important paper of all, containing the signatures of Prague's factory workers. We came too late. The newsboys were already assembling in the yard of the printing house. The chief machine-minder went up to the rotary machine, patted it, spat on it, and switched it on with the words:

"Here goes—for Dubcek!"

S——, who kept following me about everywhere, opened a freshly printed copy, soiled his jacket with newsprint, and started looking for his eleven hundred signatures. They were on the paper that had got left behind in the office. Before he could do me any physical harm I asked him to take them to the Radio.

At seven that evening the TV cameras went into action. Jiri Hanzelka and I took turns reading the Message. When we finished, the girl announcer had tears in her eyes, reminding us that the period we were living in was not exactly full of merriment. But we were alive, and so I took Z—— to dinner. Shortly after midnight we walked home from the Golem, past Children's House. Outside

265

there was a large crowd. In the morning a young man had put a table, which he had borrowed from the department store, out on the pavement, and now he already had seven thousand signatures and several eager assistants from among the passers-by. We bumped into the actor Litera, who had just returned from a performance at the castle of Karlstejn and told us that during the intermission Charles IV had put his spectacles on and read the Message out to the audience, which rewarded him with tumultuous applause.

On Saturday I tried in vain to write a film script about a divided Prague, with the Americans on the left bank and the Russians on the right. In the afternoon there was again someone at the door. It was the young man from the Children's House. They had collected twenty-two thousand signatures and he wanted to know where they were to take them. I phoned the television people, and they told me that Dubcek would be arriving in half an hour's time to record tonight's speech. Z____ came in, and we left at once for the TV studio, taking the signatures with us.

I looked at the sheets of paper I had been given.

"Perfect," Z____ said. "People have even given their full addresses—this can later save the security men a great deal of work."

"Don't be monotonous," I said.

I was most impressed by the paper that came from the employees of the U Rozvarilu restaurant. It was covered with stains which gave one an idea of the day's menu.

The TV executives were all waiting outside on the pavement. Z____ asked how many people were in the retinue of the First Secretary of the Party in these stormy days. Then a single official Tatra arrived, and out of it stepped Alexander Dubcek—by himself.

We all squeezed into the studio. On the bottom monitors we could see Slovan Bratislava playing a soccer game, the top ones showed us Dubcek. He spoke faster and made more slips of the tongue than usual. One of the technicians said with compassion:

"He's hurrying so he can get to the football match on time. What kind of a life is that, I ask you?"

In the small buffet next to us sat a slightly inebriated youth who kept shouting that Dubcek could go to hell. We thought the same of him. It was good to know that he could say things like that with impunity. It was less good to know that he knew it too.

Again we looked at the monitors and saw the First Secretary bent under the weight of the huge pile of paper they put in his arms. I wondered how much those signatures actually weighed. Dubcek then hurried off to remove the TV make-up. I greeted him as he passed me. He must have had the feeling that he had seen me before somewhere, and he asked me what I had done to my finger. I replied that someone had stepped on my hand, for I could think of nothing better to say on this historic occasion.

We then drove home again, to watch the news on TV. The whole country was signing.

"Isn't it fantastic!" I said. "Forty-eight hours ago there were four of us in the office and we felt pretty scared."

"I still do," she said. "You see, I wonder what that amiable gentleman we met at The Cloisters is likely to be signing at this very minute."

I again took her out to mingle with people. The Children's House department store had provided a room and an adding machine. The President of the National Front, Kriegel, had just been here and gone, having lost his wife in the milling crowd. Before that another visitor had been Smrkovsky, who had assured the people gathered in front of the store that anyone who betrayed the regeneration process would be remembered for a hundred years, and it certainly wouldn't be he. Tourists from the friendly countries stared wide-eyed and added their signatures. I got involved in the discussion. Z——— stood by, listening without protest, until well after midnight. One man asked me what would happen if the Russians invaded us. I told him that although I prided myself on a fairly vivid imagination, this was something I could not picture without concluding that I had only dreamed the past twenty-three years. He would not be put off, however, urging me to try, just for the sake of argument, and then to tell him what we were to do if it did happen.

So I told him that if it did happen we ought to pretend we had noticed nothing.

On Sunday afternoon the radio announced that the plane carrying the Presidium of the Central Committee of the Communist Party was about to leave Prague for an unknown destination. The thriller had begun.

The volunteer corps from the Children's House had extended its activities to Hradcany Square, the National Theater, Wenceslas Place, and the Prague railway stations. People were returning home from their weekend in the country, and in the last eight hours there had been as many signatures as during the whole two preceding days. They now totaled 71,566. The corps had its own group of translators, which kept foreign tourists and newspapermen informed in eight different languages. Sandwiches, mineral water, and beer had been provided free of charge for the volunteers by the U Pelikana restaurant.

During the hour between half past eight and half past nine no fewer than nine thousand people signed the Message. I met almost all my relatives and friends, including my children. We drove them home.

Again the news. The closely observed train carrying the Presidium had left Kosice for an unknown destination. I tried to picture railway coaches full of Politburo members. I also thought that with such confidence behind them, our Politburo did not have to hold its meeting miles away from anywhere.

Then it was midnight and we had to think about where to put those piles of paper overnight. Before we had decided, Z_____ arrived with my huge travel bag. The adding machine was employed for the last time, and the result it gave was 85,507. I wrote this down, but then a woman jumped out of a tram, wrote Tichackova Anna, Prague 5, Na Skalce, and still had time to jump in again before the tram left the stop. And so I wrote 85,508. Then someone knocked on the door and what was to be the very last signature was added by Major A. Hynek from the Ministry of Defense—85,509.

It now seemed to me that the bells should be ringing, and that we should have champagne, and general merriment. But we were all very tired and we could not stop thinking about that train. Helped by Z_____, I picked the travel bag up with my good hand, thanked all those present, and went home. We weighed the papers in the bathroom—those 85,509 signatures weighed forty pounds and four ounces. For all of them I said good night to Helen Kubickova, Pionyru 1713, who happened to be lying on top. Z_____ dragged the bag across to the sofa.

"Do you think," she said, "that so many people have ever slept together in one room?"

"What's Dubcek going to do with this lot?" I rejoined sleepily.
She sat on top of the bag and thought about it.

"I guess what we need is a chest. A pretty, painted one, from the Moravian-Slovak border so that there should be no national jealousy. We should put the papers in this chest and the chest in his office. And whenever anyone came and started arguing, all Dubcek would have to do would be to get up and open the chest."

"Fine, I'll suggest exactly that. Aren't you sleepy? I am."

"You know what?" she said. "I think I'm happy."

"Well, you've certainly picked a fine time for it." I replied.

In the morning she took the bag to the Literární noviny office. The radio said the conference was being held in Cierna. The evening communiqué stated that the talks would continue next day. I could wait no longer. I should already have been in Nuremberg, to arrange for the autumn's premières. When I was finished, Z____ was to join me and we would set off together on our holiday by the sea.

I crossed the frontier at night and worked until late that evening. Then I switched on for the news. The talks weren't over yet. I phoned a friend from the Municipal Party Committee, to whom I had said goodbye only yesterday.

"Why is it taking so long?" I asked him.

"Can you come to the office in the morning?" he said in a voice hoarse with sleep.

"Is it really so urgent?" I asked unhappily.

"Yes, you really ought to come," he said significantly.

I scribbled notes of apology to my colleagues, at three I said good morning to my customs officials, and at seven got Z____ out of bed. She almost had a stroke when she saw me. Shortly after eight I strode into my friend's office.

"What's up?" I asked.

"Oh, nothing much," he replied. "We have no news as yet."

"Is that why I had to come all the way from Nuremberg?"

"Oh, did you call from Nuremberg, then?"

I thought I'd kill him, but then I was glad I had returned. A holiday under these circumstances was unthinkable. I should only have stared unseeingly at the landscape and at Z____. I spent the whole day at the Municipal Party Committee headquarters, together with a large number of people who had come here for exactly the same reason—to seek information at the source. The statesmen of our modern country, however, had worse communications than a Scout troop with its own amateur transmitter. Every day some member of the Party delegation would come over the air, so faintly as to be almost inaudible, to say that they all sent their best wishes and were looking forward to being with us again.

It was not until Thursday that the surprising news came about the forthcoming conference of the Six in Bratislava. On Saturday television cameras showed us the group of Soviet and Czech leaders; ours were smiling, Brezhnev raised Svoboda's and Dubcek's arms in the air. The alliance was again radiant, like a rainbow in springtime.

As the faithful went to church on Sunday I drove to the Central Committee building. I had guessed right: here they came, one after the other, straight from the airport. Cernik, Smrkovsky, Kriegel, Mlynar, Jakes, and so on. The Slovaks had remained in Bratislava with their families. Dubcek, they said, had gone to bathe. They were tired, but even at close quarters looked satisfied. They would not go into details about the talks. Smrkovsky and Cernik said the same thing, almost word for word:

"It was tough, but we managed to convince them."

Only Kriegel remained taciturn and grave. When I met him in the washroom, he replied to my question in three words:

"It was terrible."

However, on Monday the tension began to ease. The remaining allied troops quickly left the country, and preparations for both the harvest and the Fourteenth Party Congress went ahead successfully. Above all Z____ showed signs of normalization.

"We're ten days late already," she complained. "Are we going on that holiday, or will it be like last year and the year before?"

I took secret counsel with my friends.

"By all means go," they all told me. "There'll be nothing doing now, at least until the Congress."

I put our departure off once more, though. There was cheering down in the square. Tito appeared at a window on the first floor of the Castle. It could not be more than a hundred feet to my window. I leaned out and waved to him. That was my way of asking forgiveness for a certain poem of mine written twenty years ago. He smiled and waved back, as if he were giving us all his pardon.

Next morning we set out at last. *Rude pravo* printed the draft of the new Party statutes. I enjoyed myself reading them, but then had to take Z——'s place at the wheel, for a hailstorm broke out and threatened to annihilate us. However, the sun came out again and the countryside around us really did look like a paradise on earth, as is said in our national anthem.

We both had coffee at the border.

"There," I said triumphantly, "you see! We're off after all!"

"Remember that foreign gentleman in the restaurant?" she replied. "Do you think he's left too by this time?"

□

Friday, 23 August 1968 / Rome
(Continued)

I   How should I know?

He   But I told you yesterday, here.

I   I'm sorry. I don't remember much about yesterday... just a moment, I'll pour myself some coffee.

He   All right. How many lumps?

I   No sugar for me, you ought to know that.... When did you get divorced?

He   Shortly before I left Prague.

I   Forgive me, but I really have to ask you this. Why?

He   I'll give you three guesses. Say "on account of the Party" every time.

I   Ah, I think I know...

He   I think you don't know. Do you remember her?

I   You seem to forget I was your best man.

He   So you were! And I yours.

I   Yes, we have been one another's witness all our lives, and yet no one will believe anything we say.

He   You got married on Stalin's birthday—for luck.

I   As for your wedding—that was almost a Party congress.

He   Well, she came from that kind of a family. Zapotocky's childhood friends. They had founded the Party and formed its first generation. A proletarian nobility in the best sense of the term. They always held it against her that she married a pen-pusher. The only mitigating circumstance was that she met me at the Party Academy and that I was working in the apparatus. She just acted stubborn and married me. But otherwise she was exactly like them in every respect.

I May I also ask you why you married her in the first place?

He Why *do* people marry one another?

I I could have sworn you would never get married. I used to envy you, thinking you simply weren't capable of losing your head like me.

He Well, I lost it good and proper when I did.

I All right. But what was the actual cause of the split, now after so many years?

He She couldn't have children.

I I see. Are you so crazy about kids?

He I don't know. Maybe. But the main thing was that she doted on the Party as other women dote on their children.

I Did she hold any Party office?

He Yes: she was my wife. The mining aristocracy has its hereditary diseases. There was TB in her family. So she worked for the Party through me. She and her clan. I used to come home worn out in the evening and it was only then that my working day would really begin.

I But surely you two should have got on extremely well. I've never heard you speak of anything but politics all your life. You've even sacrificed your talent to it. You could have been a far better writer than I today.

He I don't feel in the least sorry about that. You see, I don't think of it as a sacrifice. I guess I am a natural, professional revolutionary. Whatever I have said and whatever I say, I mean it with all my heart.

I Well, where was the problem in that case?

He In that I was a revolutionary for everyone else, but not her. She would never believe that I was really sincere. For people like you I was a dogmatist, for her a revisionist.

I But that's absurd!

He Maybe it is and maybe it isn't. Perhaps she was right. You and I spoke about this very thing this afternoon.

I   Oh, come! You're an educated, thinking man. You can't see the world through the spectacles of nineteenth-century revolutionaries. This is the age of the scientific-technical revolution. If the Party wishes to survive, it will have to take this into account. We, who want the Party attuned to present needs, are right.

He   Don't let my being drunk fool you. I'm drunk because I *know*. And my knowledge fills me with utter skepticism. Those spectacles of theirs are far more accurate than you think. Where did the thinking from which we derive our present-day conclusions come from? It originated in good old Europe, which exported it in a few ships across the ocean. We're convinced that it has taken root throughout our planet, and yet we're nothing more than a ridiculous group of white men who have managed to cultivate a small clearing in the jungle and feel like conquerors as a result. The trouble is, the jungle is full of creatures that are at home in it, who have their own traditions, their own laws, and their own ideas about the world of the future, and they vastly outnumber its supposed masters. How many people are there who think along lines similar to yours and mine? According to the world atlas, five hundred million. One to five. But how many of us are there really? My wife did not think the way I do. Nor her family. Nor her whole class. They're far closer to the two and a half thousand million proletarians in Asia, Africa, and Latin America than they are to us, you know. You and I are shocked because thousands of tanks have rolled into an ancient European city under cover of the night and fog. We're broken because they resemble the tanks that liberated us twenty-three years ago. But that was only a legend, again created by our own minds, nurtured on Andersen's fairy tales about the wicked dragon and the noble knight. They did not liberate us then, just as they did not occupy us now. All that has happened is that slowly, almost imperceptibly, step by step, decade after decade the world which was here long before we were has come closer to us, the world which built Chinese walls and Aztec palaces and Egyptian pyramids at a time when the Ice Age was coming to an end in Europe. When we were still at elementary school, America was in a panic because Orson Welles had written a radio play about a Martian invasion. We were afraid to go to the toilet in the dark. Today we, as well as the Americans, laugh at this, we compete in the production of hydrogen bombs and in the conquest of space, we have NATO and the Warsaw Pact, and we go to sleep at night with the soothing knowledge that we have created a wonderful, infallible balance of power. Only in a mere twenty years there will be ten thousand million people on this earth, and there will be ten of them to each of us. The only thing that is still not certain is whether the capital of Europe will then be Peking or Kinshasa. That is why you ought not to be surprised that the politicians or the poets of a tiny country which is doomed to extinction anyway are today arrested or perhaps even liquidated in broad daylight. Just as I am not surprised that in a foreign city far from that country of ours I get beaten up by a former friend whose young lady I have dropped off at the Piazza di Popolo because she expressed a wish to go for a walk by herself.

□

2 XII 63 / Prague

You
born on the threshold
of the immense crazy maze
—which bears the sign the Twentieth Century
led me unerringly
toward the warmth and light
marked our path
over a million well-scrubbed parquets
Whenever I got lost
you hoisted a thousand washed shirts
on every yardarm
and lit fires
smelling of doughnuts and Christmas pastry

You mended my socks and my heart
with small firm stitches
I can wear them to this day
With the salvo of your sleepness nights
you warded off a horde of fevers
with your two knitting needles
you pierced the world crisis
and conducted the world war standing by your stove
changing water into tea and earth into bread

At midnight I drove again to the hospital, turned the car to point my headlamps at her window, and flashed them several times. She used to say that whenever the pills failed to help and she could not go to sleep, she would watch a film about my childhood on the ceiling of her room. I wanted to please her by screening one for her myself. In the morning I phoned from the theater to ask how she was. They told me she died at midnight.

I said nothing, carrying on with the direction of the play like a well-oiled machine. I kept talking all the time, though, because as soon as I stopped I could not help wondering whether my last farewell had come in time.

I did not even call E_____. After our last taciturn meeting, she had not come to see me, had not phoned all that time when every day I went straight to the hospital after rehearsals, spending long hours in that small white room so as not to miss a single occasion when she woke up for a short spell. I had a desperate feeling that I must ask her about many important things which no one but she could tell me. But she was invariably so tired from her sleep that I refrained from asking.

That was why I now kept putting my hand in the inside pocket of my jacket, in which I carried a letter she had sent me that summer when we were filming on location. I had never opened it. Maybe it contained some completely ordinary piece of news. But she had already been incurably ill and I believed that the letter held a message far more important than any that I received from other sources. I meant to open it when I was in trouble and had nobody to turn to for solace and advice.

That afternoon I went to see about her funeral, and then I spent some time with the children. They cried a little, and before long the flat was full of their arguments and laughter. Perhaps it was better that way. My feeling of loneliness grew, however. I went home and for the first time in years wrote a little poetry.

I always thought you were
immortal and invulnerable
Your face I glimpsed
through childish ailments
fear
passion
disappointed love
like the star in my sky
and your hand swept aside
the dark and fire and sorrow
as easily as if they were the bead curtain
we had in the bathroom
Who could have guessed
that you too had your heel of Achilles
a tiny invisible spot
through which one day would creep
death

The maisonette, still unfamiliar despite four years, seemed to be crushing me. I wandered about, trying to find something to occupy me, but if yesterday there still might have been some sense in my thoughts or my work, today I could find none. At last I understood that today of all days I could not be alone.

The Viola had an air of revelry about it, as always before St. Nicholas' Day. I found a single empty stool by the bar and sat on it, drinking Czech whisky and listening to the fragments of conversation around me. A girl was sitting with her back to me. I could see her close-cropped hair. She seemed to be talking with everyone and yet with no one in particular. Suddenly she turned to me and said:

"Why so glum when all about you are merry?"

It was just like all idle conversations of this sort. But today that was exactly what I needed.

"I'm afraid to be alone at home," I replied.

"In such cases female company is deemed advisable."

Her slightly arch manner of speaking did not sound forced but instead lent her a pleasantly humorous air. I followed suit.

"Where is one to obtain said company?"

"One must look for a girl who does not belong to anybody."

She did not seem particularly beautiful to me, but she had fine features and frank, friendly eyes. In her thick pullover she looked more like a boy. I always found it difficult to get acquainted, conducting conversations such as this to a certain point and then switching to politics or art. It was in fact due to shyness, but the impression I gave was one of ostentatious lack of interest, so that contact was soon lost. This time I crossed the borderline in no time.

"Does the girl present belong to anyone?" I asked her.

"Well, since I'm talking to you now, I guess I belong to you."

"In that case would you have any objection to keeping me company?"

"Objection overruled," she replied.

"All right, let's go, then," I suggested.

By the cloakroom I ran into an artist I know.

"Careful," he whispered in my ear. "You're in for a night of intellectual discussion or for a slap in the face. She's famous for it!"

Nothing could have been better. I only hoped he was not kidding. She went to my place as matter-of-factly as if she had been in the habit of going there every day. When I unlocked the door she glanced at the card with my name on it and asked:

"What do you do when you're doing something?"

"I write," I told her.

She burst out laughing, but refused to tell me what was so funny. We emptied a bottle of vodka and looked down from the terrace at the night trams and Faustus House. She hopped about in my bathrobe, which she had put on in place of an overcoat, regaling me with one story after another. It seemed to me that the terrace was full of gay people all of whom I knew intimately. Thanks to this I felt a relief I had not known for many months, despite the fact that this was still the day on which death had taken my mother.

"What do you do?" I asked her.

"I'm looking at the city."

"And what do you do when you don't happen to be looking?"

"Nothing."

"I see. But surely there's something that interests you. Isn't there anything you want to be?"

"Yes," she said. "I want to be happy."

□

Friday, 23 August 1968 / Rome
(Continued)

He waved to me and flew off in the elevator like an unhappy modern Faustus. At that very moment I thought I had the answer. I again saw the eyes of the man who had leaned across the table to kiss her hands.

IF SHE IS ANYTHING LIKE YOU, SHE CAN WAKE ME AT TWO IN THE MORNING!

It was a quarter past two. I put my foot down hard on the accelerator. I heard the screech of brakes and the offended hoot of a horn, but the car behind did not catch up with me. I relied on my instinct, climbing the hairpin bends up to the Villa Borghese and choosing one of the roads across the park at random. It did not surprise me in the least to discover the neon sign of the Parco dei Principi Hotel in the second turning. It was a luxury hotel, and even at this late hour the door was opened by a white-gloved bellboy. I was met by two pairs of courteously reserved eyes as I laid the Canadian Czech's visiting-card on the receptionist's desk.

"Yes," said the receptionist in English, "he is in."

"May I speak to him?"

In place of a reply the man looked meaningfully at his watch.

"I am a friend of his," I said.

The receptionist smiled apologetically.

"He has a visitor, sir."

My pulse began to beat faster.

"But he assured me I could call on him any time I wished."

He had no reason to disbelieve me, and so he ventured to the borderline of indiscretion.

"I don't think he would be glad tonight."

Several seconds went by. I was unable to concentrate on any single thought. Turning round I saw the open doors of an elevator in front of me.

The porter beat me to it, placing himself between me and the door. His voice was now courteously menacing.

"Sorry, sir."

Taking him by the arm I swung him aside. Caught completely unawares he staggered back, coming to a halt against his desk. I jumped inside the lift and pressed the top button. I was in a long corridor with many doors on either side. The second lift arrived a few seconds later, discharging the porter and receptionist, their faces showing a mixture of astonishment and rage. I started running, calling out his name as I went. Before I had reached the end of the passage, the first doors were already opening. I flailed my arms in the air and kicked out so violently that no one dared come near me.

"*Scusi, signori e signorini*, I'm calling the police," exclaimed the receptionist.

He scuttled off toward the lift, and it was then that I saw her. She was standing in a doorway, dressed in a man's dressing gown the sleeves of which she had turned up the way she did when she was with me. My arms flopped to my side, but no one moved. Everyone was staring at us in absolute silence.

"Come back!" I said hoarsely.

"No," she answered. "You left me in Perugia. I no longer have a country; I don't want you either. You and your lot messed up everything you touched. You can do what you like, kill me if you feel like it. I hate you. I hate the lot of you!"

I stared at her slim hands, half-hidden in the sleeves of the dressing gown, seeking shelter. I knew that this was the end of me, and my eyes filled with tears....

The porter, who was still standing between me and the open door of the lift, turned his head discreetly aside. Slowly I walked away, and as I passed his desk the receptionist said:

"Take it easy, sir."

The white-gloved bellboy opened not only the hotel door but also the door of my car for me. I delved in my pocket and handed him the rest of my banknotes. His mouth fell open and he just stared in speechless surprise. I slammed the car door myself. The Hotel Parco dei Principi vanished in my rear-view mirror like the last lighthouse of a continent to which I was never to return. Tears streamed down my cheeks. The last time I had cried had been five years ago, looking through the glass partition of the mortuary. I had encountered death so many times in my life that I had never given any serious consideration to my own. True, on a number of occasions, driving along the narrow Bohemian roads and seeing the lights of an approaching vehicle careen toward me through the rain or fog, I had said to myself:

"Here comes my death!"

But that was only make-believe. The lights invariably flashed past and the road ahead was again clear, taking me to dinner, to applause, failure, or love. I had had to load my car with books and bathing suits, I had had to cross half of Europe in search of the sea, kisses, and a long-deferred vacation, for death to set its trap at the end of a sunny day, in this land of wine, eucalyptus, and cicadas, to deliver me to transitoriness just when I had come to the Eternal City. I passed road signals and lights to find my road out of life.

In those moments when the world of men passed in review before my eyes for the last time perceived by me as in a tear-stained haze, I suddenly thought I understood everything that had hitherto seemed incomprehensible. I saw that right from the beginning I had built my life on illusions and self-delusion, creating a fantasy world out of my wishful thoughts, a world that again and again collapsed about me like a house of cards as soon as it came in contact with reality.

I LOVE YOU BUT DON'T WANT YOU TO GIVE YOURSELF TO ME IN THIS NIGHT OF FAREWELLS AND BLOOD! THAT WOULD BE LIKE A SACRIFICE.

I had left her, going out to join the rising which needed me as little in the night as it did next morning. Perhaps it was to my cowardly escape that she owed the sexual hunger of which she never managed to rid herself.

I TOO AM THE REVOLUTION! IF YOU WANT ME TO, I'LL TEACH YOU TO LIVE!

She did want me to, but I was unable to answer any of the questions that tormented her, because I did not know the answers myself. She had to leave her home and sail round the globe to hear them from a Cuban doctor.

NO ONE IS SAD ON SUCH A SHIP, MY DEAR! ON SUCH A SHIP NO ONE IS ALONE!

Yet I did not know how to dispel her fears and her loneliness, even though I brought her under my roof. Her constant battle for a place by the stove and her way of arranging the cutlery seemed to me ridiculously insignificant when compared with the grandiose struggle of the classes and races of this world. She gave up her large flat and good name for a small certainty that was hers alone.

WHEN YOU GROW UP I'LL TELL YOU ABOUT THEM DURING A GLORIOUS SPRING IN WHICH ALL MEN WILL BECOME BROTHERS!

Now he was sleeping uneasily, clutching the flag with which he had spent the previous day bravely protesting against the self-same tanks to which I had dedicated my first published poem.

I WANT TO BE HAPPY!

Is that really so selfish a wish as I had thought? Or is it rather a courageous expression of the true creed of human existence? Surely this is the key to everything! How can a man who has not succeeded in improving the lot of a single individual he has come in contact with hope to improve the world?

She argued with me, reproached me, but her arms were devotedly waiting for me every night to save me from having bad dreams.

I drove about the city, looking for that lovely roadsign of my childhood games:

GO BACK TO SQUARE ONE!

But it was too late to seek the leopard's skeleton in the white snows of Kilimanjaro. I was not Jan Hus and therefore was not able to place myself in the hands of the cold-eyed man waiting at the stake. Yet I was not Comenius, either, to accept the hospitality of my would-be benefactors at the University of Iowa and there culminate my life and work. I could neither turn to God, whom I had abandoned, nor had I yet found Marx, whom I was seeking. All I could do was continue on my way toward the Via Appia, where I would be able to step on the accelerator, put my head on the wheel, and sleep.

The car with a flashing light which had driven alongside me for some time now accelerated, overtook me, and forced me to stop by cutting in dangerously right in front of me. I was too exhausted to feel any fear this time. I only reacted more slowly than I would have done normally and brought the car to a halt at the very last second, my license plate lightly grazing their running board.

"*I suoi documenti, per favore!*"

The other policeman was getting the breathalyzer ready. I pulled my passport and my handkerchief out together. It was clear to me that I could easily have committed not one but a dozen traffic offenses. I quickly mopped my face with the handkerchief, which was at once drenched with perspiration.

"*Viene della Cecoslovaccia?*"

"*Si.*"

"*Perche la sua macchina non porta la targa del paese?*"

I could not understand what he was driving at, but I saw what he wanted when I walked round the car and discovered that someone had taken my CS plate as a souvenir. I shrugged my shoulders helplessly. However, their voices lost all trace of official severity.

"*Non si sente bene?*"

He gesticulated to explain his meaning by placing his hands against his temples as if suffering from a headache.

"No," I replied, and my voice sounded as if it came from the grave.

They exchanged a few words. Then the more high-ranking of the two asked me where I was staying.

"*Dove abita?*"

But I had by now lost my ability to guess the meaning of Italian by its similarity with Latin.

"*Non capisco,*" I said.

"*L'albergo?*"

That was a word I knew. I told them the name of my hotel. He apologized, climbed into my Renault, and opened the other door for me to get in. The police Fiat led the way and we followed. I was now completely done in, and so I rested my head against the seat and closed my eyes. My mind was blank. I stopped thinking and soon dozed off. I was awakened by a touch on the shoulder. He helped me out of the car, made sure it was locked, and handed me the keys.

"*Grazie,*" I said, being incapable of longer speech.

"*Non c' e di che. Buona notte. Tanti saluti alla Cecoslovaccia!*" He leaned closer to me, adding very softly: "*Sono socialista.*"

The hotel was open all night, the porter's lodge empty. I could not find my key, but then at last remembered that I had left it in the door of my room. I hoped I would discover that the room had been completely burgled, for I was afraid to see her belongings there again. Dozens of objects I had hated because they had for years cluttered up my writing desks, my beds and my chairs were now waiting for me like so many mines which would explode the past as soon as I caught sight of them. I relied solely on my weariness to save me from the impact.

There was a light under the door—I must have forgotten to switch it off. When I opened the door I stopped dead in my tracks. It looked as if not a burglar but a lunatic had been at large in my room. My shirts, underwear, socks, and handkerchiefs had been draped all over the place, on the windows, bedposts, washbasin, on the chairs and wardrobes, even on the lamp. The floor was covered with books, magazines, notebooks, photographs, and a large number of sheets of paper on which a single face had been painted in many different techniques and sizes: my own. In the midst of all this disorder lay a naked female body, curled up and showing no signs of life. I stepped forward, but before I could reach her she opened her eyes and cried out. She pulled me down toward her, her hands wandering over my head, my shoulders and hips as she repeated over and over again a single warm word from the good old times:

"Sweetheart, sweetheart, sweetheart, sweetheart."

Piecing together her words, riven by sobs, I learned that she had walked back to our hotel and stopped at the restaurant downstairs to buy a liter of Frascati, with which she wanted to join us in our sorrows. She just managed to catch a glimpse of me as I jumped into the car and drove off like a madman. She ran after me, bottle in hand, all the way to the corner, shouting so desperately that even Roman windows were thrown open.

"I thought you were on your way home and were leaving me behind."

The whole business now seemed utterly absurd to me.

She had been stranded there with her bottle of Frascati and all our luggage, which had become meaningless, alone in that squalid room, in a foreign city, with not even anyone's address or telephone number.

"But you had *his* address, didn't you?"

"Oh, you fool, you silly, cruel, wicked fool, my dearest darling, did you really think I would run out on you?"

I gave her a confused resumé of my mad nocturnal odyssey, and she vacillated between laughter and tears as she listened.

"They told me he had a visitor and would not care to see me."

"He must have found a Czech woman at last. You have one already, so you can thank your lucky stars."

"I do."

"And you can repeat after Capek: there's always a tiny little possibility—that remained even during the Deluge."

A well-known text was suddenly remembered, and I gratefully accepted my cue.

"What possibility is that?"

"That the Newts will start fighting among themselves and become extinct!"

"And what then?"

"And there will only remain that old fossil impression of Andrias Scheuchzeri."

"And then?"

"A few people will survive on ships or they will evolve once more out of the apes and then will discover fire and write the Legend of the Deluge, and then perhaps create a new civilization."

"And then?" I asked, replying for her: "You don't know what will happen then...."

"Then is a long way off," she said. "First you must sleep with me...I want to have a child."

This was the opening of a scene we had played many times before. After her cue should have come my reply that I was not a cat and did not have a number of lives, that I was forty and did not want to have children the same age as my grandchildren and that I had never insisted that she link her life to mine. Instead of all this I picked her up in my arms and carried her across the jumble of our belongings and destinies, carried her to the region where human immortality begins. I knew that I was treading the same path as hundreds of thousands of my fellow countrymen who were lost this night in the Labyrinth of the World and, like me, were trying to find their *centrum securitatis* where our sorely tried nation might find a haven to wait out the storm and then rise again like the phoenix from the ashes.

And lo, I heard a Voice that spake thus to the Pilgrim:

GO BACK WHENCE THOU CAMEST, INTO THE ABODE OF THY HEART, AND CLOSE THE DOOR AFTER THEE!

[The end of The Story]

◨

24 September 1968 / Prague
(From the diary of the writer PK)

I saw them as soon as we broke through the thick, low-lying cloud and came in for the landing. The long lines of tanks were standing in the meadows and fields, on every hilltop. They did not try to conceal them in the woods or under camouflage nets; the arrogant self-confidence of an army that knows it is master of the land and the air.

The runway was lined with Army helicopters. Their crews were billeted in tents pitched next to the aircraft. There they sat on the wet grass and stared at us.

Both the secretaries of the Writers Union were waiting for me in the Airport building. At the beginning of summer we would still have embraced one another, but now in the autumn of 1968 such embraces had fallen out of favor. On the way into town they read me an article in the East German Communist organ Neues Deutschland, which had been quoted in this morning's Rude pravo. In it I was described as the head of the counterrevolutionary emigrés in West Germany.

Less amusing because of their sinister implications were the documents found in the building of the Writers Union and the Academy of Sciences after the Warsaw Pact troops had evacuated them.

The buildings had been occupied without resistance: the commanders had asked the employees to leave, and they did. I now held in my hand a piece of paper on which a certain Comrade Davydovsky gave the reasons for recommending that First Lieutenant J. A. Orlov be decorated.

"Comrade Orlov, J. A., showed determination, courage, and initiative when fulfilling the task of occupying the building of the Czechoslovak Academy of Sciences. He carried out a maneuver to the rear of the building and, by his decisive action, gained control of the left wing of the building. In the course of the day he took over the entire building and organized its defense."

During the war a similar phrase had covered a considerable number of dead and missing.

For a long time I stopped thinking of anything because I was intent only on looking at Prague. The people I saw standing at the streetcar stops seemed grave, more dignified and self-confident than ever before. The streets were still stripped of names, the houses without numbers. The asphalt of the city's roads had been turned into one endless "street gazette." Many of these inscriptions had been freshly painted over, as they evidently contravened the Moscow agreements. The rest consisted of four names, repeated over and over again: Dubcek, Svoboda, Smrkovsky, Cernik.

I was to meet Cernik that very morning at eleven. I left my suitcase at the Writers Union. With its vice-president Jan Prochazka I exchanged greetings reminiscent of the tough heroes of his films, with a sentimental heart concealed under a rough exterior.

"Hello," I said. "I recognized your texts on the radio even when they were not signed. But your Moravian vocabulary has grown a little coarser lately."

"Hello," he replied. "I don't know what it is, but a month ago I was awakened one night by some noises in the street and ever since my gall bladder has been bothering me."

In front of the government's presidium building I found a couple of those men who now patrolled the whole city. One was an elderly policeman, the other a very young soldier. Their function was of course largely symbolic, like all our armed forces. Still, the very fact that they stood there alone was not without significance.

Cernik did not keep us waiting long. He entered the room and, speaking with his distinctive Ostrava accent, addressed us by our Christian names just as he did when we met him in July.

I read him the proclamation signed four days ago by the Czech participants of the Frankfurt Book Fair. This text, which had roused Neues Deutschland to such indignation, contained these counterrevolutionary thoughts:

"We, Czechoslovak writers and cultural workers who happened to be abroad at the time of the invasion, share the nation's confidence in the present State and Party leadership. This confidence is also shared by those who are now leaving Czechoslovakia to continue their planned artistic activity. All of us are abroad legally, we are Czechoslovak citizens and, regardless of political affiliations, support the endeavor of the government and the Central Committee of the Communist Party of Czechoslovakia. We are socialists and our home is in Czechoslovakia, where we intend to return and from where we again want to travel abroad freely and continue our work, which helps to bury the specter of the cold war."

"They asked me to show it to you first," I told him. "The non-Communists especially did not want to do anything that might make your position more difficult."

He looked at the paper with the signatures of the writers Fuks and Skvorecky, the poet Hirsal, the actor Valtr Taub, the artist Pravoslav Sovak, and others.

"Don't publish it yet," he said.

"But surely, this is proof that Neues Deutschland is lying!"

He nodded, but repeated:

"If you can, let it ride for the time being."

It had been left to me to decide whether to publish or not, but I felt my first twinge of disappointment. Cernik started speaking about "the August events." The unusual term he used instantly revealed the narrow confines drawn for us by the Moscow protocols. I could not help thinking of the proclamation issued in the days when the guns of foreign tanks pointed at this building as well as at many others:

"Our nation's resistance to the illegal occupation of our beautiful socialist homeland is growing daily. Our citizens demand the withdrawal of the forces of occupation, the release of our representatives, and the full legalization of the work of the properly constituted organs of the Czechoslovak Republic." Signed: on behalf of Parliament Valo, on behalf of the Trade Unions Polacek, on behalf of the government Lubomir Strougal.

Now the tanks had gone, but our vocabulary showed the white spaces where their tracks had rolled over it. The released representative went on with his analysis, which was precise, carefully thought out—and depressing. To my astonishment it was based on an argument I had heard once before, on a night last August. According to this thesis, Czechoslovakia was not the center of the world but a mere pawn on a chessboard upon which the merciless struggle of the Kings was being waged. I realized that this persevering man, unmarked by the small private hell he had endured since our last meeting, was determined to do everything to keep that pawn in the game. Maybe at a price that I would not be prepared to pay. He took leave of us cordially.

"See you," he said to me.

But I was almost sure he would not see us for a drink again.

The company that met over lunch at the Writers Union was one I had already considered doomed. Jan Prochazka, Karel Kosik, and Ludovik Vaculik were tired, yet bristling with energy, hurt but undefeated. I had the marvelous feeling that they formed a firm component of the nation's life, undefinable but important, somewhere between the family and the fatherland.

When I stepped inside my barber's shop, the attendants could not believe their eyes. Mr. Ptacnik, who has been jealously looking after my head for the past seventeen years, gave expression to their astonishment:

"I'll be damned! We thought you'd stay abroad!"

"Really, Vaclav," I told him reproachfully, "just look at my head. I couldn't walk about any longer looking this way."

That was probably the only argument that I could use with any hope of success. I was being shampooed when I was called to the phone. Mr. Ptacnik went in my place and came back with a message.

"They want you to call 099, someone called T____."

And then he was annoyed with me because I told him I was in a hurry, which offended his professional pride. 099 was the number of the Central Secretariat of the Party. I only knew T____ very slightly, yet he urged me to come and see him at once.

"Get over here as quick as you can, they're looking for you."

The large house on the embankment was again as coldly impersonal as it used to be before last January. T_____ at once switched on his radio, as people used to do in the days of bugged telephones.

"He's heard that you're back and would like to speak to you."

He did not have to tell me more. Then he led me up rear staircases and side passages, explaining the reason for this succinctly:

"There are all kinds of people here these days, not all of them exactly nice."

We ended up in a small office, whose occupant told me that I would have to wait a little.

"He is just seeing the Soviet commandant, who's come to lodge a complaint. He's here all the time now."

The "little" wait lasted an hour and a half. I was just about to give up when Dubcek came in without knocking, mercurial as always. He fanned the smoke-filled air with his hand.

"Why, you'll suffocate before long! Do open a window."

His eyes were puffed, the eyelids red. No sooner had he sat down opposite me, however, than he began to question me eagerly. His main interest centered on the people who were still abroad. I read the Frankfurt proclamation once more.

"That is not the voice of emigrants," I told him when I had finished. "They're simply people who can't stomach certain things. Don't drive them into a blind alley. That would be unjust to them and a luxury for this country."

"We'll do everything we can to enable them to return. On the other hand they must understand the position of those of us who're at home and not make it any harder for us. After all, fourteen million people can't emigrate and we have to see to it that they can live here where they belong."

He told me about one of his associates who had bravely stood his ground in August, only to give way to a sudden depression and go off with his whole family to Vienna.

"I sent him a message to say that he should take it easy and come home. He wrote back to ask what guarantees could I give him. So I sent him another message: if you want to be safe, you can sleep in my flat."

I laughed, but I felt no gaiety. What guarantees could anyone in this country give anyone else nowadays? His secretary came in and turned to me reprovingly.

"Comrade Dubcek's lunch is getting cold—this is the second time we've brought it."

It was three in the afternoon. I rose at once, but Dubcek remained seated, as if he had heard nothing.

"Tell me," he said, "do you think Werich will be back? I can't imagine what things would be like here if he stayed abroad."

I knew nothing about Jan Werich's whereabouts, but I had no doubts on this score.

"He'll be back all right. He has known for some time that he doesn't belong only to himself. Just like you."

"How do you mean?"

I started telling him about my experiences abroad, trying to put in a nutshell the effect this last spring and summer in Czechoslovakia had had on the European Left.

"The progressive part of the left-wing movement realized that what happened here last January represented a great opportunity for them as well as for us. In August they witnessed a crucifixion which, contrary to the usual pattern, failed to come off. They are horrified and delighted simultaneously—and you cannot be surprised that your name has come to be a symbol to them."

He tried to protest, but I would not be interrupted.

"You have become a symbol that exists irrespective of you. I know you are a politician, I know that there is nothing to be done but to make concessions; they didn't send half a million troops here to give us the time of day. But even concessions have their limits, beyond which they turn into defeat. Forgive me for saying this, but if your name were to become the symbol of capitulation, it would be a tragedy not only for Czechoslovakia."

"We'll go on implementing our post-January policy," he said. "There's no other way for us."

That reminded me of something. I could not remember what it was.

The secretary came back to warn Dubcek that his lunch was getting cold once more. He took not the slightest notice, continuing to speak, to listen, and to laugh. The longer I was with him, the more convinced I became that it was not so much that he wanted to hear what I had to say—what could I tell him that he did not know already?—but that he felt the need of an ordinary conversation. There were moments when, in the midst of laughter, he would visibly fall prey to weariness and skepticism.

"We were up against such power . . . ," he said all of a sudden dismally. "No one can imagine."

And immediately afterward, with a sigh:

"If only I could be a bricklayer for a year or so!"

I again saw that tiny pawn on the terrible chessboard of the world, and I was seized by utter hopelessness. But he by this time was again enthusiastically reiterating his conviction that a society which had shown such stamina and discipline would be able to overcome any crisis.

"Perhaps there's one good thing about all this," he added, smiling. "Since we'll not be able to talk so much, maybe we'll start working a little harder for a change!"

Behind the jest grinned the specter of censorship. I was about to start arguing, but I could no longer bear the sight of his secretary, gesticulating behind his back to indicate that at least I ought to have the sense to know when to stop. And so stop I did, though heavy-hearted. Dubcek repeated:

"We'll go on with our post-January policy!"

On my way home I tried to remember what this sentence reminded me of, but I failed.

A little later a young man whose voice was changing led me into his sanctuary and showed me his latest canvas. A poisonously green cube in a composition of pastel-colored arches.

"What's it called?" I asked him.

" 'An Individualist,' " he replied. "It's meant to show that harmony that's imposed and not voluntary can be dangerous to life."

For the first time in several years I had no comment on one of his experiments.

"Is it very bad?" he asked me cautiously.

"On the contrary, I'd say it's very good."

"I've been promised a hundred and fifty for it, but if you like it, you can have it," he declared grandly.

I accepted the picture. He looked at me distrustfully.

"What're you laughing about?"

I changed the subject. How could I explain to him that I had just become a father?

It was a quarter to six. I rang the telephone exchange of the Parliament and could not believe my ears when I heard Smrkovsky's characteristically deep voice.

"Hullo," I said in astonishment.

"Hullo, who is it?"

I told him and said I'd like to see him whenever convenient.

"Well, why aren't you here, then?"

"Tell me," I asked him, "since when have you been a telephone operator at the National Assembly?"

"I guess they've all gone home. Nobody worries about things like that just now."

The soldier and the policeman standing on guard outside the Parliament building let me in without a card.

"This is good," said the policeman, much amused. "I've just read somewhere that you are the boss of the exiles!"

"If occupation can be fraternal assistance," I told him, "why can't exiles be at home?"

I entered an office on the second floor. This was only the fifth time we had met but I felt I had known Smrkovsky all my life. He embraced me so hard that my bones all but cracked. Coming from him I did not mind it. Then I burst into laughter. He was wearing a dark suit and a splendid silk tie on which had been embroidered the State emblem and, in gold thread, the words Truth Prevails.

"They made this to welcome us home," he said. "So I'm wearing it."

Somehow it was like being back in the last century. Yet it seemed quite in keeping with the situation. We had once again reached the very bottom and it was necessary to cling to the basic certainties.

"Are you also convinced that we can carry on?" I asked him after we had toasted each other with a glass of brandy.

"I don't know whether we can," he replied. "All I know is we must."

"But how do you see this in practice? Have we really any leeway left at all?"

He nodded, looking lost in thought.

"Time," he said.

"Yes, only time can also work against us."

"I understand . . . apathy, the breaking up of our unity. . . ."
I looked him straight in the eye.

"Or perhaps loss of confidence. This country is not likely to stand any more politicians who serve foreign interests."

"Well, I'm not going to be one of them!" he declared resolutely.

A girl secretary appeared, bringing him a file of papers to sign. I had to wait. A TV set was playing behind his chair. When I entered the room, Smrkovsky had turned up the sound; that, clearly, was a regular custom these days. Now he found the noise getting on his nerves and so he turned it down completely. It was half past six; they were showing some educational film for children. I watched huge spiders soundlessly moving about over his head, weaving a web out of threads as thick as cables. A Kafkaesque backdrop.

I was tempted to question him about his experiences on that August trip to Moscow, but I refrained. I concluded it would have been as tactless as to ask someone about his serious illness. When I was about to leave I said:

"Thank you."

"Whatever for?"

"For remaining unchanged."

To my great surprise he replied with my own thought.

"The other day I went to the National Theater and I realized that I'm nothing more than an actor helping to play out the national destiny. And I am going to play my rôle whatever the ending."

I tried to remember which restaurant in Prague had the best beef with cream sauce, and then drove in a borrowed car to the Brussels Restaurant in the Letna Park. There was not a single guest in the large dining room. The waiters stared at me, as surprised as the barbers had been before them.

"Are you closed?" I asked, disappointed.

They explained that although the curfew had been lifted, people still did not go out much after dark, and especially not into the parks. These were full of foreign nationals who, instead of a passport, carried automatic weapons. I did not enjoy my meal. But then a look at the paper told me that one of my plays, The Clown, was on at the Vinohrady Theater. I got there just after the intermission. I leaned against the box parapet which had supported me for the past eighteen years. They silently greeted me from the stage. I closed my eyes. Now at last I was truly at home.

Then the trusting clown was fenced in by the bars of the cage and all that remained was to open the gate that let in the tigers. The clown kept flicking his whip happily, ingenuously repeating for a hundredth time his greatest wish:

"I want to put eight white Lippizaners through their ... whatdyumacallit? ... paces."

WE'LL GO ON IMPLEMENTING THE POST-JANUARY POLICY!

That was what the sentence I had heard this afternoon had reminded me of.

And then I moved toward the house I had seen at a distance all day, every time I crossed one of the bridges over the Vltava. Now I drove across the city to get there. At ten in the evening it was as deserted as a stage set after the performance. Suddenly a Soviet armored troop carrier came out of a side street and turned so that it was directly behind me. In the small white Fiat I would have been quite justified in feeling like a scared rabbit in front of its powerful headlights. Strangely enough, my feelings were completely different. The fin-de-siècle gables of Paris Avenue, with the silhouette of the Old Town Hall peeping out behind them, that was my native ground, the stage I was accustomed to, on which I could never know stage fright. I took a familiar short cut, past the Golem restaurant now submerged in darkness, turned right twice, and when I again emerged onto the main road, I found myself right behind the armored car. I flashed my lights and proudly passed it.

My hands trembled as I unlocked the door. Setting down my suitcase I switched on the light. The pink-and-white faïence chandelier glowed under the blue ceiling, which looked just like the sky without stars.

Carefully arranged on top of my writing desk were some small bits of metal. It took me a little while to realize that they were bullets.

The windows had been repaired. I went up to the corner window and, pulling up the blind, opened it.

Prague, which was spread out below me in all its horizontal and vertical beauty, from the grassy slopes of Petrin to the twin spires of the Tyn, from the surface of the Vltava to the top of the St. Vitus Cathedral, left me breathless. I was overcome by the homesickness of all those who tonight were falling asleep far away from this city. I wanted to do everything in my power to enable them to return.

In the palm of my hand lay the ten small messengers of death, but above the roof of the castle opposite, the Presidential flag fluttered fearlessly, like the wing of a huge dove.

---

25 January 1969 / Prague–Karlovy Vary
(From the diary of the writer PK)

When the music stopped and the first speech began, the bells of Prague all started pealing at once. The sound was muted and soft as it reached the deep well formed by the narrow courtyard of the Carolinum, yet it was enough to drown the words of the speakers and I was able to rewind the films of memory.

Pre-Christmas Basle was Swiss in its affluence, German in its noisiness, and French in its gaiety. Nothing of this was reflected in the flat I visited on behalf of the Czech artistic unions and the Academy of Sciences. The sitting room, uncarpeted and curtainless, contained only a television set, a table, and three chairs. The beds next door had been lent by the Red Cross.

I sat facing Dr. Sik, member of the Central Committee of the Czechoslovak Communist Party and former Deputy Premier, the man who used to be called the father of our new economic system. The press of the five Warsaw Pact powers denounced him as a treacherous emigré while his friends at home sent him messages to say that his return was not desirable at present. I had been sent to see him in order to ascertain his stand, which could then be set against the assertions of our opponents. We could not very well afford to lose people of his caliber without resistance—that was too much of a luxury, if not downright suicide. Since I now had the opportunity of talking to him in person I could not help putting to him a question that was of foremost interest throughout Europe.

"Were we really on our way to a new form of capitalism?"

I brought back his reply on tape.

"I have discovered during my lecture tour that not only in the East but also here in the West people were under the impression that we were concerned solely with the recognition and reintroduction of a market economy, that we therefore wanted nothing more than to achieve the same effective production and high consumption they have in the West. As they themselves are waging a struggle against the industrial consumer society and its serious shortcomings, people in the West—and in particular the young— saw in this a retrograde step. Now that I have had the opportunity of giving them a detailed explanation of our aims I meet with great interest bordering on enthusiasm. While to ensure effective economic development was a must for our country, our primary aim was to create the kind of socialist society that is nowadays known as democratic. We wanted to change the present state of affairs, where a minority still dictates its will and interests to a majoriy of the nation. That minority, in a capitalist society, is formed not only by the proprietors but also by the very powerful economic technocracy, which forces the whole society to live according to the interests of the producers and thus gives it its materially limited consumer character. We wished to create a theory of a truly direct democracy, in which neither the capitalist technostructure nor the interests of a small group of State and political bureaucrats would predominate, a society whose true interests (that is, the interests of the consumers as well as the producers) would be respected. Where people are not masters of their social relationships, they are equally not masters of the forces of production. Power has been wrenched from them, is opaque and stands above them; they have no influence over it. Just as there is a certain alienation in an industrial consumer society, it also exists in a centrally directed bureaucratic society, for people do not have the feeling of true freedom—they do not feel that they are masters of their own destiny. If we were to create a society free from this alienation, we should give new hope not only to the East but also to the West. It would bring new hope to the progressive forces of all mankind."

The funeral procession marched slowly between the silent cordon of hundreds of thousands of onlookers. I saw a single policeman, completely surrounded by the crowd. What was to prevent that immense mass from being set in motion, breaking up the procession that was walking through the city six abreast, and releasing an avalanche that could have provided the pretext for some more brotherly help in the shape of tanks? Nothing but a thin line of students from the department of philosophy with paper owls in their buttonholes and a coil of string in their hands, probably the thinnest on the market.

Perhaps it was meant to show the nation's leaders that in this country the bond of confidence was more powerful than truncheons and tanks.

Normalization progressed apace, and it was both remarkable and depressing. It is only fair to say that from the time of that August hurricane until this moment, the captains had guaranteed the safety of all those who remained on board. However, if one compared present reality with the hopes of last spring, one could not help being despondent. It was enough to read the Slovak Pravda, printed on 20 August. In it Dr. Husak was quoted as saying in a speech to the foundry workers of the Slovak town Zdiar:

"The fact remains that in Slovakia the regeneration process has come to a halt halfway. While in the Czech lands there have been important changes in the leadership of every organ, in Slovakia hardly anything has changed, and if so then only in a minor degree. How can anyone believe that the people who for the past fifteen years have held the same posts and used the same old methods will change overnight and suddenly be able to work differently? The process of democratization must in Slovakia too affect the broad masses of the nation. It must affect every single citizen!"

The people who had "held the same posts" for fifteen years were now to stay in those posts, being protected by a special clause in the Moscow agreement. On the other hand, those who for fifteen years had been preparing the ground for the Czechoslovak spring were on their way out with the autumn. Vasil Bilak, whom Dr. Husak had criticized by name and who had been deprived of his post by the Congress of the Slovak Communist Party, remained Secretary of the national Central Committee. Zdenek Hejzlar, who shortly before August became Managing Director of Czechoslovak Radio and who had helped to keep the legal free radios going during the first few days of the occupation, was again forced to resign, as he had been fifteen years ago when he was Chairman of the Youth Union. Minister of the Interior Josef Pavel was again devoting all his time to his strawberries, whereas his ill-famed deputy Salgovic, back in his official capacity, raised a glass to welcome the federalization of Slovakia. In his Christmas television speech Dr. Husak unexpectedly suggested that a Slovak candidate should replace Smrkovsky as President of the Federal National Assembly. For this he was applauded by the Czech hard-liners, who as recently as last August spat at the mention of his name. Perhaps he only accepted the unpleasant rôle prescribed for him by the Soviet author. Perhaps he too was playing that great game of the little pawn. Politicians, after all, have to compromise. Writers don't. I wrote him a strongly-worded open letter, joined by the one-million-strong union of metal workers. Dr. Husak devoted his next speech to an attack on right-wing pressure groups, so that the arguments made famous by Antonin Novotny were now repeated in Slovak.

The history of the nation continued, and with it that of the nation's literature. A new round had begun. And I was in the ring once more.

The Jan Hus monument in Old Town Square was swarming with young people until it seemed to be cast of youthful bodies. HE WHO SPEAKS THE TRUTH RISKS HIS HEAD; HE WHO IS AFRAID OF DEATH LOSES THE JOY OF LIFE. The dead Jan Palach, his pupil from the same school, was not afraid of death, yet he had lost the joy of life. Unlike the Master, he had lit his own pyre. His action defied judgment. Nevertheless, I could not help thinking that whoever left us now, whether beyond the frontier of life or the frontier of our country, was needlessly evacuating the small area of space and hope that he had been defending.

On Tuesday we had gone to Prague Airport to await the arrival of Professor Sik. It was the only day when all of Europe was fog-covered. He asked by teleprinter whether he ought not to come by car. From a small room next to the customs shed I replied that it would be sheer lunacy to do so. In my heart of hearts I was glad he had been prevented from coming; the days between the death of Jan Palach and the funeral had been literally charged with gunpowder. But the desire to return home, which had made up for the missing furniture in that Basle flat, had been stronger than fear. He announced that he would come by train, arriving at midnight at Prague's main railway station.

In my exchange over the teleprinter I had used the cover name of Dr. Peter, under which I had for a long time managed to evade the newspapermen in Switzerland last August. As I was about to leave the airport, an unknown young customs man told me that the security police were on their way to pick up my messages. I took the original so as to be able to prove what I did and what I did not say, and I asked him to give them my compliments.

That evening I was invited as a witness to the flat of the playwright Vaclav Havel. On the strength of certain information, he had discovered a bugging device in the ceiling of one of the rooms. It seemed that we had two separate State Security forces. We decided to make things hot for one of them, and for the Minister of the Interior as well.

The former Deputy Premier and author of the new economic system arrived at midnight, unaccompanied but moved, because all the way from the border he had been warmly greeted by customs officials, railwaymen, and his fellow passengers. Instead of his former friends the politicians, he was met by a group of scientists and writers, most of whom he did not even know. The train was almost empty. No wonder that four gentlemen were left on the platform, having waited in vain for someone to meet. In their disappointment they followed us as we drove away from the station.

A surprise awaited me the following morning. A meeting of the Central Committee of the Writers Union was being chaired by its President, Professor Eduard Goldstucker. Obviously moved, he expressed his thanks to the poet Jaroslav Seifert, who had only since August come out of his political retirement and his hospital room to deputize for him until the anti-Semitic campaign of the fraternal press of the Warsaw Pact powers ceased.

That very day Professor Sik and Professor Goldstucker took their oath as members of the Czech National Council. From that moment on it would be very difficult for anyone to go on alleging that they were emigrants and traitors. On Friday, the day before Jan Palach's funeral, they both left Czechoslovakia once more for an indefinite stay abroad, to prevent their presence in the country from becoming the cause of fresh consequences.

The rain changed into a downpour, but no one showed the slightest inclination to put up an umbrella. That said a great deal. The funeral was also a demonstration of strength. Our greatest weapon was stubbornness. I closed my eyes as the rain streamed down my face. In Paris Avenue I raised my head on some sudden impulse and saw something I shall never forget. Behind every window in those tall, fin-de-siècle houses candles had been lit, many of them held by children.

On 15 January a public meeting was held to commemorate the first anniversary of the beginning of Dubcek's reforms. Only the people on the platform were different. Of the politicians only Frantisek Vodslon, member of the Central Committee of the Communist Party, had dared to turn up. But, just like last year, we openly replied to every single question put to us by members of the audience. The reaction of those thousands of young people in the hall spoke volumes for their dignity and inner freedom; this seemed to me at this moment of far greater worth than the freedoms granted by magnanimous rulers. How far removed from the emotional atmosphere and mass hysteria of my young days the long-haired boy walked up to the microphone to say that Czechoslovakia could not be the center of the world as long as Vietnam was part of that world, and that our anger toward the occupiers must not become anger toward nations.

"If we become silly nationalists," he said, "we'll be exactly where they want us to be!"

Applause. One of the last questions I was called upon to answer was this:

"After last January you started to claim that you were building socialism with a human face. Please explain what kind of socialism you had been building before then."

The signature read okay. I could not see him among all the hundreds of equally young faces, and therefore I looked in every direction in turn as I made my reply:

"My dear son, it is precisely because I hope to find the answer to that question that I am now writing a large book which I hope to give you next May as a present for your sixteenth birthday."

It was typical of him that he had not asked at home but here, in public. By doing so he gave me a proof that it was not only possible to talk with him but, indeed, imperative.

The head of the funeral procession reached the School of Philosophy. It was twenty-two years since I had first crossed its threshold. The orchestra was playing the national anthem. All Prague stood still. I recalled the funeral of our Great Leader and it seemed to me that I was a hundred years old. This time instead of the factory sirens the church bells were still ringing. Many of them had rung like this at the execution of the Czech noblemen after the Battle of the White Mountain. Some of them pealed during the sermons of Jan Hus.

FOR WHOM THE BELL TOLLS?

For a nation that knows how to rise from the dead.

The hearse carrying the coffin drove away. The crowd of hundreds of thousands dispersed in a matter of minutes. Hats were taken off to greet last year's Chairman of the National Front Frantisek Kriegel, the only man who refused to sign the Moscow agreements, one of the four members of Parliament who had later voted against the treaty legalizing the temporary stay of foreign troops in Czechoslovakia.

I drove straight to Karlovy Vary. Although it was early afternoon, all cars had their lights on. All cars except one. This was a lorry under whose canvas could be glimpsed the country-boy faces of young soldiers who were clutching weapons in their hands because someone had fooled them into believing that they were in enemy territory. I hoped I would be able to meet them ten years hence, in their own country of course.

I reached Karlovy Vary literally skidding through the fog on the icy road. A group of local hard-liners, which had been formed following the example of Jodas and Co. in Prague, spread the rumor that I had come to Karlovy Vary to found an anti-State organization which had the West's backing and was intended to pave the way for those vile enemies of the revolution, the social democrats.

Excellent, I said to myself. Seeing that the only real-life social democrat I know is Gunter Grass, they will no doubt conclude that I am also preparing the annexation of the Karlovy Vary region by Germany.

I did not intend to give this any more attention. I was almost certain that this rumor had been invented by the same people who were simultaneously spreading another rumor in Switzerland— to the effect for a change that I was an agent of the Czech secret police. In view of the fact that there had never yet been a writer-agent in the history of Czech literature, this gave me a slight feeling of pride.

As for the social democrats themselves, it struck me as absurd that they should often figure as our archenemies, more so even than the imperialists, while they considered us their greatest foes in return. If there existed a hot line between Moscow and the White House, there should at least be an ordinary mail service between the various heirs of Karl Marx; after all, they badly needed to learn from each other's mistakes.

I entered my room in the writers' pension which had been my home away from home since last autumn. The sofas, chairs, and carpet were all strewn with the manuscript pages of this book. Its first version was intended to provide information for all those who were trying to understand the somewhat complicated life story of my generation. It in fact began and ended with the arrival of Soviet tanks in Prague. I deliberately divided it up into three levels. One of these is the history of the Czechoslovak spring 1968. In this part I play myself, while in the other two appears a man who merely resembles me. I have done my best to record the authentic state of my mind in the various periods of the past and present. Some of the pages caused me acute embarrassment when I wrote them (and understandably even more so when I read them). Yes, I can truthfully say that on occasion I felt thoroughly ashamed. Is it possible that these naïve, bombastic phrases had once been uttered aloud? Alas. But it was impossible to leave them out if this Diary was to have any meaning. It was meant for readers with a sense of fair play; no other readers interest me.

The writer Jan Prochazka was sitting in the dining room of the mutilated Pupp Hotel, out of which a local architect had attempted to create a Czech Hilton by adding an annex which made the whole place look like a grandmother in miniskirts. Jan Prochazka was sitting in the dining room and enjoying life, for the first time since his operation drinking the wine of his native Moravia. With the good sense of the farmer he had once been and still remained in his writings he had made use of the political intermission for a thorough overhaul of his physical self. Now he was again ready for the fray. As usual.

Over my dinner I had a quick glance at a month's accumulation of mail I had brought with me from Prague. It included a letter from Mr. Kulhanek. Each year, he sent me his bill for the work he did in my garden, accompanied by his highly individual commentary. Since his annual report coincided once every four years with the inaugural address of the American Presidents, I called them all A Report on the State of Nature. I finished reading the latest one and became speechless. I handed it over to my friend.

The letter was written in a rough hand and with a profusion of grammatical errors. It contained the thoughts of a man who for over sixty years had rarely been away from the barn and the cowshed, formerly his own and now belonging to a farmers' cooperative. Jan Prochazka, formerly a farmer, now a writer, read the letter through and said proudly:

"The Czech nation will not perish."

Here is the full text of Mr. Kulhanek's letter:

"Dear Mr. Kohout,

I inclose a list showing wat I did in 1968. This old year is almost over. Wat a year it's been. The winter pretty mild. Spring came very early. The thrushes and other birds arrived at the beginning of March, a fortnight earlier than last year. In March we planted root vegetables and other kinds of early vegetables. The soil in the fields was ready for the spring sowing. Also early in March the farsisia bushes began to bloom (which don't happen other years). Early cherries were in bloom at the beginning of April, then later in the month the greengages, damson plums, then apples and pears. The flower bushes also were in a hurry, 'cause the spring's so early. Everything that flowers early showed itself better and more beautiful than wat flowers late. The early vegetables had finished growing at the end of May and could be used in the kitchen. Also the early cherries were ripe. The corn grew well in the fields. The bees were pleased by the good wether and were kept busy polinating and carrying honey home to there hives. This was very useful to us. By the end of June all semi-early plants had almost grown, and also the corn. July is the month when the corn is ripe, and some of the early fruits. From the beggining of March to the end of July the wether was good touching the moisture and temperature.

continued on page two

Therefor everything did well, corn as well as fruit and vegetables. Until this time the rich harvest deserved that we give thanks to a higher power. After the January resurection and with twenty years of serfdom behind us, we breathed more freely and lived more hapily. You too Mr. Kohout came more often to Sazava than other years. Didn't you think it was a bit better than other years?

Then comes August: much horror and disapointment. That which gave us joy is now changed into fear and darkness. Everything stopped and we waited wat was to be. These horrors slowed down the work because of the uncerenty. As a result many goods are not to be had in the shops. Also coal is very short. Work on the land was delayd too. It was only thanks to the mild autumn, with no frost and snow, that it was done at all.

I think I've wrote enough and so I will stop.

I work in your garden as normal every month.

Please forgive the handwriting, my hand is heavy and also it is getting a little stiff with age.

> Bedrich Kulhanek
> farmer
> Xaverov near Sazava
> 27 December 1968

◻

Tuesday, 20 August 1968 / San Marino
(The beginning of The Story)

A postage stamp appeared in the long stretch of flat landscape, a postage stamp with a rock and three castles on it. I felt I was driving back into my childhood, where it had graced my father's stamp album.

"Rocca Guaita, Rocca della Fratta, Rocca Montale..."

"What's that you're humming?" she asked me.

"An anthem I composed when I was a little boy and wanted to be Garibaldi when I grew up."

"Oh, that's a new one on me. I thought you only wanted to be Cyrano de Bergerac, an Evangelical pastor, a leading man in the theater, a Red commissar, and lately a national martyr!"

"Oh, Garibaldi came long before all those," I explained condescendingly. "And *he* was preceded by a fireman, Mikhail Strogoff, and Mr. Chroust."

"Mr. Chroust? Who on earth's that?"

"That was our local stationer."

"Now at last I see why you spend hours looking at pencil sharpeners and erasers in every chain store we go into."

"That's right," I said. "And that also is why I have always bitterly regretted that I wasn't the son of a working-class or peasant East German family, since in that country small-scale private ownership is flourishing. If the good Lord and Professor Sik succeed in doing the same for us, I'll set up a little stationer's shop and will have at last reached my long-desired goal."

She leaned against the car door and watched me in some astonishment. The sun was setting directly behind the mountain. The three black castles now looked like the scenery of a puppet show. I could hear my mother's large hand-bell announcing the start of a performance. At the first crossroads I turned right. Z____ grabbed the wheel.

"You've taken the wrong turning! Rimini is to the left!"

"Yes, I know. I know everything there is to know."

"We're supposed to be heading for the seashore, remember?"

"Of course we are, but that's tomorrow. Now we're going to dine."

"Why can't we dine in Rimini?"

"That is impossible, my child, for the night is nigh, and the hour is that between the dog and the wolf when the streets of Rimini are haunted by the spirit of the clever but cruel *condottiere* Malatesta, who stabbed his first wife, poisoned his second, strangled his third, and then took in marriage his beloved mistress Isotta. San Marino, on the other hand, is the home of benevolent merchants and shepherds, who since time immemorial have given shelter to fugitives. And it was they who, in the fifteenth century, defeated Malatesta of Rimini, unable to bear his wicked deeds any longer."

"Well, your story shows that Rimini is the proper place for us to go. Perhaps there you might propose to me at last."

"It's your turn to be strangled, my dear."

"But at least I'd have time to take a dip in the sea beforehand."

"Sorry! In obedience to your wishes I have covered hundreds

of kilometers in a southerly direction. I have conquered for you the dull city of Linz, dreamy Salzburg, proud Grossglockner, and Venice, the pearl of the seas. Now you must allow me to take the real beginning of our vacation into my experienced hands. I have laid careful plans for this day, plans which I shall only reveal to you one by one with devilish cunning."

She laughed.

"You're becoming quite amusing," she said.

"You wait. Beginning tomorrow I'll make you split your sides."

"Why beginning tomorrow?"

"Because, my love, today I am starting out, with one month's delay caused by a certain confusion within the socialist camp, on the second half of my enviable life. In spite of my youth, I can with a clear conscience terminate my political career and leave the well-being of our community in the care of your admirable generation. For my own part I intend to devote myself to wine, dance, song, the breeding of dogs, and the writing of my memoirs before I forget them. Wherefore I ask you to bear with me this night and once more thoroughly celebrate my fortieth birthday."

We drove past a metal structure which carried an inscription saying welcome to the Republic of San Marino. I stopped outside the first likely-looking inn.

"Why don't we drive straight up?" she asked, gazing at the winding *strada panoramica*.

"Luck is like women," I told her philosophically as we walked onto the terrace. "Why throw ourselves upon it heedlessly when we can savor it slowly, thus protracting our pleasure until it makes our head reel with delight. Hey there, lad," I said to the waiter in Czech, "the queen I am escorting is worthy of your best attention, which will moreover not go unrewarded. Bring us all your spaghetti milanese and bolognese, lavish on us your ravioli and your pizzas, fish out for us all the *frutti di mare*, not forgetting to provide us with *vinum et panem*. The games we'll organize ourselves!"

He divined that he was witnessing an extraordinary occurrence and was back with a carafe in a flash.

"Thank you for being so patient with me," I told her. "In return, I can now hand over to you my homeland—an earthly paradise where the flower of spring is once more in bloom, to quote our national anthem. After dinner we'll drive up to the Casino and break the bank. Out of our winnings we'll purchase a stick and give expression to our joy by banging the shop shutters. Finally, I'll hire the most beautiful suite in the hotel and tomorrow morning lay at your feet the entire South, from the Apennines all the way to Dalmatia. For I would have you know that at long last I am free and happy."

(Continued at the beginning of the book)

About the Author

Pavel Kohout was born in Prague in 1928. He was one of the inspirations and most forceful fighters for the ideas of the "Prague Spring." He spent his youth and university years in his native city. He began his professional life as a radio journalist and reporter; later he became cultural attaché at his country's embassy in Moscow. Since 1955 he has concentrated exclusively on writing. However, his writing has not been an end in itself, but rather is bound up with a political and social involvement that is trying to prepare the way for a humane socialism. In German-speaking countries Kohout is particularly well known for his plays, among which are *Josef Schweik, Around the World in 80 Days, Such Love,* and *August, August, August.* His dramatic works have been published in two volumes by C. J. Bucher.

DATE DUE

GAYLORD			PRINTED IN U.S.A